As Long As It's Pink

Don Gres⋯ ⋯ London, ⋯ ⋯ 1⋯

As Long As It's Pink

The sexual politics of taste

Penny Sparke

An Imprint of HarperCollins*Publishers*

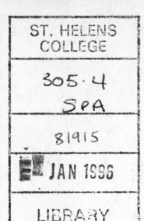
To the memory of my mother

Pandora
An Imprint of HarperCollins*Publishers*
77-85 Fulham Palace Road,
Hammersmith, London W6 8JB

1160 Battery Street,
San Francisco, California 94111-1213

Published by Pandora 1995
1 3 5 7 9 10 8 6 4 2

© Penny Sparke 1995

Penny Sparke asserts the moral right to
be identified as the author of this work

A catalogue record for this book is available from the British Library

ISBN 0 04 440923 0

Printed in Great Britain by Woolnough Bookbinding Limited,
Irthlingborough, Northamptonshire

Contents

Preface

It's surprising how long it can take to see what is staring you in the face. In the 1960s, a decade which for me represented an incredible opening up of possibilities, I was preoccupied with what I saw to be the liberating forces of pop culture, especially on the world of material things and visual culture in general. The possibility of finding a personal style to represent my emerging identity was a crucial part of growing up. The availability of styles, whether of dress, interior decor, or of music, also rep-resented a complete break with a past which had been characterised by fixed rules and static social and cultural identities. In the '60s, or so it seemed, all that could be thrown to the wind with a toss of the hair, a change in the length of a skirt, or a splash of orange paint on the wall. Like many of my female contemporaries I also played lip-service to the emerging political agenda of the women's move-ment, aware of the many issues of inequality but unaware that they had anything to do with my dedication to style.

When, in the 1970s, I became a historian of modern design, my earlier preoccupations influenced the way I began to think about material culture. Still committed to the idea that things have the power to affect the lives of ordinary people, with the potential to be both 'expressive' and 'liberating', I intuitively veered away from – and indeed sought ways of undermining – the dominant rhetoric of Modernism. To me, that movement seemed committed to a much more 'high-minded', authoritar-ian, and heavily politicised programme of architectural and design intervention and reform, based on rational principles of collectivism, standardisation, and social egalitarianism. I pinned my faith, instead, to the more open-ended, individualistic and essentially 'pleasurable' mast of 'post-modern' ideas expressed in the writings of the architectural and design historian and critic Reyner Banham, and in the work of the Italian designers, especially that of Ettore Sottsass. Here I discovered the same liberating and joyful optimism that I had found in pop. Perhaps, also, although I didn't consciously recognise it at the time, I found there an experience of the material world which could be characterised more obviously as stereotypically 'feminine' rather than 'masculine'.

As the 1980s progressed I almost lost that sense of optimism as the idea of 'design' seemed to become overlaid with attributes suggesting that 'things' were, after all, simply part of late capitalism's snare, powerless to liberate in other than the most superficial and illusory of ways. The visual culture of modernity, separated from its ideological underpinnings, and indeed of postmodernity as well, seemed now little more than a seductive trap, destined to reinforce rather than to challenge the status quo. However, my continuing fascination with, and underlying faith in, things led me to resist judgments of this kind, and to search instead for a means of understanding and interpreting the complex meanings of material culture, both past and present.

My own researches led me to an abundance of material rich in potential meanings but largely uncharted. I was puzzled by the gaps in knowledge that emerged: why had so few people looked at mass-produced artefacts as cultural forms? Why were there no serious books about refrigerators and cars? Why was there so much work available about architecture and so little about interiors? So few good books about shop and shopping? So much written about Fordism but nothing about Sloanism?

These vast areas of knowledge relating to the material culture of this century were still 'hidden from history'. What's more, the little that *was* documented was all linked, in one way or another, to the 'heroic' buildings, objects, ideas and people (mostly men) who made up the story of modernism. Anything that did not come within its remit had simply been ignored. Why was this the case?

The first obvious ideological route to explore was that of the domination, of one class over another. The modernist architects had all belonged to the educated middle-class, committed to prioritising culture over commerce, idealism over pragmatism. Although intended to improve the lot of the working class community, theirs was essentially an elite, middle-class movement, its aesthetic embedded within the high-minded moralising that characterised the public face of that particular social group. Modernism was committed to a notion of the 'rational' and the 'good', the latter defined according to the criteria which promised the democratisation of everyday things, namely mass production. Within Fordism modernism located the way ahead.

It was in contemplating the importance of the production process for modernism that I made the sudden realisation that it was not class alone, but, more significantly, gender, that underpinned this misrepresentation of our material culture. Prioritising production meant underplaying the role of consumption, an undisputedly feminine arena. Suddenly things fell into place that had not made sense to me before. My own preoccupation with popular culture, for example, could be seen now not just as a 1960s pop formation, but rather as a measure of my empathy with what has been seen as a characteristic of feminine culture throughout this century. Standing outside the dominant masculine experience of modernity, I realised, feminine culture, linked with the everyday, the commercial and the aesthetically 'impure', had been relegated to the margins.

From assuming that everything changed in 1959 I now went back to explore the ways in which my mother and her mother before her might have experienced 'feminine culture', in particular the world of things through which they had located themselves. The search coincided with a shift in my own ex-perience of being female. Motherhood, rapidly succeeded by the death of my own mother led to a sharply focused emotional understanding of the continuity of feminine culture and experience, passed down through generations. Unlike masculine culture, which is largely inherited through mainstream institutions, its feminine equivalent is handed down through such marginal domestic skills as knitting and sewing, as well as through the shared enjoyment of popular culture – in my mother's case, Hollywood films. I realised that my intuitive feelings about material culture had come through continuity rather than, as I had thought, disruption and change. My interest in the 'post-modern' and my suspicions of the 'modern' were consistent with a commitment to the continuity of feminine culture as it has been formed, and marginalised, over the last century and a half.

From this point onwards everything I already knew, and everything that I subsequently uncovered, about the world of material culture in this century confirmed my conviction that gender lay at the heart of an understanding of why things are as they are and that we are as we are, to a significant extent, as a result of the gendered material world that we encounter and negociate every day. This is the subject of my book. In conceiving, researching and writing it I must thank an enormous number of people. Above all, my colleagues on the joint Royal College of Art and Victoria and Albert Museum History of Design MA course over the last decade – Gillian Naylor, Christopher Frayling, Charles Saumarez-Smith, John Styles, Paul Greenhalgh, Jeremy Aynsley and Christopher Breward – have provided a vital forum for discussion which has been enormously stimulating and has given me an opportunity to test many of my ideas; students on the course over the same period have reinforced this environment, several among them – Claire Catterall, Kathy Hogan, Vicky Reed, Alison Clarke, Margaret Ponsonby, Scott Oram, Rebecca Preston, Alison Harry, Susie McKellar, David Attwood, Lisa Hurst and others – having themselves contributed significant pieces of useful and original research to this area; visiting speakers to the course over the years — among them Christine Battersby, Ben Fine, James Obelkevich, Mica Nava, Rachel Bowlby, Christine Morley, Bill Lancaster, Frank Mort, Julia Porter, Amanda Vickery, Nick Barker, Daniel Miller, Pat Ayres, Sonia Bowlby, Tim Putnam, Nancy Troy, Sonia Livingstone and Tim Breen – have all served as tremendous sources of inspiration. I am also indebted to the pioneering work undertaken by 'feminist' design historians, among them Pat Kirkham, Judy Attfield,

Cheryl Buckley, Anthea Callen, Suzette Worden, Lee Wright and Angela Partington, who have opened my eyes to so many issues in this complex area. The work of Alison Light and Carolyn Steedman has also been immensely helpful in demonstrating that the academic and the personal need not reside in two different universes. That the Royal College of Art gave me a term free from teaching made it possible for me to finally write the book, for which I thank those concerned as well as those colleagues who took on an extra workload as a result. I would also like to thank the secretaries in the department of Humanities at the RCA, Barbara Berry and Gill Plummer, who ensured that I was not interrupted too much while the writing was in progress.

The book would not have appeared at all had it not been for the unfailing enthusiasm and support of Jane Bradish—Ellames and of Sara Dunn and the production team at Pandora. On a more personal front – and, after all, this is in many ways a very personal book, I have to thank numerous friends and members of my family, especially my husband John, with whom I have debated many of the ideas contained here and without whose patience and help the hours to write it could not have been found. Above all, I thank my three daughters, Molly, Nancy and Celia who, although little, were also understanding and supportive. After all, it was their Barbie dolls, their love of gilt and glitter, and their inexplicable but nonetheless unquenchable thirst for the stereotypically feminine that finally spurred me to put pen to paper, armed with the firm conviction that feminine culture can be fun.

The Architect's Wife

'It is evident that women's "character" – her convictions her values, her wisdom, her tastes, her behaviour – are to be explained by her situation.

– Simone de Beauvoir[1]

Sometimes what seem like the most trivial of tragedies are the most poignant. In Nicholas Barker's television series, *Signs of the Times* (1992), television cameras entered 'ordinary' people's living spaces and asked them to talk about their lives. One woman, married to an architect for whom white walls, minimal decor and Venetian blinds were de rigueur, explained how she sometimes went into the children's bedroom – the only room in which curtains were 'permitted' – and softly wept. A middle-class woman shedding tears for curtains in her domestic space may seem absurd in today's society in which tragedies of enormous global and personal significance are beamed into our living-rooms. And yet it was a televisual moment which moved a considerable number of people, especially women. It hit a nerve.

Signs of the Times focused on the concept of 'taste', that highly personal, and yet collectively negotiated agent of aesthetic discrimination which is 'at work' continually, influencing the food we eat, the music we listen to, the books we read, the way we adorn ourselves and the manner in which we modify the physical spaces we inhabit. Through the objects and styles which represent it, taste communicates complex messages about our values, our aspirations, our beliefs and our identities. Deprived of the curtains she so desperately wanted, the architect's wife was being denied the right to form, and to

This ornate curtain arrangement, in conjunction with the ornamental use of bric-a-brac and flowers on the window-sill, is a visible reminder of the continued presence of the nineteenth-century domestic aesthetic ideal, which prioritised comfort and display, in so many of today's homes. (Photograph by Martin Parr. Magnum Photos Limited)

express, her own identity. Indeed, her sorrow was, perhaps, less trivial than it seemed, compounded by the fact that this was clearly a 'woman's problem', part of that relentless oppression that has been women's lot for so long. On one level, the story of women in this century can be recounted as a list of achievements in gaining some kinds of equality with men; on another, there are still many areas of women's lives in which inequalities and marginality still cause daily grief and feelings of powerlessness.

One of these areas, I would argue, is that of the aesthetic dimension of women's everyday lives. Stereotypically 'women's tastes' still stand outside the 'true' canon of aesthetic values of the dominant culture, this in spite of the fact that many women would be quick to disassociate themselves from those tastes -characterised as they so often are by gilt and glitter, soft pastel colours, rich textures, 'frilly' decorative effects, and a general sense of 'cosiness' – claiming that they have learnt to understand 'good taste', why Venetian blinds are more 'culturally advanced' than curtains. With remorse, I recall my own feelings of irritation with my mother's insistence on covering every available surface in her living-room with glass ornaments. While I continued to give her such bibelots at Christmas and birthdays, knowing that they would please and delight her, I found even the process of wrapping them up distasteful.

Educated in the neo-modernist climate of the '60s, and geared to believe that being equal to men meant being the same as them, my world and my value-system were far removed from my mother's. Hers had been formed within a tradition of 'feminine domesticity' which reached back to the Victorian era. Her glass ornaments carefully positioned on top of the television, the mantelpiece and the pelmets were the direct descendants of the 'knick-knacks' that embellished many a Victorian middle-class lady's parlour. What's more, they carried with them strong traces of the meanings of those earlier decorative items. The extensive draperies, padded chairs, naturalistic patterns, and cluttered surfaces of the Victorian parlour, combining comfort with display, had their ornamental and symbolic equivalents in the 1950s living-room. And like them, they were perceived by mainstream masculine culture as trivial, tasteless and even dangerous.

However, there was one crucial difference between the 1850s and the 1950s. The Victorian domestic world had been valued as a complement to the masculine world of work and the key to social, economic, cultural and moral stability; a hundred years later, it had lost both its cultural kudos and its moral authority. By the 1950s, domesticity had become a more marginal, private phenomenon, and domestic tasks – the exercising of taste being one among many – occupied a lowly position within the hierarchy of things. My mother's bibelots were a testimony, both in my aspiring eyes and to society and culture at large, to the degraded status of home-making in general, and of feminine taste in particular.

Between 1850 and 1950 domesticity, and along with it 'feminine taste', was displayed from the centre of things by modernity and its cultural ambassador, modernism. By the second half of the nineteenth century, the enormous transformations – social, demographic, economic, aesthetic and psychological – that constituted the onslaught of modernity carried tremendous influence in Britain and the USA. Its effects, however, were assimilated differently by men and women. The 'separation of the spheres'[2] relegated women to the world of domesticity, and all that went with life in that emotionally charged environment, dominated by morality, social aspiration, the exercise of taste and display, and kept men in the much more 'rational' world of work, progress, technology and utility. This dramatic physical and psychological separation of men from women led, inevitably, to the emergence of a set of polarised value systems and ways of relating to the world. The masculine experience of modernity dominated and eclipsed its feminine equivalent, rendering the latter marginal and trivial. Taste, not surprisingly, was relegated to the feminine sphere where it became the primary means through which women negotiated that private, 'alternative' face of modernity that touched and transformed their lives.

Women's experience of modernity was indubitably different from that of men. The literary historian, Alison Light, has suggested that it was represented by such seemingly minor and 'invisible' innovations as that of the disposable sanitary napkin[3] rather than by the much more visible public advances in the fields of industrialisation, communications and transportation. Entering into and assimilating modernity was also, for women, a much more gradual experience for one of their duties in the era of modernisation was to act as guardians of the past, maintaining a sense of continuity by keeping one foot in the pre-industrial world. In this way they provided an anchor to ensure that modernity was encountered with a set of values that was both tried and tested. The inevitable conservatism that accompanied that role created an 'archaic' version of modernity which became associated exclusively with women for well over a century. Stereotypically, their role was perceived as one of applying the brakes to the technological frenzy of male progress, earning them a reputation for being reactionary and anti-progressive. Indeed, it wasn't until the years following the Second World War that the feminine world of domesticity became modernised in a significant way, finally giving women the possibility of encountering modernity on their own terms. By that time, architectural and design modernism – the material cultural representatives of masculine modernity – had been 'softened' by the femininising force of the commercial marketplace. The radical message of modernism was already wearing thin and its appropriation by women proved too much for it. The monolith began to crumble and a new 'post-modern' set of cultural possibilities began to rise to the surface, holding out a hand to women and their culture of conservatism.

Nowhere has this conservatism been more visible than in the home, that bastion of reactionary values. Indeed, the idea that 'woman's place is in the home' has dominated discussions about feminine culture and provided a focus for many of feminism's key texts in the last few decades, albeit with different explanations attached to it. For Betty Friedan, for instance, author of one of 'second wave' feminism's key texts, *The Feminine Mystique*, domesticity resulted in the 'problem without a name',[4] a form of indescribable psychological angst which hovered over the suburban housewife, cut off from the community and the world at large. Sheila Rowbotham, on the other hand, judged domestic labour a form of exploitation, blaming society for believing that 'because housework does not fit into the prevailing notions of work it mysteriously becomes not work at all'.[5] For her, the problem was less psychological in nature than economic: housewives were expected to be unpaid labourers and society remained determined to view housewifery as a form of leisure activity.

Many supporters of the women's movement of the 1970s shared the belief that women's domestification whether essentially psychological or material in nature was the key to women's oppression and inequality. 'A growing mass of evidence,' Anne Oakley proclaimed, 'points to the conclusion that progress towards sex equality is hampered by women's domestic responsibilities, even when legal and other institutional barriers have been removed.'[6]

Although domesticity was unanimously declared the oppressor, there was little discussion about the reasons why it had become such a dominant cultural force. Nor were there many attempts to unpack the subtle and various ways in which it had impregnated, and continued to impregnate, women with a set of values and attitudes which informed a complete way of life, influencing their outlooks, their aspirations and their expectations. Women simply could not throw off the shroud of 'femininity' and enter the so-called 'liberated' world of men. The complex workings of the domestic ideal could not, and indeed still cannot, be overturned with the simple relegation of duster to the dustbin or the purchase of a business suit.

Recent writings on gender have moved beyond this earlier femininist stance and have begun to explore the subtle ways in which stereotypical notions of femininity and masculinity have been constructed and linger on in our cultural system, subliminally influencing our daily lives.[7] The concept of the home has once again been highlighted, this time as a key factor in the formation of the stereotypical idea of femininity that has dominated cultural life in this century. By prioritising certain values over others, the domestic ideal, and all that goes with it, has had a crucial influence upon the ways in which women have formed relationships with the world around them. Those relationships have been endlessly examined by sociologists, psychologists and psychoanalysts, keen to find out why women think and behave in the ways they do, but less attention has been given to the cultural forces which have helped to form the idea of femininity.

Central to that cultural dimension, but largely ignored, is the aesthetic arena of women's lives. Since industrialisation this arena has been largely constituted by the taste and consumption decisions which have determined the nature and appearance of the home and its contents. And these decisions have, for the most part, been made by women. Choosing one wallpaper rather than another is a complex activity, influenced by a number of factors, not least among them the role that the consumer believes she should be performing and the values that she wishes to express. As ideals are translated into forms, they are transformed into the material backcloths of our lives which, in turn, play a part in helping to reinvigorate, substantiate and indeed to construct those same ideals. This circular process is central to an understanding of the way in which material culture – the objects and environments which surround us – intersects with culture in general. While the material and aesthetic culture of the home is both a mirror and an embodiment of the values underpinning the ideal of feminine domesticity, that ideal also plays an active role in forming and reinforcing those values. Women's taste, and the decisions they take are key in the process of selecting objects for the home. And in making that selection, women are also constantly choosing – whether consciously or unconsciously – either to accept, or to reject, stereotypical constructions of femininity. Over the last century and a half that choice has played a part, however minor, within the wider context of sexual politics.

In the early years of the last century, with the production of domestic goods taking place increasingly outside the home, the parallel expansion of consumption extended the influence of feminine taste into the public realm and gave it an obvious and key role within economic life. This has compounded the problem of women's cultural inferiority and the marginalisation of their tastes: not only has their reactionary domestic culture come under repeated attack from influential taste-makers and design reformers over the last 150 years, the notion of consumption has also provided a sitting target for many cultural critics in this century. Patriarchal culture has scoffed at women's curtains and devalued the activity of going out to buy them.

Very little scholarly writing on consumption has addressed the question of feminine taste, or seen it as part of the broader discussion about sexual politics. Until recently cultural theorists have tended to view consumption as a form of manipulation, the commodity out to trap the unsuspecting consumer.[8] The only alternative to this essentially negative account of consumption has been that of anthropologists who have studied it as a form of social ritual, a means of achieving social cohesion.[9] However, their accounts, like those of their fellow social scientists, have underplayed the role of gender.[10] A number of social, economic and cultural historians have addressed feminine consumption as it emerged in the late-nineteenth century with the growth of department stores and mass retailing.[11] While some have perpetuated the idea that women's role in this was entirely passive, others have offered a more positive view of feminine taste, seeing it as operating outside the value judgements imposed on it by masculine culture. The evocation in these writings of the sensations of pleasure and aesthetic delight go some way towards an understanding of consumption in specifically feminine terms. While these accounts have emphasised the physical and aesthetic sites of consumption and their role in stimulating a response from consumers – a response rooted in the values of the domestic sphere – they have stopped short of a description of goods themselves as objects of feminine taste. This book takes those objects as its starting point. It bases its argument on the assumption that they alone – the curtains and the glass ornaments – have represented and embodied masculine and feminine values in action – that is, the dynamic tension between gendered values as they have moved through the cycle of production, consumption and use. Only objects experience that cycle in its entirety and only they cross the bridge between the separate spheres.

Like people, objects have lives and their meanings change in response to the different contexts within which they are found. At the same time, they carry their accrued meanings to each new context, transforming and enriching it in the process. While many scholars have tried to break the codes of objects, few have grasped the importance of the object's life span.[12] Only the British cultural theorist, Dick Hebdige, in his analysis of the Italian Vespa motor-scooter,[13] which moved from being a mainstream mass cultural object in one country to a subcultural icon in another, has made fully explicit the importance of recontextualisation in decoding objects.[14] In focusing on an object which was consumed by a predominantly male subculture, however, Hebdige side-stepped the vital question of gender raised by the vast number of goods within main-stream mass culture which are designed and made by men in a masculine cultural setting and consumed and used by women in a feminine context. The gender relationships within mass-produced goods are complex. Within sexual politics objects have a clear role to play: like barometers, they measure the extent to which masculine values dominate culture at any one time, and feminine culture's resistance. They also reflect the way in which masculine and feminine values meet at the inter-section between production and consumption, negotiating the power relationships between them.

Interestingly, the moments of feminine 'resistance', as represented by the objects of mass production and mass consumption, have not kept in step with radical feminist action in this century. At moments of feminist achievement – the 1920s, for example – objects were often at their most mascu-line while at moments of feminist inactivity – the 1950s come to mind – many objects were extremely feminine. This can be explained by the fact that mass-produced objects, which repre-sent and embody stereotypical notions of femininity, have tended to be seen by radical feminists as oppressive construc-tions of patriarchal culture from which, they believe, women should free themselves if they want to achieve equali-ty with men. The evidence from objects suggests, however, that the relationship between women and gendered goods is more complex and ambiguous than this, and that it can be seen to have liberated women as much as it has oppressed them. Any account of the relationship between gender and taste has to take place on the level of the stereotypical, rather than the actual, attributes of the two sexes. Within the epochs of modernity and postmodernity gender identity has been estab-lished to a significant extent through negotiations with the stereotypes that have been presented through the mass media. They play, therefore, a key role in the construction of gender. Within the context of feminine domesticity, stereotypical images of women and of the home were conflated and turned into a single ideal. In response to that ideal women have formed their own individual and collective identities. By incorporating, in material form, the stereotypical attributes of femininity and domesticity, objects of consumption have also played an important part in the cultural construction of gender. Through the exercise of their tastes women have selected and arranged objects in their domestic settings and in doing so have both formed and reinforced their own gender identities.

The question of how mass-produced objects are imbued with stereotypically gendered attributes is, of course, central to this discussion. Once industrialisation had removed much 'making' from the home, and standardised factory production had come to dominate the manufacture of individual items for specific customers, large numbers of goods had to be 'designed' for customers whose individual characteristics were unknown to their makers. The nineteenth-century designers and manu-facturers of goods destined for the domestic sphere worked with an image of the customer, usually female, firmly in their minds, catering, as closely as possible, for her psychological, symbolic and aesthetic needs. Conscious that fashion, novelty and comfort were general requirements, they translated those concepts as faithfully as they could into goods. In doing so, they aligned the concept of design, as it functioned within production, directly with that of taste, as it operated in the arena of consumption. While the spheres of production and consumption were clearly gendered, the aesthetic values of goods on the marketplace reflected the primacy of the latter. The shift from a world in which the female consumer played a central role to one in which rationally conceived, standardised mass production began to dictate a new aesthetic and role for the domestic object came with the marriage of technological and economic modernity to cultural modernism. Motivated and justified by a commitment to democratic ideals, architectural and design modernism imposed on goods and their design a stereotypically masculine aesthetic, not only because it was undertaken by men but because it was now embedded within masculine culture. Thus taste was super-ceded by design which, in turn, set out to remove all aesthetic autonomy and authority from the hands of women.

The terms of the struggle, which still goes on today, as the architect's wife knows to her cost, were not simply those of the aesthetic characteristics of objects – their shape, colour and decoration – but the ways in which the two sexes used and related to objects in their everyday lives. With the separation of the spheres came a split between the realms of aesthetics and utility: within the feminine sphere objects became, first and foremost, symbols, sacrificing their utilitarian features to their symbolic functions. Thus, while a chair remained an object for sitting in, its primary function within the domestic context was not only to represent, but also to embody in a material manner, the idea of comfort.[15] In sharp contrast, within the masculine sphere, objects were defined increasingly as tools. In its attempt to assert the pre-eminence of masculine culture, and the role of objects as its representatives, architectural and design modernism set out to rid them of their feminine content. It achieved this by removing them from the contexts for which they were intended, and by defining them instead in terms of their internal properties. Thus a modernist chair became an exercise in an examination of 'chairness' which did not take into account, and indeed forcibly set out to deny, the role of that object within the feminine, domestic context of comfort and display. Such was the power of feminine culture, however, allied to that of the marketplace within which it found a home, that the aesthetic role of the object survived and the modernist 'style' became, by the middle of this century, a familiar characteristic of the everyday environment. In turn, masculine culture embarked on a campaign intent upon devaluing and trivialising what it saw as an unacceptable 'feminisation' of modernist ideals.

While on one level the links between women, commerce and the marketplace succeeded in pulling mass-produced objects away from the exclusive control of masculine culture, on the other, they reinforced the marginalisation of feminine taste. Defined as part of mass culture, it suffered the fate of other cultural manifestations of the mass media, such as romantic novels and TV soaps, generally perceived as trivial and potentially damaging because of their sentimentality and lack of sophistication. Like them, the objects of feminine taste have, in this century, have frequently been deemed inferior to those of high culture. The material culture of feminine domesticity – expressed by such reputedly 'vulgar' items as coal-effect fires, chintzy fabrics and potted plants – has frequently been singled out for condemnation or, at best, sarcasm, termed as 'bad taste' or 'kitsch'. The aesthetic and ideological opposition to modernism demonstrated by these objects served to divorce them from the world of 'legitimate' culture and its 'good taste'.

By the early years of this century, the concept of taste, once whole and feminine, was no longer a unified one. The split into 'good taste' and 'bad taste' was the result of a male-directed moral crusade which began with the mid-nineteenth century design reform movement and which moved into modernist architectural and design theory as well as modern cultural criticism. It was, in reality, little more than a thinly-disguised attempt by masculine culture to set the cultural terms of reference for modernity such that women, with their new-found power as consumers, would not take over the reins. Surprised and threatened by women's suddenly increased authority in the marketplace, masculine culture attempted to redress the balance of gender power by condemning and devaluing the alliance between aesthetic, commercial and feminine culture. In its place they posited a high cultural model which aligned itself with universal values and the pure logic of function. In his insistence on Venetian blinds rather than curtains, the architect in *Signs of the Times* was perpetuating a tradition of male domination, the puritanical control of the material environment begun over a century and half earlier. His wife did have something to cry about after all.

PART ONE

Feminine Taste and Design Reform, 1830 – 1890

CHAPTER ONE

'An Institution of God Himself':

The Domestic Ideal

'Her sphere is in the household, which she should "beautify"
and of which she should be the "chief ornament."'
　　　　　　　　　　　　　　　　　　　– Thorstein Veblen[1]

T he stereotypical idea of 'feminine taste' that still
pervades our western, industrialised culture – that
trivialised set of aesthetic preferences that we all asso-
ciate with frills and furbelows, 'unnecessary' display and
ornamentation, and an 'excess' of gilt and glitter – has its roots
in the last century. More specifically, it has its foundations in
the period when the concepts of 'woman' and 'domesticity'
became, effectively, one and the same, and when a notion of
'feminine taste' embedded in domesticity extended its influence to the activity of 'consuming'. The emergence of that
notion was rooted in the particular combination of circumstances – economic, technological, social, cultural and political
– which brought about the Industrial Revolution (in reality, a
slow process which took place in Britain between the late-
seventeenth century and the late-nineteenth century, and a
little later in the USA). In addition to transforming the means
of production and the lives of most people, it also produced a
new image of femininity, within which taste, linked to domesticity and consumption, played a new and fundamental role.
At this time feminine taste was seen as a necessary, and indeed indispensible, component of economic, religious, social,
cultural and political life. Far from being trivial, marginal and
undervalued, it was rooted in the very structures that enabled

that society to function as it did. Its subsequent destiny as the butt of so much criticism was a result of gender tensions within Victorian society which led to the subsequent marginalisation of women from mainstream cultural life.

The art historian, Rozsika Parker has claimed that 'twentieth-century concepts of femininity are still deeply embued with Victorianism'.[2] Our contemporary image of domesticity is also rooted in the Victorian era. The indissoluble link between the concepts of femininity, beauty and the home has never been stronger than it was in the middle years of the nineteenth century. Thorstein Veblen's belief that woman's place was in the home, not only as the chief 'home-maker' but also as an aesthetic component of the environment – part, indeed, of the display itself – reflected that century's linked ideals. This idea has been echoed by many writers: historians Leonore Davidoff and Catherine Hall explained that 'they (women) were themselves the ultimate expression of taste, for beauty was best expressed in the female form',[3] while the art historian, Debora Silverman, has described women as being 'elaborated with and as the elaborators of beauty'.[4] The notion that woman's role was that of a 'beautifier', not only by her actions but by her very presence, demonstrated a belief in the metaphorical transference of feminine attributes from woman herself to the home and its objects. A chandelier could, as a consequence, be described as 'delicate',[5] an epithet long associated with femininity and the female body. Needless to say, for the Victorians, these feminine attributes were considered to be 'natural' features of the female sex, a result of her essential biological and physical characteristics. Beauty, it was generally agreed, was a fundamental attribute of women and, therefore, women, rather than men, were ideally qualified to inject it into the domestic setting. 'Women', according to Davidoff and Hall, 'would be the purveyors of taste'.[6] Deep-rooted ideological structures were being translated into the world of things, and in the translation, taste had a crucial part to play.

The idea that women was the personification of beauty in the home, and the chief beautifier of the domestic environment, lay at the heart of what has been called the 'Cult of Domesticity', a phenomenon which dominated British and

American cultural life in the mid- to late -nineteenth century. It was rooted in the desire of the mid-Victorian middle-class family to establish an escape route for itself from the ever-present world of commerce and the harsh realities of the marketplace. In this period of relentless industrialisation and rapid urbanisation the demands of commercial life were becoming increasingly stressful for society's middle class, threatening to undermine other aspects of existence. 'Home,' explained Davidoff and Hall, '(was) the basis of a new moral order in an immoral world of the market'.[7] The Cult of Domesticity resided at the intersection of religious belief, politics, commercial activity and family life, serving to bring together all these facets of existence by making the family, and within it the idealized image of woman, a vital component not only of the moral community but also of successful business practice and national prestige. 'The idealized position of women was a central theme in nationalistic claims to English superiority advanced by radicals and conservatives alike,' wrote Davidoff and Hall.[8]

A similar situation existed in the USA where, by the mid century, the Cult of Domesticity had had the same impact. There, however, its expression was overtly political, demonstrated by the boycotting of British-made goods before the American revolution and, later, in the role of the domestic sphere in socializing citizens.[9] What has been called 'Romantic Evangelism'[10] was also linked to the home, thereby intensifying its role as a highly significant institution. The political, religious, emotional and social roles that were associated with the American home in the early nineteenth century benefitted women enormously, enabling them to operate in the public as well as in the private sphere, and making possible the emergence of what came to be called 'domestic feminism', a phenomenon which has been described by the historian Glenna Matthews as

a vital part of the American political landscape for decades. Arising in the antebellum period because the valorizarion of home gave women a powerful new tool for legitimating their claims to cultural influence, it succeeded so well that it generated what can only be called a backlash among male authors in the late-nineteenth century. These attacks notwithstanding women continued to use the home to serve their political purposes until well into the twentieth century.[11]

While in the United States the home became an overt site for sexual politics, this was less evident in Great Britain where fewer claims were made for the public significance of the private sphere. Nevertheless, the centrality of domesticity to political and national life in both Britain and the USA served to raise it, in this period, beyond the level of the local, the mundane and the trivial to which it was later consigned.

On a local level the home also served to persuade and reassure other members of the middle-class community of a family's level of gentility and respectability. It was the chief bearer of middle-class status, a social rank which was becoming increa-singly significant in Britain in the early years of the century and a little later in the USA. According to the historian John Brewer, '1 million out of a population of 7 million in eighteenth-century England [could] be described as of the 'middling sort'.[12] By the early nineteenth century, however, Catherine Hall suggests that '20–25 per cent of the total population . . . [were] middle-class'.[13] This was a world

peopled with farmers, merchants, manufacturers, tradesmen and professionals. Their fortunes rested on either the manufacture and sale of an immense variety of material goods – from Derbyshire stockings to Birmingham candlesticks, from Gloucestershire cheeses to Suffolk lawnmowers, from Yorkshire woollens to Kidderminster carpets; or the production and sale of material and cultural services – the clergyman tending the spiritual welfare of his flock, the dentist caring for their teeth, the physician and the surgeon their health, the lawyer their property, the architect their buildings, the novelist and poet their imaginative fare, the essayist their moral and political diet.[14]

The fluid nature of society at this time meant that many people were acquiring new middle-class identities and needed visible displays of their new status: the domestic sphere provided the ideal opportunity. The demands of this complex social ritual were, however, often at odds with the moral dictates of society which required the middle-class family to demonstrate the qualities of thrift and modesty in their daily affairs. It was the role of the housewife to ease the tensions that were created by these conflicting demands and to create a domestic setting which fulfilled both requirements simultaneously. The mid-Victorian, middle-class home was a highly feminized phenomenon: within its walls women had a major responsibility both to ensure that it was an appropriate moral milieu for the family and that it displayed the 'proper' sense of taste. This is not to say that the domestic ideal was solely a middle-class affair. In spite of the fact that working-class women (and indeed single middle-class women) were more likely to participate in the wage economy at this time – many of them working in the textile factories, for example – the cultural ideal of domesticity penetrated their world as well. Despite industrialization creating ever new wage-earning opportunities away from the household for these women, traditional family relationships remained and the wife's domestic responsibilities were in no way diminished.[15] The sexual division of labour continued to assign to her the management of household matters. The idea of doubling household duties with work outside the home existed only for working-class women. Within middle-class homes it became increasingly the norm throughout the 1830s, 40s and 50s for wives to devote themselves exclusively to housewifery and to keep well away from paid work. To engage in such labour would have undermined their position in society.

At this time large numbers of middle-class families in London and the provinces moved their homes out of the city centres into the new suburbs in order to create a physical space between work and home and to protect the domestic arena from the potential contamination of commercial life. Sociologist Janet Wolff has described the Manchester suburb, Victoria Park, in this period, pointing out that women were committed to life in the home

Thirty-five ... large houses were constructed in Victoria Park between 1837 and 1845 ... James Kershaw, one of the earliest residents of Victoria Park (he lived there from 1838 to 1859) [was] typical of those setting up their homes there. He was a partner in the calico-painting firm of Leese, Callender and Co., having started life as a warehouse lad. He was a member of the Council of the League, an Alderman from 1838 to 1850, Mayor in 1842–3, and MP for Stockport from 1847 to 1859. Interestingly . . . before moving out of the centre of Manchester, Kershaw had lived in Great Ancoats Street, where his wife carried on a business as a linen draper . . . She certainly did not . . . [continue her occupation] from the new address, and it is most unlikely that she travelled into town. Although the extent of surburbanization should not be over-estimated (many middle-class families remained in the more central urban areas), where it did occur, the move to the suburbs entailed a clear separation of home and work, and a firm basis for the ideology of the home as haven, and of women as identified with this private sphere.[16]

Wolff's account is one among several focusing on the suburbanization of the English middle classes in this period.[17] Davidoff and Hall have provided equally detailed information about the inhabitants of Edgbaston, a suburb of Birmingham, profiling the life of a certain 'James Luckcock of Birmingham . . . a radical Birmingham Jeweller'.[18] Having risen through the ranks of the jewellery trade and become a manager, Luckcock was able to purchase property in Edgbaston and to move there with his family in 1820. He described the pleasure and fulfilment that came with that move, 'I have all my heart could wish. The house and garden planned by myself, the situation picturesque, secluded and charming; the aspect, a southern slope; the soil deep and highly productive; and the whole plantation rapidly rising to beauty and perfection.'[19] The stress on the importance of beauty as a quality of this haven was marked, as was the high level of idealism attached to his move. There are significant differences between Luckcock's masculine world and that of his wife which was characterised by her anonymity and 'domestic obscurity'. Like Mrs Kershaw she too had 'worked briefly in the family enterprise, but when circumstances permitted, retired to the home'.[20]

Although the significance of the home and all that went on

in it touched the public world of politics and commerce, its everyday reality revolved around the private world of the family. It functioned simultaneously as a sanctuary for the husband and as an arena for the moral education of the children, for social life, and for establishing status. The gendered split between the worlds of the private and the public lay at the heart of the gendering of taste. With the demise of the small, family-based, production unit, a widespread form of manufacturing before the advent of the factory, women became less and less involved with the process of production and increasingly involved with the activity of consumption.

The rural cottage industries of the pre-industrial eighteenth-century, among them wool and cotton weaving, had been family units, centres both of production and consumption. The household had been the locus of work and the family's residence. In the urban setting and on the farm the married couple had often worked together and, while there had been, as elsewhere, a clearly defined sexual division of labour, women had also played an important productive role in such activities as spinning, sewing, lace-making and straw plaiting.[21]

The pre-industrial American home had also been a production unit, albeit once again, with sexually defined tasks within it. As the historian of technology, Ruth Schwarz Cowan, has explained,

the division of labor by sex in household work seems to have no rhyme or reason to it, but it was unquestionably a real fact of social existence before industrialisation, just as it is today. Men made cider and mead; women made beer, ale and wine . . . women mended clothing that was made out of cloth, but men mended clothing . . . that was made out of leather. Women had some tasks with which they filled the interstices of their days (sewing, spinning), but so did men (chopping wood and whittling).[22]

Some historians have delved back many centuries in attempts to show that a woman's role in pre-industrial times had been less separate from, and more equal to men's. Alice Clark, writing in 1919, has claimed that 'the transition to capitalism . . . disenfranchised women of their medieval and early modern equality' and that while

> under modern conditions, the ordinary domestic occupations of English women consist in tending babies, and young children . . . in preparing household meals, and in keeping the house clean . . . in the seventeenth century it [the domestic role] embraced a much wider range of production; for brewing, dairy-work, the care of poultry and pigs, the production of vegetables and fruit, spinning flax and wool, nursing and doctoring, all formed part of domestic industry.[23]

In the early nineteenth century laws affecting the employment of young children in work outside the home changed the responsibilities of the housewife. And with the introduction of large machinery into textile manufacture and the building of factories to house them, women, hitherto involved in the production of textiles, could not easily combine childcare with work outside the home. These practical exigencies, combined with ideological ones, nurtured the conviction that it was unthinkable for women to enter the public sphere. This extended beyond the idea of work itself to their exclusion from coffee houses and other public and social places.

Within certain feminist texts about the separate spheres there is an implicit suggestion of a pre-industrial golden age when men and women worked and lived in harmony with each other. Much has been written in support of, and in opposition to, this idea. Some writers have claimed, for example, that women had been destined to life in the domestic sphere from as long ago as Ancient Greece and that industrialisation did not bring about an abrupt change. There has also been much debate about whether or not domestic life was necessarily oppressive for women.[24] Consensus reigns, however, over the view that the nineteenth-century Cult of Domesticity was a gendered ideology and that the creator of domesticity was female. The concept of the 'separate spheres' – at least as an ideal if not as an all-pervasive reality – is central to an analysis of women's experience at this time. Where the question of taste is concerned the separation of the private from the public, and the emergence of two distinct ideological systems, was fundamental. Women's essentially private sphere was characterised by its involvement with the life of the emotions; their lives defined by their role in creating social status; their responsibility for the creation of a moral framework for the family and for ensuring the appropriate level of gentility and respectability. Above all, they were defined by their roles as guardians of the aesthetic dimension of life. Men occupied a parallel universe defined by a commitment to work, rationality, utility and universal values.

These stereotypically gendered characteristics and values were not new, of course, but, in this particular cultural setting and with the physical separation of men and women, they took on a new and heightened significance. For the Victorians, this division was considered a result of 'natural' causes. A belief in men's and women's different natures, rooted in their biology, lay behind the Victorian sexual division of labour. Later in the century Thorstein Veblen was to elucidate these differences:

The sexes differ, not only in stature and muscular force, but perhaps even more decisively in temperament, and this must early have given rise to a corresponding division of labor. The general range of activities that come under the head of exploit falls to the males as being the stouter, more massive, better capable of a sudden and violent strain, and more readily inclined to self-assertion, active emulation and aggression.[25]

His account was informed by Darwinian evolutionary theory which had become very influential by the end of the century, premised as it was on the idea that women were further down the evolutionary chain than men. This was widely promoted in the second half of the century by those who believed that women needed to conserve all their energies for the task of reproduction. The idea of essential, biological sexual difference also underpinned comments about the effect on women of work outside the home. Friedrich Engels, for example, believed that it 'unsexes the man and takes from the women all womanliness'.[26]

The cultural division of public from private did not mean, of course, that women were the sole inhabitors of the private sphere; men and children spent much of their time there as well. But within the house itself there were gendered spaces. The architectural historian Marc Girouard has shown how this operated in the aristocratic and upper-middle-class home:

As well as an extremely complex and often impractical arrangement of rooms, so that children, servants, mothers, and fathers should only coincide at approved times and in approved places, Victorian houses also contained 'an increasingly large and sacrosanct' male domain, whose nucleus was the billiard room. The domain often expanded to include the smoking room and the gun room, and sometimes adjoining dressing room and study.[27]

In the suburban home the dining-room was considered the husband's domain while the parlour, or drawing-room, and the bedroom (the equivalent of the aristocratic boudoir) were considered part of the woman's sphere, the former for formal social occasions and the latter for privacy and for more intimate meetings with female members of the family and close friends.

Middle-class Victorian women's values were formed, therefore, largely as a result of their domestic roles and expectations. The moral and practical exigencies of their duties brought with them a set of behaviours and attitudes which

Robert Tait. 'A Chelsea Interior'. 1857. In this depiction of Thomas Carlyle's drawing-room, his wife, seated amidst the rich, variegated patterning of the interior upholstery and decor, occupies the centre stage indicating her vital role in this domestic setting. (The National Trust Photographic Library)

characterised their everyday lives. Much of this was stereotypical in nature but it had no less an impact on the way women were expected to, and undoubtedly frequently did, behave. This also extended to the realm of the aesthetic. Indeed, in the middle of the last century the moral and the aesthetic were seen to be inextricably linked. The 'good' was also the 'beautiful' and woman, the embodiment of beauty, was also the personification of morality, responsible for the moral dimension of family life.

Unlike morality, which was expressed in behaviour, beauty found a direct material form in the objects and arrangements which made up the domestic interior. It was contained and expressed in the way in which middle-class Victorian women chose objects and arranged them within their homes. The values held by women became transformed, through the exercise of visual discrimination, or 'taste' decisions, into domestic environments which were both mirrors and embodiments of those values and sustainers of the status quo. The domestic values which dominated this stereotypical picture of middle-class Victorian life were complex in nature. We have already seen how moral exigencies could mitigate against the demands of social display, but these were not the only conflicting forces influencing a Victorian 'angel in the house' when she came to exercise her taste. Above all else, she had to make her home a sanctuary from the outside world. In physical and psychological terms this meant that she had to provide a comfortable environment which did not threaten or create dis-ease of any kind. The equally important requirement of the mid-Victorian housewife – that of demonstrating that she was in tune with the latest fashion – could, in certain circumstances, however, cut across the provision of comfort. Through its unfamiliarity, 'newness' could sometimes induce psychological discomfort; the housewife had to ease this tension and ensure that the goods and decorations she brought into her house did not create disturbances of any kind. Conflicting demands meant that difficult decisions had to be made. Exercising taste and consuming, or organising the consumption of, goods undoubtedly took up a great deal of time and energy. As a consequence, the widely held belief in the idle, leisured Victorian wife was more myth than reality.[28]

Most documenters of the Cult of Domesticity have ignored the way in which it manifested itself materially and aesthetically. Davidoff and Hall devote a chapter to 'the creation of the middle-class home' in which they outline the importance of the garden to the suburban villa, and make general observations about the appearance of the domestic interior:

by the 1830s, a range of modifications and additions had unquestionably added both comfort and gentility. The nineteenth-century taste
which favoured lightness and space was giving way to the heavy
upholstered cluttered effect of the mid and late Victorians. Cowper's
sparse domesticity, the sofa, shutters and tea urn, had now
burgeoned with carpets, curtains, redesigned grates, mahogany
furniture, wallpaper, chintz covers and bedsteads.[29]

But theirs is little more than an impressionistic account and
fails to explain the reasons for the change in taste that they
describe. They ignore the link between the material culture of
the home and the dominant ideology at work at the time.

Understanding the dynamic, two-way relationship between
the Cult of Domesticity and the material and aesthetic culture
of domesticity necessitates looking closer at objects, interiors
and styles in order to see how ideas were translated into forms
and environments.

The idea of comfort, for example, is linked with the idea of
the sanctuary and haven, suggesting safety and security. In
material terms, this was more likely to have been represented
by old, old-looking, or traditional goods, by objects which
recalled the past and the rural, rather than the future and the
urban. The idea of physical comfort could be expressed, for
instance, by cushioning, soft textures and surfaces, and soft
blends of colours, by gentle curved forms and patterns rather
than harsh, geometric ones, by visual references to the natural
world rather than to the man-made world of technology. The
language of forms, patterns and material interior environments is, and was, a subtle one. It offers a wide range of
possible selections made on the basis of taste. Taste, in turn, is
influenced by the socio-cultural and ideological context which
helps to form it. The desire to create a comfortable environment in the mid-nineteenth century would inevitably have led
the home-maker towards goods which, singly and/or collectively, spoke the language of comfort. Once consumption
became the dominant means of acquiring objects, home-makers
were largely dependent upon the availability of goods in the
marketplace to create the sanctuaries that cultural ideology
demanded of them. This, in turn, meant a dependency upon the

supply system of manufacturing, design and sales.

In order to turn effectively, the wheels of production and consumption needed oiling by a system of 'taste-formation'. The most obvious form of 'taste-making' for the middle classes at the time was that of social emulation, or, more specifically, gentry emulation. The gentry was associated with leisure and idleness and therefore with conspicuous wealth. The idea of displaying material goods as a manifestation of social status, derived most probably from the earlier aristocratic enthusiasm for collecting objects – antiques and curios – and making a showcase of them. Davidoff and Hall write that:

undoubtedly some details in housing and furnishing came from gentry emulation. For example, there are hints that visiting professional men, the local attorney calling to draw up a document and stopping for a glass of wine or the doctor attending a prestigious patient, noted and imitated the accoutrements of upper-class style. The homes of local gentry were regularly opened to a select public, providing a glimpse of taste to be followed even if it was electroplate rather than solid silver which graced middle-class sideboards.[30]

Seldom did emulation mean exact copying but resulted rather in an approximation of what was being copied. In this way the language of material goods acquired dialects which communicated, at a glance, the social standing of their owners.

In addition to gentry emulation other forms of nineteenth-century taste-making included books and periodicals written to tell middle-class women how to behave in society, and how to embellish their homes and gardens. In Great Britain *The Magazine of Domestic Economy*, first published in 1835, was joined by Mrs Peel's *Book of Household Management* (1861), *The Englishwoman's Magazine* (1852), *The Young Ladies' Treasure Book* of the early 1880s and Mrs Haweis's *Art of Housekeeping* (1889). The works of the domestic ideologues – Mrs Ellis, Harriet Martineau and Hannah More – were seminal, as were the landscape gardener and architect John Loudon's writings for home and garden.

In the USA there was a huge expansion of advice and home decorating books in the 1850s. These followed a number of earlier examples, among them Frances Parkes's *Domestic Duties* of 1829; Lydia Maria Child's *The American Frugal Housewife* of the same year and, most influential of all, Catherine Beecher's *A Treatise on Domestic Economy* of 1841. In 1869 it was republished under the new title of *The American Woman's Home* this time co-authored by her sister, Harriet Beecher Stowe, author of *Uncle Tom's Cabin*. In the same year Julia McNair Wright published *The Complete Home*. The USA also saw a spate of 'domestic novels' at this time which served to reinforce the values linked with the Cult of Domesticity; among them were Catherine Sedgwick's *Home* (1835). The periodical *Godey's Lady's Handbook*, in print from the 1830s onwards brought regular information about manners and furnishings into the American domestic sphere. The landscape architect, Andrew Downing, was America's equivalent of Loudon.

The most rapid growth in the number of advice books in Britain came in the 1860s, culminating in Charles Eastlake's highly influential *Hints on Household Taste* of 1868. At this period women were not only making choices about interior decor but also beginning to participate in it as well. Men also played a part, but in a strictly delineated role, as Davidoff and Hall suggest:

Men took an active part in setting up the home ... they often planned and maintained the garden, or at least the masculine sections of it. Men were responsible for buying certain items: wine, books, pictures, musical instruments and wheeled vehicles. They accompanied their wives to buy furniture and carpets, while both men and women painted and papered rooms. In the 1820s, a civil engineer in a West Midlands ironworks made drawings for alterations to the house, shopped with his wife for furnishings in Birmingham and carpets in Kidderminster and papered the rooms.[31]

Taste, linked primarily with consumption, was seen as a primarily passive phenomenon, contrasted with the more 'active' world of production. It could be argued, however, that it was a highly active agent complementing the few remaining 'feminine accomplishments' – such as embroidery – which still went on in the nineteenth-century home. Indeed it is arguable that consumption and home-making were *themselves* forms of feminine accomplishment and that the over-emphasis upon male production in the workplace in most social-historical accounts of this period has clouded our picture of feminine culture, thus helping to marginalise its role in nineteenth-century productive and cultural life.[32]

The role of feminine taste in sustaining mid-nineteenth century culture should not be underestimated. It played a vital role in the domestic sphere in its primary function of supporting and complementing the public world of commercial and political life. Taste – that is, the capacity not to be vulgar – was not simply a means to an end, it was also valued in and for itself, implying that a housewife had enough time on her hands, or servants to help her, to involve herself with activities of an aesthetic, not merely a utilitarian, nature. Thus taste made visible became an important social sign. The creation of a beautiful home was more important than the creation of a mere home, a site for leisure rather than labour, a mark of middle-class gentility. In a description of an American housewife's work produced by a certain Abby Diaz in 1875, 'arranging flowers' was included alongside many more practical tasks such as 'setting tables; clearing them off; keeping lamps or gas-fixtures in order; polishing stoves, knives, silverware', evidence of the significance of such seemingly 'useless' activities in domestic life at that time.[33]

As the century progressed the idea of gentility became less linked with rectitude and religious zeal and more with material display in both Britain and the USA. As a result, taste became increasingly central to a housewife's self-definition and the deployment of it in the household more fundamental to her social role and position. It had to be apparent in the material accoutrements of the home, most of which were acquired on the open marketplace. Artefacts and interiors – the 'paraphernalia of gentility' – represented, and indeed even helped to form, the domestic ideal.

CHAPTER TWO

'The Things which Surround One':
The Domestic Aesthetic

A house is a dead give-away.
– Elsie De Wolfe[1]

Taste is molded, to a very large extent, by the things which surround one, and the family taste is trained by the objects selected by the homemaker. There is, therefore, a distinct obligation in the home to set the highest standards of beauty ... Since art is involved in most of the objects which are seen and used every day, one of the great needs of the consumer is a knowledge of the principles which are fundamental to good taste.[2]

So wrote two American 'taste' advisers, Harriet and Vetta Goldstein, in 1932. Their words could have been published a century earlier as they applied equally to the mid-nineteenth-century housewife whose job it was to 'beauti-fy' the home. A century earlier, however, the term 'taste' was more likely in advice books than the elaborated 'good taste'. Used alone the word 'taste' implied the presence of 'goodness' and 'beauty'. In the mid-nineteenth century a housewife either had, or didn't have taste, and her home either did or didn't manifest this. This monolithic notion of taste was rooted in an earlier historical period when only the elite had had the means to participate in the world of taste and fashion. With the democratisation of the capacity to consume goods with which to demonstrate social status – as opposed to being judged by the number of cows in one's possession – came the need on the part of the custodians of the dominant culture to create two categories of taste – good and bad – as a form of social and cultural distinction. It was a means of distinction which, by the end of the nineteenth century, was to have overtly gendered connotations.

Within the culture of mid-Victorian, middle-class domestic femininity, ideological values were made manifest in the physical reality of the home. To a significant extent it was the design of artefacts – their forms and appearances determined during their manufacture in the public sphere – which led to this link between the ideological and the material. Within the feminine culture of domesticity there were many connections between appearances and values which provided an insight into the way people led, or rather were expected to lead, their lives.

Taste was an active agent within the consumption and disposition of goods, and within the process of domestic display. Design can be seen as a passive respondent to its demands. Adopting this perspective permits a regendering of the conventional discussion about material culture in this period and a reassertion of the importance of the feminine sphere, marginalised by an emphasis upon 'design' at the expense of 'taste'. Inevitably, however, discussions about taste and design overlap each other. In mid-Victorian Britain and America, the goods which made up the material culture of domesticity – those objects with which the housewife chose to represent her ideal image of home – were mostly made and 'designed' outside the home. Once consumed by the housewife and brought inside they were arranged and integrated into an interior setting according to her aesthetic preferences. Thus, in this context, the term consumption encapsulated the whole process of selection and use, and the concept of taste necessarily complemented that of design. Nonetheless, an analysis of the aesthetic content of the goods and interiors of the mid-century, middle-class home suggests that taste was controlling design and not vice versa.

As we have seen, many middle-class family homes, both in Britain and the USA in this period, could be found in the new suburbs. One of the main appeals lay in the large gardens which came with such houses. James Luckcock, for instance, sought a 'small comfortable house, and a good sized garden'.[3] In America, suburbs constructed from the 1870s onwards included Shaker Hills outside Cleveland; Chestnut Hill outside Philadelphia; Ravens- wood outside Chicago; and Queens outside Manhattan. Los Angeles also developed 60 new communities to accommodate the expansion of its population from 6,000 to 100,000 between 1870 and 1877. The main selling point, and undoubtedly a central appeal of the new suburban housing, was its links with nature. This was reflected in the materials and designs of the houses themselves: 'Picturesque site planning and natural building materials evoked a return to nature, to a lost innocence and an earlier stability'.[4] This was evoked in the use of 'rough limestone, wide clapboards, cedar shingles, green patina on slate tiles' in addition to colours which 'simulated the hues of nature'.[5] The recurring rhetoric surrounding suburbia stressed its role as a safe secure haven from the immorality and pressures of city existence and the stresses and strains of commercial life.

The same appeals generated the British rush to the suburbs begun a few decades earlier. London's population more than doubled between 1800 and 1840 and Henry Mayhew wrote in the *Mornington Chronicle* in 1850, that 'Since 1839 there have been 200 miles of new streets formed in London, no less than 6,405 new dwellings have been erected annually since that time'.[6] Unlike their American equivalents, most British suburbanites rented rather than owned their new houses. Writing rather disparagingly about the new London suburbs the architectural historian, John Gloag, explained that:

North, south, east and west of London, mile after mile of streets were lined with these drab houses, each with cast-iron railings and front gates of identical pattern, bay windows and porches with fussy Gothic trimmings, and drain-pipes carrying water from gutters and bathrooms disfiguring the facade.[7]

Gloag's reactions were typical of a generation of historians and critics brought up on a diet of anti-Victorianism. Notwithstanding, his account is perceptive, highlighting as it did the central values which underpinned the construction of the Victorian suburban home – the emulation of the grander rural dwellings of the

aristocracy, and the function-
ally- and sexually-defined
areas within them.

Above all, Gloag focused
on the central concept of
'comfort' which lay at the
very heart of the mid-
Victorian home, both in
Britain and the USA. The
language of domesticcomfort
depended heavily upon its
references to the natural
world. Whereas the realm of
technological progress which
lay outside the sphere of the
home was linked to the idea
of culture, that of nature
stood boldly in opposition to
it, suggesting a lost innocence, a rural idyll which had
to be retained if Victorian
citizens were to maintain a
balance between the spiritual
and the material aspects of
their lives. Ironically, this will
to spirituality was expressed
in the home in an overtly
material manner through the

consumption of goods and decorations which evoked nature in
a variety of ways.

The furnishing and embellishments of the mid-Victorian
home served to bring nature inside the domestic sphere. Potted
plants and the addition of a conservatory filled with greenery
achieved this literally, as did collections of flowers and small
plants in bay windows. Many housewives also brought 'real'
nature inside in the form of shells and other natural objects
used as decorative items. In *The American Women's Home*,
Catherine Beecher and Harriet Beecher Stowe encouraged the
use of natural objects in the forms of

A Victorian Drawing-Room, 1800-1897. This heavily draped and ornamented British middle-class interior from the late century has bric-a-brac adorning every available surface, demonstrating the way in which such spaces were still being used to combine comfort and display.
(Hulton-Deutsch Collection)

picture frames of pinecones, moss and seashells; hanging baskets for plants; climbing ivy trained around the cornice; a large terranium furnished with ferns, shells, trailing arbutus, and partridge berries which offered a 'fragment of the green woods brought in and silently growing'.[8]

Gwendolyn Wright confirmed that such advice *was* heeded when she observed 'displays of shells, seeds, corals and other objects of natural history' in the American Victorian suburban home.[9] Aquaria filled with fish and a profusion of water plants were also a popular feature and they were frequently given the same kind of decorative treatment as an intricately carved piece of furniture, festooned with ornament inspired by natural forms and images. Stuffed animals also appeared in abundance from snakes encircling tree stumps to the more conventional hunting trophies.

John Gloag pinpointed a similar obsession with plants in and around the British house and quotes the advice literature of the time:

'whenever it is possible, climbing plants should be trained up the house and round the windows' said *The Young Ladies' Treasure Book*, adding that 'More than any invention of carving, friezes, stucco, paint, or outward adorning, does nature's greenery decorate the house'.[10]

Glass domes covering plants and other natural items were also a familiar sight.

The domed glass case, under which ferns and and other plants were used in conjunction with a small table supported by a pillar resting on claws or a solid base, and was known as a Wardian case. It was a popular item in Victorian furnishing, introduced in the mid-nineteenth-century, and named after Nathaniel Bagshaw Ward who, in 1829, discovered accidently the principle which led to this method of growing and transporting plants in glass cases.[11]

These inclusions of nature maintained the ideological imperatives of the Cult of Domesticity, suggesting a sense of continuity with the not too distant past. They also served as educational tools with which the housewife could introduce her children to the value system which underpinned their culture and they helped to create the image of domestic comfort which required familiar forms and soft, organically-derived decorative effects in the household.

Flowers were, without doubt, the most popular natural items in the Victorian home. In her account of nineteenth-century embroidery Rozsika Parker recounted an attack on an embroiderer's work by a certain Reverend T. James because of her representation of flowers: ' ... gigantic flowers, pansies big as peonies; cabbage roses which deserve the name, suggesting pickle rather than perfume; gracefully falling fuchsias big as handbells'.[12] Embroidery's dependence upon flower imagery had early origins but it was in the seventeenth century that flower gardening and embroidery became the particular province of women while professional embroidery was still controlled by men.[13] By 1740 the verbs 'to embroider' and 'to flower' had come to mean the same thing,[14] as the heroine in Samual Richardson's novel *Pamela* demonstrated, 'Mrs Jervis shewed my master the waistcoat I am flowering for him'.[15]

The strong link between women's chief accomplishment – embroidery – and flowers in the eighteenth century indicates the central role that flowers came to play in homemaking. It was clearly the housewife's role to cultivate flowers and to bring them into the house. In the decoration of the mid-Victorian house they were an essential element as well as a strong symbol of femininity, reinforcing the idea of the home as a feminine sphere. The American art historian Katherine C. Grier has pointed out the Victorians' enormous interest in the symbolism of flowers:

Entire chapters of domestic manuals were devoted to explicating the meaning of 'finger-rings' or the 'language of flowers', (a term used in the period). Richard Wells' *Manners, Culture and Dress*, an advice manual that was reprinted often in the 1890s, listed in one chapter the meaning of 318 flowers and plants presented as gifts. A deep red rose signalled 'bashful love'; and an iris signalled 'melancholy'.[16]

If nature itself entered the Victorian home in a variety of forms, it was also present in the two and three-dimensional decorations and furnishings. Mrs Trollope's advice book to middle-class Americans – *Domestic Manners of Americans* – talked of 'little tables, looking and smelling like flower beds',[17] undoubtedly elaborately carved, with flowers, leaves and other natural motifs covering their surfaces. The idea that furniture – tables, chairs, cupboards, and beds – could be both utilitarian and symbolic was a *sine qua non* of the Victorian interior and a recognition of the importance for feminine culture of object symbolism. Through the familiar carved forms which embellished their surfaces and their structural components they spoke a language of opulence and propriety at the same time. 'Much of the furniture,' explained Gloag, 'was monumental in effect, and copiously decorated with carving in high relief: flowers, fruit, animals, fabulous creatures and human figures, incongruously assembled, skilfully executed and exhibiting a basic confusion of ornament with design'.[18] In condemning this exuberant form of decoration, he was ignoring its fundamental role in creating the kind of environment expected of the housewife. Her ability to construct an image of comfort depended upon her including the required symbols in as great a quantity as possible. What has subsequently been condemned as 'Victorian clutter' marked the housewife's attempt to fulfil, to the best of her ability and through an effort of visual discrimination, the ideals that society and culture expected of her. That suitable items of furniture were available to her can be seen as a reflection of the manufacturers' and designers' close understanding of these needs.

Natural imagery ran riot over the surfaces of many of the home's two-and three-dimensional artefacts, from chamber pots to wallpapers. Patterns, used everywhere to soften lines and to enhance a sense of comfort, favoured the naturalistic and drew on many sources. Textiles, ceramics and glass were all subject to this form of elaboration, made possible by new printing techniques in their respective industries. Mrs Orrinsmith, for example, referred to a carpet on which 'vegetables are driven to a frenzy to be ornamental'.[19] While, inevitable, stylistic shifts occurred in home decorating from the early to the late-nineteenth century – the naturalism of the early and mid-century giving way to a greater degree of stylisation and aesthetic simplification – the obsession with imagery from the natural world remained constant.

The psychological comfort provided by familiar, reassuring motifs in the home was fundamental to the image of domesticity which, in turn, was linked to the idea of virtue and respectability. It reinforced an essentially conservative culture, committed to social convention and obsessed with propriety. These meanings were also communicated through the level of comfort provided to ease the body as well as the mind. The mid-Victorian interior was characterised by a preponderance of upholstered furniture, and by a liberal use of draped textiles to increase a sense of privacy and to soften the environment, both visually and to the touch. The depth of upholstery increased considerably after the invention of the coiled spring in the 1820s.[20] Borrowed from mattresses, it helped create the bulky, elastic, corpulent appearance of many mid-Victorian easy-chairs and settees, a corpulence which evoked an immediate sense of physical comfort. Buttoning served to emphasise that effect, giving an impression of objects almost bursting out of themselves. The Chesterfield sofa was the exemplar of this *par excellence*; it was described by Rosamund Mariott Watson as 'an indirect descendant of the Empire sofa, with the comfort kept, but all the grace left out of [that] obese, kindly-natured couch ... about as comely as a gigantic pin-cushion, and as little convenient in a room of moderate dimensions as an elephant; plethoric and protuberant with springs and stuffings.'[21] Chesterfields were joined by many other similarly 'comfy seating objects', from dining chairs with upholstered seats to easy chairs – with high and low backs, with and without arms, and intended for male or female sitters – and circular ottomans. Even rocking chairs were given the same veneer of comfort.

American furniture responded to the challenge of the coil spring and other technological advances in a very similar way. From the 1870s onwards it witnessed the appearance of large numbers of seats boasting spring-seat upholstery. Whether they were physically comfortable or not is beside the point; their purpose was to provide a visual image of comfort through technological means. If this tells us little about the actual level of physical comfort in the Victorian home it tells us a lot about the perception of a popular desire for that quality to be visually apparent. Grier has described upholstery springs as 'one more expression of the sensibility of softening that reached its fullest popular expression after 1950'.[22] She also stressed the way in which upholstery affected the sensorial nature of the interior, 'upholstery operated by influencing the sensory character of the parlor, affecting vision and tactile sensation in particular. Textile furnishings softened the world of sensation. They obliterated the edges of hard furniture surfaces and mediated, through structural padding, the contact of the body with seats.'[23]

The idea of a 'sensibility of softening' found further expression in the widespread use of draped fabrics. Writing in 1881, Janet E. Ruutz-Rees explained that 'So many delightful possibilities are concealed by a curtain; not to mention the skillful hiding of defects made feasible with such means, or the softening of angles and happy obliteration of corners.'[24] Mid-century parlours in Britain and the USA combined velvet, damask and lace draped at windows and doors and across items of furniture as a means of emphasising the privacy of the spaces and of concealing corners which were considered the epitome of discomfort. These heavy fabrics muffled sound, softened light and increased the level of quietness in an interior, thereby exerting a highly civilising influence.[25] At the same time they served to shut off the outside world, thus reinforcing the separation of the spheres.

In addition to the main window and door coverings, smaller objects were also clothed in fabric to soften their hard surfaces and make them part of a unified interior spelling out a single message: comfort. Small tables were covered with silk, velvet or cotton with cloth lambrequins attached to them, complete with fringes and tassels. Cushions were thrown on to sofas, themselves becoming softer and softer in the period from 1850 to 1910. Shelf lambrequins were introduced in the early 1850s in America. Housewives devoted considerable effort to making such items in needlepoint, adding crocheted and macramed details to them. Handwork such as this served to sustain women's production in the home. The intensity of detail and the level of craft that went into decorative interior arrangements was remarkable. Women also made small assemblages of

birds' feathers and other natural objects, which were positioned on shelves already festooned with needlework lambrequins. The visual detail in these small assemblages was repli-
cated in other arrangements in the same room, demonstrating
the degree to which materials and objects were seen by the
housewife not as individual units within an interior but rather
as part of a decorative whole. The distinction between production and consumption in the Victorian interior was eroded as
objects acquired in the marketplace, such as pianos and chairs,
were transformed in the domestic setting by their aesthetic
integration with pieces of needlework and other objects,
natural and otherwise, both made and acquired by the housewife, and with 'artistic' arrangements also created by her.

Gwendolyn Wright described the level of 'making' that
went into creating this kind of display: 'these [natural] objects
she [the housewife] skilfully juxtaposed with her own hand-
made creations or "household elegancies" which might include
crocheted lambrequins, hand-painted cabinets, rustic furniture,
shadow boxes, Easter eggs, screens and easels bedecked with
ribbons and flowers.'[26] Making *and* consuming were, therefore,
both vital, almost inseparable, aspects of the work of the
housewife in the last century.

Within this emergent 'consumer culture' more and more
goods could be bought in shops and used in these decorative
arrangements. In typically disparaging tone, once again John
Gloag explained that, in addition to the,

retail furniture houses could supply there were other shops to tempt
them [Victorian women] crowded with a costly and glittering profusion of pâpier maché articles, statuettes, bronzes, glass, and every
kind of 'fancy goods' that could be classed as 'art workmanship'.[27]

In the late century the idea of domestic comfort found a
direct form of expression in the idea of the 'cozy corner', a
concept with oriental origins. Gloag illustrated two examples
from the 1890s, represented in an advertisement by Oetzmann
and Company, a London-based furniture retailer. The corner
was a mini-environment consisting of a padded corner sofa,
complete with a stuffed cushion and crettone drapery, and with

a decorative mirror and shelf above. A potted plant stood to one side of Gloag's example. In other instances 'Bagdad' curtains were draped across such corners, suspended on a metal rod, to reinforce the idea of privacy and a retreat from formal parlour behaviour.

Comfort, however, was not the only message of the Victorian interior, nor the only preoccupation of the house-wife. Another face of the domestic interior looked to the more overtly forwardlooking world of fashion and novelty as ways of expressing the new social position of its inhabitants. This created obvious links between the material and aesthetic culture of the home and the marketplace. In Charlotte Brontë's novel, *Jane Eyre*, published in 1847, the heroine described the subtle combination of comfort and fashion in her refurbishment of Moore House:

The ordinary sitting-rooms and bedrooms I left as they were: for I knew Diana and Mary would derive more pleasure from seeing again the old homey tables and chairs and beds, than from the spectacle of the smartest innovations. Still some novelty was necessary, to give their return the piquancy with which I wished it to be invested. Dark, handsome new carpets and curtains, an arrangement of some carefully selected antique ornaments in porcelain and bronze, new coverings, and mirrors, and dressing-cases for the toilet tables, answered the end: they looked fresh without being glaring. A spare parlour and bedroom refurbished entirely, with old sage, and carpets on the floor. When all was finished I thought Moor House as complete a model of bright modern snugness within, as it was, at this season, a specimen of unitary waste and desert dreariness outside.[28]

While the idea of comfort carried with it a stabilising pull with its nostalgic interest in the natural world, and a desire to

The Parlour of the Dr. J.G. Bailey's House in Santa Ana, California, circa 1876. Filled with artistic bric-a-brac, and combining such typical objects of display and comfort as a cut-glass chandelier and lacy curtains, this American interior from the late nine-teenth-century shows how similar such spaces were to their equivalents across the Atlantic. (Courtesy of the Bowers Museum of Cultural Art, Santa Ana, California)

create an unchanging, familiar environment to soothe and protect, an engagement with the world of fashion pushed the domestic sphere in another direction – that of change and ephemerality. The housewife who sought to express her family's social status by showing that she understood the vagaries of fashion and kept up with its stylistic changes had to keep one eye on the taste-making publications and another on the homes of her peers to see what was around the next corner.

The fashion system had its roots within the system of mercantile capitalism and was expressed first, and most fully, in the area of dress, especially women's,[29] followed by domestic furnishings and decoration. Fashion is synonymous with change and its function is both social and ideological. In addition, it acts on behalf of the individual and the group.[30] The need to participate in the furnishings fashion system was dictated by the social and cultural requirements of the Cult of Domesticity, which expected the new middle-class to emulate the gentry and display signs of what Veblen was later to call 'conspicuous leisure'.[31] To participate in fashion signified a distance from the world of necessity and an ability to indulge in a level of luxury.

By the eighteenth century gender differences in dress had taken on a special significance, and with industrialisation men began to renounce fashionable dress to adopt instead a kind of standardised uniform for which the working dress of the aristocracy and the gentry provided a model.[32] The idea of fashion as display was now seen as a predominantly feminine pursuit. Clearly men *did* continue to participate in fashion through the nineteenth and twentieth centuries, although in a less ostentatious manner. However, the cultural stereotype associating women exclusively with fashionable display and its condemnation of feminine culture for its more trivial preoccupations was born in this period. This stereotype – of women playing a role in the fashion system and of men operating in a different sphere – has been enormously influential in defining gender differences and inequalities in this century.

In the nineteenth century the coincidence of these shifts in the gendering of dress coincided with the emergence of separate spheres. Women and fashionable dress combined to create a new concept of femininity, to which domesticity also contributed an important element. It was a short step from dress as a form of fashionable display to furnishing and home decoration as a manifestation of conspicuous leisure. And just as the fashion industry geared itself increasingly to concentrating on the female consumer, so the domestic furnishings industry inevitably followed suit.

What this meant in material and aesthetic terms was quite complex. In creating a home for her family, the middle-class housewife was communicating an image of herself, both to herself and to others, as well as simultaneously positioning herself within a social group and in contradistinction to other social groups. The language of display was both shared and individual at the same time, and its creation a mixture of work and pleasure. We have seen the extent to which women exercised their aesthetic sensibilities in creating decorative details in the home which helped them construct their own self identities, and communicate to their peers and others the level of their families social aspirations and achievements. Gloag focused on exactly this practice when he wrote disparagingly that

men might well have complained that the home was always being disrupted by expensive novelties, that new fashions constantly intruded, and shelves and brackets and tables were cluttered up with knick-knacks, fancy goods and examples of 'art-workmanship' sheltered by those glass domes, 'for the covering and preservation of clocks, statuettes, wax flowers, alabaster, and other ornaments and articles of vertu'.[33]

His emphasis upon the idea of 'art-workmanship' reinforced the fact that this practice had little utility value but a high level of aesthetic significance as one the key ways in which women expressed their tastes.

The Victorian housewife had a number of strategies to emphasise the importance of display in her interior; the sheer quantity of objects, patterns, colours and surface embellishments was one, while another was attracting the eye to certain objects. Display was exclusively a visual affair: cut glass

decanters reflected and refracted light and highly polished
metal and wood surfaces jostled for attention. Newness had an
enormous appeal while bright colours and rich textures also
served as attractions to the eye. The new analine dyes were
particularly useful in producing dazzling effects.

As we have seen, comfort and display often pulled the
Victorian housewife in two different directions and made
demands upon the task of exercising her taste. These divergent
requirements had quite distinct cultural roots.[34] The need for
comfort was essentially Anglo-American while the fashion
urge came from France where elegance and refinement were
the order of the day. With the latter also came, especially in
the USA from the 1840s onwards, an aesthetic vocabulary
derived from eighteenth-century French taste which introduced gilt and pastel colours to the middle-class Victorians.
The work of the American furniture designer John H. Belter
exhibited characteristics of what was dubbed the 'Rococo
Revival', providing a model which was widely imitated. This
fashion was received with some ambivalence by many
American social commentators, among them Harriet Beecher
Stowe who, in 1871, published her book *Pink and White
Tyranny*, which focused on the fashion for French taste. It
described just such a rococo interior:

'The house was furbished and resplendent – it was gilded –
it was frescoed – it was à la Pompidour, à la Louis Quinze and
Louis Quartorze, and à la everything French and pretty and
gay and glistening'.[35]

This overtly French taste, linked with gilding and pastel
colours, represented an ideal means of display in the domestic
interior. Nowhere were these aesthetic strategies more evident
than in the parlour. It was here, along with the bedroom, that
feminine culture and its accompanying aesthetic were given a
free rein. It was the least utilitarian and most symbolic of the
house's spaces, the place where social ritual was most enacted.
There was display in the dining-room also but, as this
remained a predominantly masculine area, restraint was called
for. What decoration there was was dominated by the 'masculine iconography of the hunt'.[36] In the parlour, however,
display was abundant and references to fashion and novelty

extensive: it was the place in which 'the housewife would show off the family's best possessions, strive to impress guests and teach her children about universal principles of beauty and refinement'.[37]

The parlour communicated through a visual language which consisted of a set of standard artefacts: in the first half of the century this included carpets, window draperies, a parlour suite, fancy chairs, a centre table, a piano, a mantle and a myriad of smaller objects.[38] Variations on these elements inevitably occurred but a general pattern was necessary to allow people to read its symbolism of social status. The subtleties of variation mirrored the dialects of a language which give away, at first hearing, the social and cultural position of the speaker. The way in which knick-knacks were arranged, combined with the elaborateness or otherwise of a particular parlour, was an immediate sign to a visitor of its inhabitant's actual, or aspired to, social status.

The parlour had to function as an aesthetic whole. It had to look as if it had been furnished all at once. This demanded a great deal of knowledge on behalf of the housewife. Before the widespread presence of advice books and retail information, the first American models for domestic parlours were commercial parlours in hotels, steamboats, railroad cars and photographers' studios. The expansion of the mass production and mass consumption of domestic goods in the USA between 1830 and 1880 made it possible for middle-class housewives to emulate the parlours in these commercial environments.[39]

All the domestic artefacts and decorations of the parlour had their roots in the traditional decorative arts; very few technological innovations made their way into the domestic spaces where comfort and display were uppermost. Inevitably, technology found its way into the kitchen but this was not an important site of expression on the part of the housewife. The kitchen was considered an essentially utilitarian space, inhabited primarily by the servant(s) and by the housewife at moments when work, rather than social ritual, was the focus of her attention. Apart from coil springs and a handful of other inventions which transformed the insides rather than the outsides of the 'paraphenalia of gentility', the

only technologically innovative object to find a place in the
parlour at this time was the sewing machine. When the Singer
company launched its first machine in the 1850s it failed to be
as successful as its competitor, Wheeler and Wilson, because
the latter company's model – lighter, smaller and simpler –
was more appealing to the domestic market. Wheeler and
Wilson's machine had a black japanned metal body with gilt
enamelled flower imagery and rococo patterns on it, an obvious draw to housewifes who could 'show off' their new technological acquisition. Singer responded by introducing a
domestic model in 1858 which was similarly decorated, thus
both companies had found a means of introducing an industrial process into the domestic sphere.

The real breakthrough came with a lowering of the price
accompanied by advertising campaigns which stressed the
appropriateness of the machine to the domestic setting. An
1867 fashion plate showed a Wheeler and Wilson machine in
what was clearly a middle-class parlour. Singer's 'New Family'
machine of 1858 was a treadle machine, the table for which
had an elaborate metal superstructure resembling branches of
a tree covered with leaves. The brochure introducing it
explained that

A few months since, we came to the conclusion that the public taste
demanded a sewing machine for family purposes more exclusively; a
machine of smaller size, and of a lighter and more elegant form; a
machine decorated in the best style of art, so as to make a beautiful
ornament in the parlor or boudoir.[40]

The use of the words, 'taste', 'elegant' and 'art' clearly
aligned the machine with femininity and the idea of domestic
display. This overt attempt to integrate a-feminine domestic
aesthetic into the sewing machine demonstrated the degree to
which manufacturers understood the role that novelty, fashion
and display played in the feminine sphere.

Participating in fashion meant that one style rapidly
superceded another in the domestic sphere in this period.
Surface changes came and went, influenced by the expanding
forms of taste-making, among them the large-scale exhibitions

of the time, among them the Great Exhibition of 1851 held in London's Hyde Park and Philadelphia's Centennial Exhibition of 1876.

One fundamental stylistic shift in the prevailing middle-class domestic idiom occurred in the second half of the nineteenth-century: the movement known as 'Aestheticism' generated a partial swing away from what were commonly thought by then to be the 'excesses' of the mid-century. Furniture grew lighter, patterns were more stylised, the palette changed, and new influences, especially from the East, came into evidence. Where the ideology linked to domesticity was concerned, however, there was no substantial change and, in many ways, this new style could be seen simply as a shift in aesthetic sensibility, yet another new fashion, resulting merely in a change in the visual manifestations of comfort and display. Although 'art' figured more prominently, the expectations of the Victorian housewife did not.

Two major changes *did* surface at this time, however. Middle-class women became more visible in their participation in home decorating, both in Britain and the USA; indeed, a handful of them moved into the professional world as home decorators, thus initiating the erosion of the separation of the spheres. And the level of criticism directed at the middle-class housewife and her taste – a critique first heard in the early decades of the century, rooted in a 'distaste' for the domestic aesthetic and by implication for the women whose tastes had created it – began to have an influence. By the late century what came to be called the 'design reform' movement had put in place a set of criteria for 'good design' which circumvented the question of taste completely and placed all discussions about the material world in the masculine sphere of manufacture.

CHAPTER THREE

'Those Extravagant Draperies':

Domesticity Contested

'We cannot ... have one taste for the drawing-room and another for the studio.'

– Charles Eastlake[1]

By the time British design reformer and designer, Charles Eastlake, was writing, the separation of the private and public spheres had also driven a wedge between the amateur world of taste and domesticity, and the professional sphere of art and design. Whereas the latter belonged to the arena of public, male-dominated institutions – among them the Royal Academy, the Society of Arts, the national museums and galleries and the Schools of Design – the former, as we have seen, inhabited an enclosed private sphere, the parameters of which were defined by religious belief and social status. In consequence, the numerous public discussions about aesthetics, especially in relation to manufactured goods, tended to lead to accusations by men about the low standards of taste in the home and the need for reform. Inevitably, the brunt of their attacks was focused upon women in their capacity as homemakers and consumers.

Eastlake called for such reform, laying the responsibility for what he believed to be the deterioration in domestic taste clearly at the feet of women:

The faculty of distinguishing good from bad design in the familiar objects of domestic life is a faculty which most educated people – and women especially – conceive that they possess. How it has been acquired, few would be able to explain. The general impression seems to be, that it is the peculiar inheritance of gentle blood, and independent of all training; that while a young lady is devoting at school, or under a governess, so many hours a day to music, so many to languages, and so many to general science, she is all the time unconsciously forming that sense of the beautiful, which we call taste: that this sense, once developed, will enable her, unassisted by special study or experience, not only to appreciate the charms of nature in every aspect, but to form a correct estimate of the merits of art-manufacture. That this impression has gained ground so far as to amount to positive conviction, may be inferred from the fact that there is no single point on which well-bred women are more jealous of disparagement than on this. We may condemn a lady's opinion on politics – criticise her handwriting – correct her pronunciation of Latin, and disparage her favourite author with a chance of escaping displeasure. But if we venture to question her taste . . . we are sure to offend. It is, however, a lamentable fact, that this very quality is commonly deficient, not only among the generally ignorant but also among the most educated classes in this country.[2]

His highly-charged, facetious attack on what he clearly believed to be the misguided nature of women's tastes was by no means untypical in this period. Indeed, many of the key 'reformers' believed that what was perceived as the deterioration of popular taste in Britain was rooted in the 'false' criteria followed by women in their task of embellishing the home.

The desire to improve public taste was not an isolated mission, however. In early nineteenth-century Britain this particular reform programme was instigated as part of the attempt to give Britain a national identity in the eyes of the rest of the world and to raise the country's profile in international trade. The 1830s and '40s saw the first trade depression since the onset of industrialisation and the government set about investigating its causes. They were quick to isolate 'design' as part of the explanation for what they believed to be the inferiority of British goods on the international market-place, especially in comparison with their French counterparts, which they considered 'superior' in this respect.

In 1836 a report by a government select committee formed to look into the problem was published. The committee had undertaken research 'into the best means of extending a knowledge of the arts and the principles of design among the people (especially the manufacturing population) of the country'.[3] This had involved taking evidence from a wide range of people, among them architects, designers, manufacturers, makers and decorators. At this level of investigation attention was focused on production rather than consumption. Many of those questioned laid the blame at the chasm between art and manufacturing and, in an attempt to remedy this, the committee recommended the establishment of a new system of art education in emulation of the existing French and German systems. Schools of 'Design' (the term was used in its original sense, deriving from the Italian word 'disegno' meaning 'drawing') were established in the main manufacturing centres in the hopes that they would begin to supply the trade with skilled artists and designers, thereby raising the aesthetic standards of British goods.[4]

Some of the witnesses questioned by the committee saw the problem as emanating less from the untrained designer than from the uneducated consumer. A certain Samuel Wiley, a representative from the firm Jennens and Bettridge, manufacturers of pâpier maché complained that, 'the public taste is bad; I could sell them the worst things, the most unmeaning, in preference to the most splendid designs and the best executions'.[5] This was reinforced by retailer J.C. Robertson who felt that the fact that designers had to work according to the 'fancy of the customer' lay at the heart of the matter.[6] The committee's response to this problem was to recommend free access to museums, libraries and exhibitions. One direct result of the recommendation was the establishment of a public decorative art collection, intended as a polemical display demonstrating the difference between 'good' and 'bad' design.[7]

The role of professional architects and designers as the best and most appropriate arbiters of taste was not in question, nor was that of government-sponsored museums and exhibitions as the means of introducing the public to the 'best' examples of design. The criteria for 'good design' that underpinned, albeit silently, the select committee's report were never once questioned. It was assumed throughout that there were fixed 'standards' in design, an aesthetic canon against which all goods could, and indeed should, be measured and judged. These standards, it was contended, should be understood and appreciated by the British public and used as a basis for decisions in regards to taste and consumption. Manufacturers, designers and retailers would then respond to the new demands made by consumers and the aesthetic standards of British goods would rise. As a consequence, the same goods would also prove more competitive on the international market and help to improve the state of the British economy.

The problem with this seemingly logical plan was that it failed to take into account the fact that two sets of value systems – those of the public masculine sphere and those of the private, feminine world of domesticity – were at work, influencing aesthetic standards in very different ways; furthermore, it would not be easy to persuade consumers, most of whom inhabited the latter arena, that the criteria for 'good design' formulated by the inhabitants of the former were the correct ones. In turn, manufacturers and retailers would not be easily persuaded to turn away from what they saw as the most direct route to profit.

Inevitably the outcome of the government's initiative was not, as it had been hoped, a sudden transformation of public taste but rather the formation of a high cultural movement injecting a new establishment-approved strand into the discourse about taste in mid-nineteenth century Britain. Its institutional base consisted of the Schools of Design and the newly-formed museums, both highly visible in their public rhetoric about the need to raise design standards and public taste. It had its own voice in the *Journal of Design and Manufactures*, launched in 1849, and was sustained by a group of powerful individuals, all connected with the establishment and who shared a commitment to the need for 'design reform'. They included among them such influential figures as Prince Albert, the President of the Society of Arts; and Henry Cole, the Director of the South Kensington Museum; others such as Richard Redgrave, originally a lecturer at the Government

School of Design, later the Inspector-General for Art in the Science and Art Department and subsequently the Surveyor of her Majesty's Pictures, also played a key role; prominent architects of the time, among them Owen Jones and A.W.N. Pugin – the architect, in collaboration with John Barry, of the new Palace of Westminster – were also involved as were celebrated writers and critics of art and design, notable among them John Ruskin, author of many books on the subject, and Charles Eastlake, by 1878 the Keeper and Secretary of the National Gallery. All in their various ways adopted the role of propagandizing reformers through their polemical writings, architectural and design practices, government reports, educational curricula; museum installations, and temporary exhibitions, to make public their ideas.

The hitherto relatively simple picture of consumption and production – an uncontested system of consumer demand being met by manufacturers and designers – was now rendered more complex by the addition of a new level of high cultural coercion in the area of design standards. In this new situation, gender played a significant role.

While details of the design reformers' complex arguments inevitably conflicted with each other – the so-called Cole group, for example, supported the idea of the designer in the manufacturing industry while Ruskin, writing a little later, and the supporters of the Arts and Crafts Movement of the second half of the century, valued more highly the work of the craftsman who performed a complete task – the protagonists of the design reform movement, extending across two or three generations from the 1830s to the end of the century, all, to a man, condemned the taste of the general British public and sought ways of ameliorating it. For the most part, they located taste within the domestic setting, seeing there the chief horrors that provided ample evidence of the need for reform. Thus, while they operated in the public sphere within the various institutions dedicated to the improvement of art, design and architectural practice and appreciation, they appealed to the private sphere to re-educate itself to an understanding of the 'correct' criteria for 'good' consumption.

In that appeal they focused their attacks upon the ideological components and aesthetic manifestations of feminine taste that sustained women's culture at that time. No doubt unwittingly, their condemnation of feminine culture, represented by women's tastes, consigned it to the marginal position it now occupies.

The most vociferous attacks were directed at the role of fashion, novelty and display in the domestic interior and at the feminine taste that valued their continual presence. There was nothing new in this: women had long been attacked for their vanity and seemingly obsessional involvement with appearance and fashionability. The outrage against these feminine traits had most often been expressed in religious, political or philosophical terms. The debate about luxury, for example, which had raged in the eighteenth century, had a strongly gendered component to it, luxury itself often being personified as 'she'. Luxury, embracing pleasure and spurning utility, was viewed as heavily feminised and women were perceived as the key consumers of the new luxury goods in the eighteenth century:

When John Foster used the Countess of Bective to give snob appeal to his carpets or Wedgwood used the Duchess of Devonshire to give social cachet to his pottery, this was the kind of latent desire they were attempting to release. These were the customers who caught 'from example the contagion of desire'.[8]

Within the sphere of eighteenth-century aesthetic philosophy Emmanuel Kant had also reinforced the idea of a gender hierarchy in his *Theory of Taste* which considered 'feminine ways and taste' to be merely a preparation for morality which, in his view, was linked with masculinity. 'Neither taste nor femininity,' were in his opinion 'principled enough to order and hence shape experience'.[9] Kant's view conformed to the general belief within the new climate of scientific rationalism that the power of reason was essentially a masculine attribute, whereas women were linked widely with the 'irrational.'

A picture of women and their tastes – their preoccupation with surface rather than with substance, with ephemerality rather than universality, with appearance rather than with

Hollyhock Chintz, 1850. With its highly ornate and naturalistic floral pattern this fabric was selected for the Great Exhibition of 1851 to demonstrate what Henry Cole described as 'false principles' of design. (Victoria and Albert Museum Picture Library)

utility, and with the inessential rather than the essential – provided a broad cultural frame for the criticisms of nine-teenth-century reformers. Implicit in their focus on feminine taste as one of the causes of the lowering of aesthetic standards was the notion that their values were underpinned in a wider, and historically much deeper, cultural discourse.

The idea of feminine superficiality was central, for example, to Pugin's comment of 1843 that 'well meaning ladies transfer all the nicknackery of the work-room, the toilette-table, and the bazaar to the altar of God. The result is pitiable . . . pretty ribbons, china pots, darling little gimcracks, artificial flowers, all sorts of trumpery are suffered to be intruded'.[10] The par-ticular target of his attack was the state of church embroidery, which he saw as being influenced by secular femininity, bearer of the superficial and the trivial. Pugin's deep commitment to the Gothic style was his means of attempting to move archi-tecture and design away from the world of the secular, the domestic and the material towards the more spiritual and universal.

Pugin's ideas were widely reiterated by subsequent reform-ers and were hugely influential in the later formulation of a 'modern' architecture and design.[11] His dismissive reference to ladies 'nicknackery' also surfaced again, notably in Eastlake's *Hints on Household Taste* in which the author proclaimed that,

At the beginning of this chapter it was observed that 'knick-knacks' were usually banished from the library. By that expression I meant to include that heterogeneous assemblage of modern rubbish which, under the head of 'china ornaments' and various other names, finds its way into the drawing room or boudoir.[12]

A little later 'drawing-room taste' once more came under attack:

It is hardly necessary to add that the so-called 'ornamental' leather-work which a few years ago was so in vogue with young ladies, who used it for the construction of brackets, baskets, picture-frames, etc was – like poichomanie, diaphanie and other drawing-room pursuits – utterly opposed to the principles of taste.[13]

Women's assemblages and amateur creative efforts were bracketed together as manifestations of their lack of aesthetic knowledge and skill. The drawing-room, or parlour, and boudoir were considered the natural sites for these aberrations and were condemned accordingly. Richard Redgrave was equally disparaging about the drawing room,

His (the furniture designer's) first consideration should be perfect adaptation to intended use; this may appear so obvious a truism as to want no enforcement, but a visit to a modern drawing-room will speedily undeceive us, for there we see a multitude of objects offending against this rule.[14]

Less involved than their wives in the symbolic role of this room, the male reformers saw it as alien territory. In fact the separation of the spheres made many experiences inaccessible to men at this time. Rather than admit this inability to interpret them, however, they chose to condemn what to them constituted the unknown, the incomprehensible and, most probably, the threatening.[15] It has been said of Andrew Jackson Downing, who knew the work of Pugin and, like him, favoured the Gothic style, that 'a parlor sent him into a paroxysm of disgust'[16] while Ralph Waldo Emerson, possibly the most influential American thinker of his time, in pursuit of his ideal of 'plain living and high thinking' also condemned domestic display and an emphasis upon material goods.[17]

Downing was also influenced by the work of John Ruskin and it is in Ruskin's texts that some of the strongest feelings directed at women and their tastes in the name of design reform can be found. In his notorious lecture 'Of Queens' Gardens', for example, he made abundantly clear his thoughts on the rightful place of women in the sexual division of labour and the separate spheres: 'Woman was made to be the helpmate of man.' Furthermore, 'it is the woman who watches over, teaches and guides the youth.' And as to the essential differences between men and women,

Each has what the other has not: each completes the other, and is completed by the other: they are nothing alike, and the happiness and perfection of both depends on each asking and receiving from the other what the other only can give. Now their separate characters are briefly these: The man's power is active, progressive, defensive. He is eminently the doer, the creator, the discoverer, the defender. His intellect is for speculation and invention; his energy for adventure, for war, and for conquest, wherever war is just, wherever conquest necessary. But the woman's power is for rule, not for battle, – and her intellect is not for invention or creation, but for sweet ordering, arrangement and decision. She sees the qualities of things, their claims and their places.[18]

Later in the same lecture Ruskin reinforced the idea of home as sanctuary: 'It is the place of Peace; the shelter, not only from all injury, but from all terror, doubt, and division ... This then, I believe to be the woman's true place and power.'[19]

In this account he justifies his belief that women's educational needs were necessarily different from those of men and, if taken in isolation, *Of Queens' Gardens* might be seen to be promoting the essential equality of men and women while outlining their 'natural' differences. It is only when we look at Ruskin's discussions about standards in taste and design that we discover what he really thought of domestic femininity.

Items made of cut glass, or 'crystal' as it was widely referred to – decanters and drinking glasses positioned on sideboards in dining-rooms, glittering table-pieces and chandeliers hanging in parlours and hallways – were among the most effective display items in the mid-Victorian household. Their ability to reflect and refract light gave them the dazzling brilliance that was frequently referred to by reformers as the epitome of vulgarity. Eastlake isolated them a decade or so after Ruskin as one of the signs of conspicuousness that he most deplored and was overt in his categorisation of them as a marker of feminine taste; he proclaimed:

North of the Tweed it is not unusual to regard 'crystal' as the all-important feature of domestic feasts; and certainly most London housewives who can afford the luxury are as careful of the appearance of their decanters and wineglasses as the glittering plate which lies beside them.[20]

He continued his crusade against cut glass by pointing out that by that time much of it was made in moulds and did not have the delicacy of its hand-made predecessors. His shift into the world of production did not, however, fully disguise his association of cut-glass objects with the showy domesticity which he so deplored, a domesticity, created by women's tastes.

In the early 1850s Ruskin had rooted his critique of the same material in the problems of its manufacture – in the fact that it was made of cold rather than hot glass, and did not, as a result, respect the material's 'natural' ductility; it was based on 'false principles'. He also expressed a sense of aesthetic disgust at the level of perfection and finish that necessarily characterised the cut-glass object, and which made it so suited for middle-class display.

Our modern glass is exquisitely clear in its substance, true in form, accurate in its cutting. We are proud of this. We ought to be ashamed of it. The old Venetian glass was muddy, inaccurate in all its forms, and clumsily cut, if at all. And the old Venetian was justly proud of it . . . all cut glass is barbarous; for the cutting conceals its ductility and confuses it with crystal. Also, all very neat, finished and perfect form in glass is barbarous: for this fails in proclaiming another of its great virtues; namely the ease with which its light substance can be moulded or blown into any form, so long as perfect accuracy be not required.[21]

In a manner typical of much design reform writing Ruskin had delivered a potent, albeit indirect, attack on feminine consumption in an argument presented in terms of the masculine sphere of manufacture, linked with the concept of 'newness'. The visual appeal of the cut-glass object provided an ideal form of social display and it was partially an intuitive response – a response, that is, based upon aesthetic and moral

Cut-Glass Salad Bowl and Servers, made by T.G. Hawkes and Company, Corning, New York, circa 1882-1892. The highly decorative and complex style of glass-cutting, known as 'Brilliant' was popular in the USA in the last years of the nineteenth-century. The conspicuousness of the objects thus worked marked them out as obvious signs of social status. (The Corning Museum of Glass)

repulsion to this 'feminine' middle-class world – that Ruskin was expressing.

Novelty, for the housewife, was all important as Eastlake indicated in his attack on women's obsession with the 'fashion-able', 'It may convey the notion of a bed of roses, or a danger-ous labyrinth of rococo ornament – but if it is "fashionable", that is all-sufficient. While new, it is admired; when old, everybody will agree that it was always "hideous".'[22]

Much of the vocabulary of design reform writing reinforced its starting point in a rejection of the aesthetic of middle-class domesticity. The words 'gaudy' and 'dazzling' appeared over and over again, revealing an emotional response to the colours and surface effects of certain materials – polished metal and the new analine dyes, for example – in the Victorian interior. Eastlake described a female shopper in a carpet shop, 'The good lady looks from one carpet to another until her eyes are fairly dazzled by their hues,'[23] and a little later he wrote of modern furniture, 'The ladies like it best when it comes like a new toy from the shop, fresh with recent varnish and untarnished gilding.'[24]

Ruskin was equally vociferous about gilding, yet another favourite of the middle class housewife,

It is one of the most abused means of magnificence we posses, and I much doubt whether any use we ever make of it, balances that loss of pleasure, which, from the frequent sight and perpetual suspicion of it, we suffer in the contemplation of any thing that is verily gold. I think gold was meant to be seldom seen, and to be admired as a precious thing.[25]

Once again, conspicuousness was seen as the enemy of taste. 'French taste', the Louis Quinze or 'rococo' style as it was referred to – the height of feminine conspicuousness – also came under attack in many reform texts. Eastlake's facetious comments about a tea-urn – 'In order to add to its attractions, the lid and handles are probably decorated a la Pompadour'[26] – bore testimony to this.

One by one the reformers isolated and targeted their attacks at the components of middle-class domestic display, showing their contempt for its neglect of the 'True Principles' which Pugin had outlined in 1841. They did not restrict their criticisms to the question of novelty and display in the domestic interior. They were equally dismissive about the material and aesthetic elements that represented the idea of comfort, the concept which was so central, as we have seen, to the mid-Victorian middle-class home.

Singled out for particular attack was the whole area of

furnishing fabrics, as Ruskin demonstrated,

I would not have that useless expense in unnoticed fineries or formalities; cornicing of ceilings and graining of doors, and fringing of curtain and thousands such; things which have become foolishly and apathetically habitual – things on whose common appliance hang whole trades, to which there never belonged the blessing of giving one ray of pleasure, or becoming of the remotest or most contemptible use – things which cause half the expense of life, and destroy more than half its comfort, manliness, respectability, freshness and facility

... I speak from experience: I know what it is to live in a cottage with a deal floor and roof, and a hearth of mica slate; and I know it to be in many respects healthier and happier than living between a Turkey carpet and gilded ceiling, beside a steel grate and polished fender.[27]

Curtain fringes had also been one of Pugin's targets. they were 'originally nothing more than the ragged edge of the stuff, tied into bunches to prevent it unravelling further'.[28] Fringes were permissible, therefore, because of their functional justification, providing they 'never consist of heavy parts'.[29]

Upholstery inevitably came under attack from many of the reformers. The bulky, 'bloated' forms of upholstered furniture represented all that was believed to be excessive in the domestic interior, in addition to the fact that it so clearly contradicted the principles of construction outlined by Pugin, and adhered to by Eastlake who wrote regretfully,

How often do we see in fashionable drawing-rooms a type of couch which seems to be composed of nothing but cushions! It really is supported by a framework of wood or iron, but this internal structure is carefully concealed by the stuffing and material with which the whole is covered. I do not wish to be ungallant in my remarks, but I fear there is a class of young ladies who look upon this sort of furniture as 'elegant'.[30]

The desire to soften the interior by covering hard shapes with fabric, a strategy which was used, as we have seen, by Victorian women to enhance the sense of comfort within and the unity of an interior, was also singled out by Eastlake,

As a lady's taste is generally allowed to reign supreme in regard to the furniture of bedrooms, I must protest humbly but emphatically against the practice which exists of encircling toilet-tables with a sort of muslin petticoat, generally stiffened by a crinoline of pink or blue calico. Something of the same kind may occasionally be seen twisted round the frame of the toilet-glass. They just represent a milliner's notion of the 'pretty' and nothing more. Drapery of this kind neither is wanted nor ought to be introduced in such places.[31]

Pugin had already expressed outrage at

the modern plans of suspending enormous folds of stuff over poles, as if for the purpose of sale or of being dried . . . the only object that these endless festoons and bunchy tassels can answer is to swell the bills and profits of the upholsterers, who are the inventors of these extravagant draperies, which are not only useless in protecting the chamber from cold, but are the depositors of thick layers of dust, and in London not unfrequently become the strong-holds of vermin.[32]

Upholstery and use of draperies came to symbolise all that was false and dishonest in the Victorian interior, along with the practice of disguising one material to look like another. Ruskin devoted many paragraphs to what he considered to be the unacceptability of marbled wood or the painting of ornament in deceptive relief. A critique of 'falseness' also underpinned Pugin's disapproving comments about objects decorated to conceal their function. He described a clock, for instance, as having been made '[in the form of] a Roman warrior in a flying chariot, round one of the wheels of which, on close inspection, the hours may be decried'.[33]

Perhaps their greatest anger was reserved for that *sine qua non* of the 'comfortable' Victorian interior – ornament. The reformers were not against ornament *per se*. They considered it, in fact, a vital component of design, but they were adamant that it should be secondary to construction and they disapproved of all ornament which they felt to be either 'dishonest' or unprincipled. Pugin and Eastlake despised the highly naturalistic forms of decoration that made two dimensions look like three, the kind of 'false relief' that was so common on the surfaces of so many household goods. They both disapproved of patterns and of naturalistic imagery which used shadows to create this effect as a form of surface ornamentation. Eastlake wrote of

The quasi-fidelity with which the forms of a rose, or a bunch of ribbons, or a ruined castle, can be reproduced on carpets, crockery, and wall-papers will always possess a certain kind of charm for the uneducated eye, just as the mimicry of natural sounds in music, from the rolling of thunder to the cackling of poultry, will delight a vulgar ear. Both are ingenious, amusing, attractive for the moment, but neither lie within the legitimate province of art.[34]

The gendered symbolism of these motifs, and the romantic nature of the imagery were of no interest to him. The principles which underpinned the 'taste' of Eastlake and many of the other design reformers derived from the language of design and manufacture, expressed in a preoccupation with construction and materials, rather than from the language of consumption for which object symbolism and context were all important.

As we have seen, nature was the primary source of inspiration for domestic ornamentation in the Victorian middle-class home. The design reformers also saw the natural world as a starting point but were unanimous and adamant in their rejection of what they called 'direct imitation'. This rejection was particularly well expressed by Richard Redgrave:

Or-molu stems and leaves bear porcelain flowers painted to imitate nature, and candles are made to rise out of tulips and china-asters, while gas jets gush forth from opal arums. Stems, bearing flowers for various uses, arise from metal leaves standing painfully on their points, and every constructive truth, and just adaptation to use, is sacrificed for a senseless imitative naturalism.[35]

Above all, nature had to be controlled, ordered and transformed through the application of a set of abstract principles. Several texts suggested ways in which nature could be tamed through the use of repetition and geometry.[36] Redgrave explained what was happening,

The true ornamentist would seem to be one who seeks out the principles on which bygone artists worked, and the rules by which they arrived at excellence, and, discarding mere imitation and reproduction of details, endeavours, by the application of new ideas and new matter upon principles which he believes to be sound to attain originality through fitness and truth.[37]

Thus did culture attempt to control nature and the masculine take dominance over the feminine.

If the meaning of the object within the social, psychological and cultural context of consumption and use was of no interest to the reformers, the emerging notion of 'consumerism' was inasmuch as it was held partly responsible for what they perceived to be the decline in the standards of public taste. Once again Eastlake was amongst the most vociferous, blaming salesmen, as well as housewives, for their low standards of taste: 'to hear a young shopman defining to his fair customers across the counter what is 'genteel' or 'ladylike' sounds very ludicrous, and even impertinent. Yet in this sort of advice apparently lies the only guiding principle of their selection.'[38]

By the 1860s consumption clearly played a central role in the housewife's duties, and it was perceived by the reformers as part of the problem of taste. A decade later Christopher Dresser pronounced that, 'It is man's duty to make money – the lady's duty to spend it',[39] thereby reinforcing the sexual division of labour. If consumerism was a burgeoning problem, it was a problem which related primarily to women.

In the last few decades of the century design reform in Britain was dominated by the work and writing of the protagonists of the Arts and Crafts movement, inspired by William Morris. With Morris, and following the example of Ruskin, also a socialist, design reform took on an overtly political face and it became capitalism itself, rather than bourgeois taste, that was diagnosed as the root of the problem of 'taste'. Only Eastlake, addressing a more popular audience than most of his fellow reformers, referred openly and frequently to the 'ladies' who were, for him, the root cause of the decline in standards. The others most likely shared this view but expressed their condemnations more obliquely. Similarly, while the 'labour without love' of industrial capitalism was the prime focus for Morris, he continued to describe the domestic arena as the main site of 'tastelessness' and the arena for reform. Like his fellow reformers, he despised 'studded chairs and more cushions and more carpets'[40] and claimed that the 'lesser arts' had become 'trivial, mechanical, unintelligent, incapable of resisting the changes pressed upon them by fashion and dishonesty'.[41] His entire oeuvre, and those of his followers, was a response to that diagnosis.

Design reform in America followed a very similar path to that in Britain. Pugin's ideas were known to Downing and the work of Ruskin was fashionable on the East Coast in the 1860s. Most influential of all British reform texts, however, was Eastlake's *Hints on Household Taste*, published there in 1872. It effects were felt most strongly in the emergence of a new style of domestic furnishings, a new fashion, which moved away from the clutter of the last few decades. Indeed, by the 1880s in both the USA and Britain, a number of popular advice books took on the tone of design reform and attacked what was now seen as the old-fashioned domestic taste, advocating the adoption of the new style which had been influenced by the designs and ideas of the Aesthetic and the Arts and Crafts movements. However, ideologically nothing had changed. This was just a subtle shift in the workings of the fashion system which was quite capable of absorbing and regurgitating its opponents. Women, among them Mrs Orrinsmith in Great Britain, could even be heard regaling against the tastelessness of the domestic parlour, as they began to enter the masculine sphere of the paid workplace. This did not fundamentally alter the gendered nature of the debate.[42]

The criteria for 'good design' recommended by all the design reformers were more or less constant during this period. Pugin's 'True Principles' – 'The two great rules for design are these: 1st, that there should be no features about a building which are not necessary for convenience, construction, or propriety: 2nd, that all ornament should consist of enrichment of the essential construction of the building'[43] – informed all the rules for good architectural and design practice. These rules were modified and elaborated by his successors but remained fundamentally unchanged. In gender terms, their significance lay in the fact that they derived from the production process – they were essentially about 'good making' and were rooted in what was called 'inner necessity', that is, in the idea that rules about 'good design' and 'good taste' could be discovered by reference to the nature of the object in question – its materials, its manufacturing requirements and its function. No reference was made to the context of the object or building, to the social, psychological and cultural frame through which it acquired, and on which it bestowed, meanings. As a result, the criteria of the design reformers cut right across those which would have motivated a middle-class Victorian housewife to make a consumption or taste decision and thereby rendered that decision invalid and illegitimate. However, the two sets of criteria continued to reside side by side within the two separate spheres which had generated them. On the level of popular culture, women continued to make choices based on the dictates of fashion and comfort, changing their stylistic preferences as appropriate, guided by the network of taste-making forces which surrounded them, while on a high cultural level a system of polemics, rooted in the masculine sphere and with strong establishment backing, pointed a new way forward. Each system, in turn, was linked back to an idealised image of the nation, the former based upon the concept of the moral family, and the latter upon a national style in the international marketplace.

In the nineteenth century the tensions between the two systems of taste remained hidden beneath the surface of the things, and the sexual politics of taste existed only in the textbooks and in the production of a handful of buildings and household goods produced for an intellectual elite. But it would not be long before these tensions became a part of everyday life in the western industrialised world. The minority voice of the design reform movement became a much larger groundswell and the controlling force over the aesthetic of the mass manufactured environment moved increasingly into the hands of designers working within industry, and away from women in their capacity as home-makers and consumers. The perceived value of 'feminine taste' on the part of society and culture as a whole was further diminished as the dominant aesthetic discourse focused increasingly on the utilitarian and the technological nature of goods and less on their symbolic and aesthetic functions. Above all, the reaction against bourgeois values which characterised progressive thought in the new century meant a wholesale rejection of the middle-class world in all its manifestations. The Cult of Domesticity and feminine taste were among the first to be pushed from the centre.

PART TWO

Modernity and Masculinity, 1890 – 1940

CHAPTER FOUR

'Everything in its Place':

Women and Modernity

'One thing distinguishes modernity from all that is past and gives it its particular character: knowledge of the eternal becoming and disappearance of all things in ceaseless flight.'
– Hermann Bahn[1]

A t the end of the nineteenth century the central role played by taste and aesthetics in daily life was being displaced by a rapidly growing preoccupation with rationality. Originating in the world of science, and reinforced by the technological breakthroughs that were changing the face of the western world, 'reason' was again becoming a force to be reckoned with, sustained by the concept of 'modernity'. The impact of the sea-change was felt in many different spheres, not least in the sexual politics of taste.

The concept of the 'modern' was to revolutionise the ways in which people thought and felt and to highlight a different set of values from those which had underpinned Victorian society. In its cultural manifestations the desire to embrace the new was motivated by a burning need to reject the old and to move beyond Victorian culture, especially in its realist and historicist manifestations. For the modernists, Victorian culture stood at the end of history. Dominated by bourgeois values, it has existed within a relatively stable universe with a known history behind it. Moreover, in locating itself, Victorian culture had referred openly to that history. Looking both backwards and forwards at the same time, it had been able to accommodate and assimilate change. Within that process, feminine domesticity and its accompanying aesthetic, articulated through taste, had played a crucial role in counterbalancing the progressive, potentially destabilising forces within that culture. Most importantly, it had provided a direct link with tradition at a time when many people's lives were undergoing enormous upheavals.

While modernity had an impact on late nineteenth and early twentieth-century western industrialised society in a multitude of ways, most of them were linked to phenomena which formed part of the masculine sphere. It was manifested, for example, in the growth of communication systems; of transportation; and in the expansion of cities, of mass production and of the mass media. These in turn simulated shifts in philosophical and political thinking. New academic disciplines in the area of the social sciences emerged, keen to interpret and make sense of it all. The cultural arena was dominated by the emergence of an 'avant-garde' which sought a new language with which to express the changes occurring around it. A *tabula rasa* was required upon which new forms and new meanings could be spelt out. Science once again provided a starting point for forays into new forms of expression in painting, music and literature. Lacking, or rather refusing, a past, many modernist experiments ritually tore apart the conventions – be they traditional perspective or architectural decoration – which, for centuries, had held culture together.

The gender implications of this were significant. In the very broadest sense, the dominance of science, technology and rationality within the prevailing model of modernity meant the rule of a masculine cultural paradigm. This was particularly apparent in modernist architecture and design. Indeed, the very concept of design, defined within modernism as a process determining the nature and forms of buildings and goods, grew out of this stereotypically masculine culture. In sharp contrast, the notion of 'taste' continued to align itself with domesticity and femininity. As such, it became increasingly marginal to modernism, representing to the protagonists of that movement all that needed to be eliminated. Their refusal to identify with the concept of taste was reinforced by its associations with bourgeois Victorianism, the prime target of attack for modernists across the whole cultural spectrum. Taste, gendered as feminine, came into conflict with design, gendered as masculine, with high culture and the authority of all its institutions on its side.

While the dominant model of modernity was masculine in nature it also infiltrated the feminine sphere in a number of ways. Attempts to rationalise the work of the household represented one instance of feminine culture yielding to the power of reason, seen, both by men and many women as well as a modernising force, while women's entry into the public sphere in their capacity as consumers was also a direct result of advances in the masculine arena of factory production. While the rational household served to minimise the role of taste increased consumption provided a new outlet for it as it was increasingly forced out of the domestic sphere.

All the existing accounts of modernity stress the dual forces of order and chaos that characterised that particular moment in history. At a popular level, the 'call to order' was represented by an all-pervading desire to rationalise everything – from office work to factory work to housework to shopping to cities to the aesthetic of everyday goods. This impulse was linked to the centrality of scientific thought as a popular faith rapidly replacing religion.[2] A *leitmotif* in many writings, from philosophical texts to advice books, it underpinned new educational ideas, and had a significant impact on the nature and appearance of the material environment. Above all, it provided an ideological framework for many different forms of cultural practice – both high and low – in this period.

On one level, this 'call to order' could be seen as a response to the encroaching chaos, fragmentation and diversification that threatened to destroy contemporary society if 'progress' was given a free rein. A compulsion to constantly renew itself lay at the heart of the modern experience.[3] Uncontrolled, this could lead to a destabilisation of society and a fragmentation of culture. The will to order, to unity, was a means of ensuring that that did not happen. The French poet and critic, Charles Baudelaire, has frequently been singled out as one of the first to isolate and describe this sense of pending disintegration. For him, it was present in city life, in the crowds which jostled each other on the streets, moving about anonymously and aimlessly, together but also alone. For Baudelaire modernity was 'the ephemeral, the fugitive, the contingent, one half of art the other side of which is the eternal and the unchanging'.[4] Art was the means of taming the ephemeral, the face of modernity that threatened, unheeded, to engulf mankind. 'Only the artist of modern life', Baudelaire explained, 'can release this beauty from its most trivial externalities'.[5] At the same time, Baudelaire was fascinated by the danger posed by 'the trivial' and he openly embraced the idea of fashion and novelty which were so central to the modern experience. For him fashion was 'a symptom of the taste for the ideal which floats on the surface of all the crude, terrestrial and loathsome bric-a brac that the natural life accumulates in the human brain'.[6] Its inherent ambiguity rendered it both repellent and appealing at the same time. For others, however, the idea of striving that accompanied the need to be fashionable was linked to a feeling of discontentment that represented the impossibility of individual fulfilment inherent in modernity.[7]

Those concepts – triviality, fashion, novelty – which, although fascinating to Baudelaire, were seen by many others as so threatening were inextricably bound up with idea of the 'feminine'. Equally, the dominance of city life located the experience of modernity firmly in the public sphere, thereby prioritising men's experience over that of the majority of women. In his influential text, *The Fall of Public Man*, published in 1974, Richard Sennett confirmed through his very title the essential masculinity of modern public life.[8] (The preoccupations of cultural modernism were mostly with the public sphere, and women were, for the most part, inevitably excluded.[9] The idea of modernity refers to a particular histori-cal moment and set of experiences whereas modernism repre-sented a high cultural response to those experiences, but the two necessarily fed off each other.[10])

By the late nineteenth century the earlier picture of the separate spheres was beginning to show signs of changes. In both Great Britain and the USA women began to move increasingly into the public arena and to become more visible. A growing body of single middle-class women entered the paid workforce alongside the large number of working-class women who were already part of it. Jobs in offices, factories and the retail sector grew apace, many of them replacing domestic service and the various kinds of home-based paid work that had been the domain of many working-class, and of some lower middle-class women only a few decades earlier. For middle-class married women, the opportunities for philanthropic and voluntary work expanded significantly, as did their desire to become involved and to find a way out of the home. In the USA, in areas which had traditionally been women's own, among them the decorative arts, this expansion was particularly notable.[11]

However, this did not mean that the sexual division of labour in the home was transformed as well. Prevailing attitudes about gender roles were such that while many women were leaving the home, they remained, nonetheless, almost solely responsible for what went on inside it. The home continued to play a vital role within national, economic, social and cultural life. Its influence spread, in fact, through society as working-class housewives strove to emulate the domestic values of the middle classes. However, it was not granted the same level of cultural significance that it had enjoyed in the middle years of the nineteenth century.

The dominant themes of domesticity were changed and the expectations of the housewife transformed by the impact of modernity. In that transformation the role of taste within women's domestic duties was relocated and redefined. Divorced now from morality, it lost its former level of cultural authority and thus became significantly marginalised and trivialised. By the turn of the century housewives were judged increasingly by the standards of their motherhood skills rather than by their ability to create a high level of display in their parlours. This change was in response to the high infant mortality rate, the falling figures in the middle-class birth rate, and the growing fear, in Britain, that mothers were not producing enough healthy children for the imperial nation. Health became the burning issue in these years, dominating all other household concerns. The infant welfare movement reinforced the idea of the separate spheres by encouraging women to stay at home with their children. By the inter-war years, the expectations of motherhood had grown to include the need to understand not only the physical needs of children but also the basics of child psychology. With these shifting priorities, taste was significantly displaced.

The themes of rationalisation and potential chaos came to the fore in women's lives as well as in men's. While men were subject to increasing rationalisation in their workplaces, its greatest impact on women was felt in the home. The force of the 'irrational', in contrast, was encountered by women in their expanded role as consumers. It took the form of 'desire', a deeply-rooted inner force which was not susceptible to rationalisation and which evaded the 'call to order'. Taste remained its key agent, a crucial means by which choices were effected. Through consumption, the ideology of feminine domesticity was reinforced in this period, taste surviving as an important element within it.

The idea of rationalising the workings of the household grew out of the 'masculine' world of science and technology imposing its value system on the feminine sphere, as well as out of women's own changing relationship with the home. For women it represented a number of different and contradictory ambitions, among them making housework easier so that more time could be spent out of the home, and professional-ising housework such that it could be granted the same status as that enjoyed by men's work in the public sphere. The entire agenda converged on the question of the desire to eliminate taste from the household. Rationality meant efficiency, profes-sionalism and skill, all of which mitigated against an emphasis upon the aesthetic component of home-making, which had emphasised the roles of intuition, instinct and amateurism. This is not to say, of course, that women did not carry on exer-cising their taste in their homes and continue to enjoy arrang-ing flowers, polishing furniture, fluffing up cushions and arranging knick-knacks on surfaces. What it did mean, however, is that none of this was any longer openly encour-aged and, more importantly, no longer openly valued by society at large. As the idea of 'display' was displaced by that of 'identity', activities such as arranging flowers became, increasingly, a means of self-identification for many women rather than a necessary social ritual.[12]

The rational household movement had a number of different faces, all united by their common interests in the world of science and technology, in their commitment to the power of reason, to the idea of professionalisation, to the renewal of the housewife's skills, not in the area of production but in consumption and organisation; and in their dedication to the idea of the simplification of housework and its manifestations. Above all, the rational home abhorred all that the middle-class Victorian home had stood for, especially its emphasis on the aesthetic and the symbolic.[13] The Victorian parlour, with its high level of display, was seen as little more than a huge dust trap. Draperies came under particular attack for their dust-holding qualities and Venetian blinds were recommended as a replacement for curtains. The colour white took on a special significance as the ultimate symbol of cleanliness. At the turn of the century in the USA, the plain whitewashed walls of living rooms and dining rooms as well as the white enamel surfaces of baths in the new, sanitary plumbed bathrooms were witness to this. The bathroom and kitchen became, in fact, the key areas of the reformed house, as Ellen Lupton has explained

While the parlor or living room is the home's symbolic heart, its 'proper' architectural focus – this center was displaced by the utilitarian regions of the the bathroom and the kitchen, which became concentrated zones for built-in construction details, costly appliances, and on-going maternal maintenance.[14]

The origins of the idea of professionalising and rationalising housework went back to the middle years of the nineteenth century, to the time when, that is, beauty and taste in the home still had enormous currency. When Catherine Beecher introduced the idea in her *Treatise on Domestic Economy, For the Use of Young Ladies at Home and at School* of 1841 it was intended as a means of enhancing the cultural significance of the home and of feminine domesticity in the fullest sense. For Beecher the home had a fundamentally spiritual purpose and the injection of reason and order into the household was meant to enhance, not to counter that role. By 1869 when she republished the book, the climate had already changed and a more progressive tone was present in the enhanced use of new technologies, among them an enclosed stove and the latest forms of heating and plumbing, and in the claim that the book was intended 'to render each department of woman's true profession as much desired and respected as are the most honored professions of men'.[15]

In Britain Mrs Beeton's *Book of Household Management* appeared in 1861. Even though less radical than Beecher's work, it also adopted a rational approach towards household tasks and activities. By the end of the century Britain had been significantly influenced by the revitalised interest in America in Domestic Economy, or Home Economics as it came to be called.[16] During the 1870s, for example, women sat on school boards promoting the study of domestic subjects for girls. In 1879, the Reverend J.P. Faunthorpe's *Household Science: Readings in Necessary Knowledge for Girls and Young Women* appeared, providing a range of information on what it called 'Domestic Economy and Household Science'. Its aim was to educate both domestic maids and housewives who could not afford the services of 'accomplished cooks and experienced housekeepers'.[17] To this end, it set out to inform its readers about the physics and biology of the household, focusing on such things as the nature of matter, natural gases, heat, blood, respiration and digestion. There were sections on clothes, recommending the most practical materials; on shopping, exhorting the reader to be a rational consumer; on household activities, such as cleaning and washing; on health; and on household accounting. Housewives and maids were repeatedly reminded that 'Cleanliness is a part of Godliness' and of the need to keep up the battle against dust.[18] Reverend Faunthorpe warned,

You should be particularly careful not to 'raise the dust' in sweeping, by moving the broom too violently; for if you do the result is a bad one. The dust only flies in the air and settles again as soon as you have finished bustling and allow it time, and you will have done more harm than good, in that case, by disturbing it.[19]

Only on one occasion was taste mentioned and that was in connection with dress. While it was not considered desirable to 'adopt any of the ugly head-coverings so fashionable at the present time'[20] and plain and serviceable boots and shoes were preferred to the 'showy and fashionable' ones available in the shops,[21] a small degree of bodily display was permitted in the form of a bunch of artificial flowers attached to a simple straw hat. The reader was warned nonetheless to 'be very particular to secure the best possible imitations of the real flowers, for gaudy distortions of nature are most offensive to persons of refined taste'.[22] The rest of the book was devoted to the idea that housekeeping was a science, which instruction would only improve: 'Everything is done in a house according to fixed law, or rule, and not anyhow'.[23]

The sentiments expressed in Reverend Faunthorpe's book were reiterated in countless similar publications which appeared on both sides of the Atlantic over the next few decades. They underpinned the curricula of Domestic Science courses in Britain and Home Economics syllabuses in the USA. The formal inauguration of the latter came at the turn of the century through the works of Ellen Swallow Richards, an applied chemist who moved into the area of sanitary chemistry, Isabel Bevier, and Marion Talbot.[24] Home Economics provided a route for these women to pursue their scientific careers. Other innovations in America included the growth of urban cooking schools; the 1876 Centennial Exposition in Philadelphia and the 1893 Columbian Exposition in Chicago provided ideal opportunities for their public display.[25] Most of these developments were instigated by women themselves as part of their campaign for equality. The model they aspired to was, in essence, a stereotypically masculine one rooted in professionalism, efficiency, order, science, technological progress and reason and, as the century progressed, that model strengthened its authority. Taste, fashion and irrationality were seen as things of the past, to be removed from the domestic environment along with the Victorian parlour and its ornate mouldings. The ideology of nationalism underpinned that aspect of the rational household which concerned itself with health. In Britain, it was the future of the imperial nation that made politicians and writers encourage the housewife to tend to the wellbeing of her family and to employ the highest level of efficiency and scientific knowledge. If the home could be seen as a site of production, as well as reproduction, it was in that of the nation itself. As Major General Frederick Maurice explained in 1903, 'the young man of 16 to 18 years of age is what he is because of the training through which he has passed during his infancy and childhood'.[26] In the 1880s scientists identified the bacteria causing typhus, tuberculosis and cholera and what came to be known as the 'germ theory' quickly became a widespread concept. Public hygiene became a dominant concern on both sides of the Atlantic and the housewife was targeted as a necessary ally and prime helper in the campaign to improve the health of the nation. Dust was considered to be the greatest evil as it was believed to harbour germs. The introduction in the first decade of the century of the domestic suction sweeper, or vacuum cleaner, was received with open arms in the battle against dust. A book of 1926, published in both Britain and the USA, devoted an entire section to 'household pests' and six pages to the question of dust. The authors explained that, 'Certain bacterial diseases . . . are air-borne; that is, the infective material may float about in the air – hence the danger of allowing the accumulation of dust.'[27] The need to eliminate dust was part of the general desire to control the environment, a strong characteristic of the masculine model of modernity which prevailed at this time.[28]

The USA envisaged a wide range of variants on the idea of the rational, reformed home in the period frequently referred to as 'The Progressive Era'. One radical movement, dubbed by Dolores Hayden 'material feminism', favoured a collectivist solution to the housewife's problems, maintaining that the single-family dwelling, with all the tasks that came with it, was the main cause of women's malaise and inferiority. This essentially gender political movement concentrated on the removal of the separation between the public and private spheres and between the domestic and the political economy.[29]

One of the movement's chief protagonist, Charlotte Perkins Gilman, a niece of Catherine Beecher, harnessed the health argument to demonstrate what she saw as the dangers of domesticity: 'Sewer gas invades the home; microbes, destructive insects, all diseases invade it also; so far as civilised life is open to danger'.[30] Her deep-seated hatred of conventional domesticity, which she believed, in true Darwinian manner, was the main reason for women's inferiority, came through this attack and she dedicated her life to proposing alternatives to it. The material feminists, Gilman among them, proposed the establishment of public laundries, public kitchens and co-operative housekeeping. Using new technologies as much as possible, they went on to propose – and indeed to influence the actual construction of – apartment blocks with communal facilities and new housing complexes. The suburban single-family dwelling, with its internal gendered spaces, was their prime target and they sought ways of creating new living spaces such that the actual material environment could facilitate change of an ideological nature. Once again, efficiency, utility and reason dominated their efforts and the aesthetic dimension of women's lives was ignored in the struggle to attain equality on men's terms. Their emphasis on de-domestification served, also, to prioritise professionalism over amateurism and to de-skill women in the area of their traditional craft and home-making activities, thus adding to the masculinisation of women's lives and experiences in this period.

However, the material feminists' idealism clashed with reality when, in the 1920s, US President Herbert Hoover initiated a huge programme of research into the construction of public housing. In pursuing this path, many of the ideas of the domestic economists were adhered to, but it was the suburban single-family dwelling that dominated the picture. In a 1932 publication entitled *Homemaking, Home Furnishing and Information Services*, brought out as part of the President's Conference on Home Building and Home Ownership, the typical family was described as having four members while 'about 15 per cent of the rural and 20 per cent of the urban families consist of three persons and 20 per cent of each have

A German kitchen containing electrical appliances manufactured by the AEG company, 1926. The exposed utensils hanging on its walls and the arrangement of items within it indicate that this was a modern, 'labour-saving' kitchen, organised according to the rational principles of 'scientific management'. (AEG)

five persons'.[31] It was clear from this that the idea of collectivism was very far from becoming a reality.

The aspect of the rational household movement which *did*
have a significant influence upon the domestic interior by the
inter-war years, at least where the kitchen area was concerned,
was the one linked with the concept of scientific management.
It was here that the influence of the factory and the office were
most in evidence as the pioneers of the movement, among
them Lillian Gilbreth (the wife of Frank Gilbreth, who along
with Frederick Winslow Taylor, was a prime mover in
scientific management) and Christine Frederick, set about
'routing' and 'step-saving' in the kitchen. Scientific management in the home, or 'household engineering' as it was also
called, directly emulated strategies being implemented in
factories of enhancing efficiency and productivity, through
minimising the amount of labour needed. In her writings,
Frederick provided a number of practical ways in which the
labour of the housewife in the kitchen, now with no servant
to help her, could be reduced.[32] Suggestions were based upon
the idea of reorganising the kitchen – preferably small and
laboratory-like – in such a way that walking between working
surfaces, the cooker, the sink, the food storage, the utensil
storage and the serving table, could be minimised. These, she
maintained, should be positioned according to the order of
actions in the task involved. Diagrams made clear what she
meant. Open shelving was advocated to save time and the
housewife was exhorted to sit on a high stool to save her back
and legs. Frederick recommended the inclusion of a butler's
pantry next to the kitchen 'to prevent kitchen odours and
noises from disturbing the dining room and to store table
china'[33] and a grouping of tools used in conjunction with each
other in the manner of the workman's bench: 'if the eggbeater,
mixing bowl and nutmeg grater are used invariably at the
preparing table, then near this surface they should be placed or
hung.'[34]

This was an extreme example of scientific method pene-
trating the home. There was absolutely no room for
aesthetic considerations as everything was governed by the
laws of efficiency and utility. In fact, so extreme was the

deaestheticisation of the kitchen that it was suggested that no one other than the housewife, the 'worker', should even enter into it. It was as far removed from being considered an area of display as a factory production line. So extreme, also, was the masculinisation of the kitchen that the housewife's tasks were defined now as completely mechanical and rational in nature; they had nothing to do with creating comfort, beauty and a sympathetic, nurturing and emotional environment for the family. Gone was the communality of the large rural kitchen and the big centre table of Beecher's day and in its place was the isolation of the efficient 'worker-housewife', intent on producing food for the family in the same way as the factory produced standardised automobiles. Of course, on closer analysis, the parallels with the factory were clearly absurd as, apart from cooking meals, the housewife's chores were not specifically concerned with production *per se* and she worked alone, like a craftsperson, rather than as a worker in the divided labour system of a factory. Those criticisms apart, the psychological implications for the housewife were clearly disturbing as they robbed her of part of her traditional role as a wife and mother, leaving only that part which could be reduced to logical components and thus made more efficient.

In spite of its obvious shortcomings, the influence of household engineering was strongly felt, both in the USA and Europe – a mark of the hold the culture of reason had on the western industrialised world by the inter-war years. Its most obvious influence was upon the avant-garde architects linked with architectural and design modernism. Through them it entered into the language of modern architecture and design, resulting in a culture, and an accompanying aesthetic, of efficiency, in kitchens and kitchen goods, which has still not been completely superceded. Not all women accepted this colonisation of masculine culture into their homes unquestioningly, of course. Many still yearned for the Victorian parlour, especially those sectors of society which had not yet experienced its pleasures.[35]

The lessons of rationalism were also extensively absorbed and, more significantly, represented in a number of different ways in the mass-produced material environment. Thus, for example, even if a housewife had never heard of 'step-saving' or 'germ theory' she was very likely to be working in a small, laboratory kitchen with the assistance of gleaming white, 'labour-saving' appliances. The goods and environments themselves, aided and abetted by their accompanying advertising and marketing material, spoke the language of the rational household, even if it was not consciously comprehended.[36] This had the potential to homogenise taste and eliminate individuality and difference. The dominance of the principles of standardisation, efficiency and utility, as the criteria for the feminine activity of home-making, threatened to devalue those alternative principles – taste, irrationality and beauty – which had constituted the domestic, and the feminine, ideal only half a century earlier. Deprived in the home setting, women had to find another arena in which to express that part of themselves which could not be rationalised. Increasingly, they found it in that one area of the housewife's duties which could not be made easier by the new appliances – shopping.

Shopping was the one domestic activity that took more rather than less time in this period.[37] Made feasible by the advent and popular utilisation of the automobile by the inter-war years, women devoted increasingly more time to consumption in relation to the amount of time spent on household production. The changes in the general picture of consumption brought about by the industrialisation of the home were numerous. They occurred over a long period but accelerated with the arrival of the new century. Ruth Schwartz Cowan has explained,

Butchering, milling, textile making, and leatherwork had departed from many homes by the 1860s. Sewing of men's clothing was gone, roughly speaking, by 1880 and women's and children's outerwear by 1900, and finally of almost all items of clothing for all members of the family by 1920. Preservation of some foodstuffs – most notably peas, corn, tomatoes, and peaches – had been industrialized by 1900; the preparation of dairy products such as butter and cheese had become a lost art, even in rural districts, by about the same time. Factory-made biscuits and quick cereals were appearing on many American kitchen tables by 1910 and factory-made bread had become commonplace by 1930. The preparation of drugs and medications had been turned over to factories or to professional pharmacists by 1900 and a good many other aspects of long-term medical care had been institutionalised in hospitals and sanitariums thirty years later.[38]

As a result of these and other changes in household production, shopping for goods outside the home became an increasingly onerous task. Not only were luxury objects acquired in this manner, it was also an obligatory means of procuring the subsistence items that were necessary for everyday life.

The exercising of taste did not play a central part in all consumption activities, of course, nor was consumption always a feminine activity. In nineteenth-century rural America, it was typically the male of the household who went into town with his horse and buggy to get the weekly provisions. There was, in addition, a sophisticated system of home deliveries and, by the end of the century, of mail order catalogues. Peddlars were also still a familiar sight in the rural landscape. Increasingly, however, with urbanisation and the advent of the automobile, women took over the role of shopping for the family's goods, whether food for the day's meals from a local source or a luxury item from the nearest urban department store.

By the late nineteenth century domestic advice books contained sections on 'rational consumption', exhorting their readers to shop wisely and not to part with their money on a whim. The Reverend Faunthorpe warned, 'Persons are often disappointed in their purchases, from the simple reason that they have spent their money without due consideration. They go into a draper's shop before they have made up their mind, either as to the kind of material or the quantity which they need.[39]

This theme provided a *leitmotif* in much writing of this nature during the last two decades of the nineteenth and the first decade of the twentieth century. By 1913, Christine Frederick could write with confidence that, 'It is a woman's privilege and duty as the possessor of the powerful weapon of purchaser that it could be used to prevent social injustice.'[40]

While over four decades earlier Mrs Beeton had already pointed out that American women were 'wonderfully clever buyers'.[41] Woman and purchasing clearly had a special relationship with each other by the turn of the century, and increasingly so once the new department stores came on the scene. 'The department stores functioned as female leisure centres,' sociologist Rudi Laermans has maintained,[42] while cultural theorist David Chaney has argued that not only were such stores largely aimed at women, they provided an important role in extending the participation in the public sphere of respectable middle-class women who would otherwise have been confined to the domestic environment.[43] The special rapport between the idea of shopping and women became increasingly strong throughout the period, such that the abstract notion of the 'culture of consumption' was frequently discussed in overtly feminine terms. Thorstein Veblen's *The Theory of the Leisure Class* of 1899 is revealing in this context. Veblen was well aware of the feminine nature of the early 'consumer society' that he isolated and described in this perceptive study of American society during the 'Gilded Age'. Indeed, it was women who personified the values of that society through their involvement in what he called 'conspicuous leisure'. Although he clearly disapproved of the value system which underpinned that society, his task was primarily one of describing it through an analysis of the mechanisms which held it in place. Conspicuous leisure, or consumption, was a central cog within that mechanism and women its key perpetrators. In addition, it was manifested through 'quasi-artistic accomplishment' such as 'household art' and the possession of the 'latest proprieties of dress, furniture and equipage'.[44]

Veblen's ultimate judgement of feminine taste was a negative one. He was nonetheless forward-looking in his alignment of the two phenomena of taste and consumption. Subsequent documenters of the culture of consumption have been less perceptive about its essentially gendered nature, tending to talk more abstractly about its causal factors and its psychological characteristics, and stressing its dependence upon the emergence of a national marketplace, upon a new class of wealthy professionals and managers, upon the influence of the

A postcard from the Paris Universal Exhibition of 1900, produced and distributed by the Parisian department store "Le Paradis des Dames". The spectacle provided by the electrical light effects illustrated here enhanced the special empha-sis upon 'feminine culture' which underpinned so many aspects of this event. (Paul Greenhalgh)

new railroad systems and forms of distribution, upon a new cultural ideal of excess replacing thrift,[45] and upon the roles of advertising and marketing.[46] Above all, they have emphasized the way in which, in the period 1890–1940 in the USA, the idea of consumption became a cultural ideal in itself, linked to

TRICITÉ

the 'individual freedom' contained in the concept of American democracy. While all these elements were central to the factors underpinning the emergence of the culture of consumption, and the mechanisms which enabled it to operate, these accounts have all ignored one of its central implications – the relocation of feminine taste in a public arena.

In the inter-war period ad-vice manuals aimed at training salesmen attempted to analyse the elements which played a part in the act of consumption. The literary historian, Rachel Bowlby, has isolated two poles of consumption – the classical (rational) and the romantic (impulsive). The latter, she has explained, '[is] often seen as having undergone a process of feminisation: [it is] 'like women' in [its] capriciousness and hedonism although without this necessarily implying that these characteristics are natural to women'.[47] The elements in 'the sale' were categorised in these same manuals as including 'Attraction, Interest, Desire and Sale'.[48] Taste was clearly important at the moment of initial attraction and, indeed, at those of interest and desire as well. Nowhere was this more obvious than in the large department stores which invested enormous effort and money to attract their customers. The level of spectacle was unequalled elsewhere, except perhaps at the large, international exhibitions. At the Bon Marché store in Paris, for example,

Everywhere merchandise formed a decorative motif conveying an exceptional quality to the goods themselves. Silks cascaded from the walls of the silk gallery, ribbons were strung above the hall of ribbons, umbrellas were draped full blown in a parade of hues and designs. Oriental rugs, rich and textural, hung from balconies for the spectators below. Particularly on great sales days, when crowds and passions were most intense, goods and decor blended one into another to dazzle the senses and make of the store a great fair and fantasy land of colors, sensations, and dreams. White sales, especially, were famous affairs. On these occasions the entire store was adorned in white: white sheets, white towels, white curtains, white flowers, ad infinitum, all forming a single blanc motif that covered even stairways and balconies. Later, Christmas displays became equally spectacular. In 1893 there was a display of toys representing an ice-skating scene in the Bois de Boulogne. In 1909 plans included a North Pole scene in the rue du Bac section, a Joan of Arc display in the rue de Babylone area, and an airplane 'with turning propellor and luminous toys' above the rue de Sevres staircase.[48]

On the other side of the Atlantic stores were no less ambitious in their display,

For the American department stores, trendy Europe also functioned as an important source of exotic inspiration. Clothes, hats and other women's fashions were often associated with Paris, the 'capital of fashion'. To obtain the desired effect of 'Parisianism', store managers imitated French salons, simulated the 'streets of Paris' and even copied the complete interior of a 'real Parisian boulevard apartment'.[49]

These exaggerated appeals to the eye marked the degree to which culture had become synonymous with consumer culture, especially as it related to the feminine sphere. The level of display that had played, and in many instances continued to play, such an important part within the mid-century, middle-class parlour had been emulated and extended into the public environment of the department store. Within this new setting the constraints and practicalities of everyday life were no longer relevant and there was scope for a full realisation of the fantasy which had resided within the parlour but which could never be given a completely free rein. Now, in the context of commerce, dreams and realities could mingle seamlessly and feminine taste could be indulged to a degree that was unprecedented in the private, let alone in the public, sphere.

In this context 'the eye' dominated the other senses. This emphasis on visual effect served to attract customers and to evoke in them a level of interest and desire.[50] The visualisers of the interiors of the early department stores set out to seduce their customers and clearly, from a commercial point of view, they succeeded in their task. From the perspective of women's culture these stores were not simply sites of manipulation but rather a refuge for middle-class feminine taste which was becoming devalued in the domestic arena under the onslaught of rationality. While rational consumption was also presented within the department store, it was clearly offset by an appeal to the irrational and to the intuitive, through the immediacy of the visual and an invitation to the exercising of taste, with its roots in mid-nineteenth century feminine domesticity.

Whereas in the earlier period a few 'feminine accomplishments' had still existed and homemaking had received a significant level of cultural approbation, by the early twentieth century both had largely disappeared, or at least seemed to have disappeared, leaving behind the idea of women as essentially passive beings. This was contrasted with masculine activity in the form of productive work. Consumption was defined as passive leisure, even by Veblen who had admitted that it was frequently an arduous task.[51] The role of taste within consumption was, as a consequence, also seen as a passive phenomenon, a response to style, the aesthetic component injected into goods at the moment of manufacture and reinforced, through display, at the moment of sale. The activity of giving meaning and form to goods was linked with the process of production rather than consumption. Taste, by implication, was seen as a passive, almost unconscious, response on the part of the female consumer to this active proposition of the designer (usually male). It was also seen as a

mass, rather than as an individualised, response to standardised goods coming off production lines as alike as two peas in a
pod. In retail, however, an 'illusion' of individualism could be
achieved by the display: this concentrated on the uniqueness
of the environment and the special effect of the ensemble of
goods in their particular setting rather than on the goods
themselves.

The determination of the aesthetic content of goods was
taken almost completely out of the hands of housewives by
this mechanised, mass production of a wide range of goods.
Thus department stores, and by the inter-war years, many
other kinds of stores as well, were selling designed, branded,
packaged goods of all kinds. It was from among these that the
housewife had to make a choice. Viewed from one perspective
the housewife can be seen to have been reduced to a passive
victim, seduced and manipulated until she was finally made to
part with her money. Viewed from another, however, middle-
class women escaped from the private sphere through
consumption and thereby entered into an aesthetic experience
which, even if only stereotypically, was their own. And it
undoubtedly brought with it an enormous sense of pleasure
such that they had never experienced before publicly.

The degree to which shopping was not merely part of
housework but also a social, cultural and aesthetic experience
should not be underestimated. In addition to the high level of
spectacle provided, and the democratised luxury on offer,
whether real or imagined, the department store provided much
else besides. At the Bon Marché, for example, visitors could go
on a guided tour of the store at three o'clock each afternoon,
and concerts were regular events. Many stores provided reading rooms and art exhibitions were not uncommon. Rudi
Laermans explains,

The leading American department stores also offered their female
clients many free services. From 1878 onwards Macy's provided
customers with writing tables and newspapers and, in 1879, this
famous New York store opened a luxurious lunch room. Around the
turn of the century, Macy's experimented with several kinds of free
courses and even a bicycle academy for women. Wanamaker realised

his cherished idea of 'public service' by such things as an art gallery (1881), a reading cabinet and a refreshment bar (1882), a post office and an information office (1884) and, from 1892 onwards, regular selections from the pictures exhibited at the official Paris Salons. His new department store in New York, opened in 1907 even had an immense auditorium, more than 1000 seats, equipped with a large organ for concerts of classical music.[52]

In the name of commerce, middle-class women could spend time not only exercising their tastes but also socialising and being entertained and educated in public.

That feminine taste was presented by department stores, stereotypically, as being linked to fashion, novelty, comfort and aesthetic pleasure reinforced the fact that, while the object of the exercise was clearly to sell goods, women were not being culturally de-feminised in the process. Unlike the rational household movement which sought to align feminine culture more closely with the value system of the masculine sphere and, in the process, to eliminate the authority of taste, women's relationship with consumption was represented, aesthetically, through a system of taste values which belonged, traditionally, to women's culture and which did not, therefore, demand a dramatic readjustment on their part. Although goods were standardised, the volume of choice increased dramatically in this period. Choices were undoubtedly made creatively and imaginatively through the exercise of visual discrimination, by then an intrinsic element of women's culture and, above all, one of her chief means of negotiating modernity on her own terms. As ever, though, women's relationship with goods was two-way and the department store was as much a part of the machinery of taste-making as exhibitions, magazines and advertising were. However, the department store reinforced, rather than denied, the place of taste within cultural life and, by implication, validated feminine culture in the process.

While, with the advent of modernity, the cultural pre-eminence of the home was being displaced, and the highly symbolic and ceremonial role of the parlour replaced by that of the more utilitarian living-room (its only remaining non-utilitarian role being the provision of an emotional base for family life, particularly in rearing children), the shopping environment was extending the physical boundaries of women's sphere and taking on a role as the key site for feminine taste.[53]

CHAPTER FIVE

'Letting in the Air':
Women and Modernism

'We have torn down the musty hangings which the Victorians
erected . . . we are determined to let in the air and to ventilate
every corner of our mansion'
— Cynthia White[1]

'As soon as the work of cleansing and sweeping out has been
finished, as soon as the true form of things comes to light
again, then strive with all the patience, all the spirit and logic
of the Greeks for the perfection of this form.'
— Henry Van de Velde[2]

The cultural responses to modernity were numerous. It
had a dramatic influence on the ways in which painting,
literature, drama, and music all redefined themselves at
the turn of the century. In response to what was seen as the
collapse of a shared social, cultural, spiritual and moral order,
and the increasing pre-eminence of science and technology, the
arts turned inwards into an analysis of their own forms. In no
area was this more apparent than in architecture and town
planning, the physical fabric and the site of modernity itself.
Not content with standing back and watching the inexorable
logic of modernity wreak havoc on the urban landscape,
members of the architectural profession intervened in an effort
to stem the flow of the disorder they saw around them. They
set out to endow architecture with a controlling power such
that it could create not only its own destiny but those of its
inhabitants as well.

The 'call to order' proposed by the supporters of the rational household movement in relation to domestic work was paralleled by a much more ambitious one in the architectural definition of the house itself. The latter programme of rational reform was instigated by large numbers of avant-garde architects in Europe, America and Britain in the period between the turn of the century and the inter-war years. It was an intense and far-reaching programme, directed primarily at the architectural structure itself, but also articulating its aims to encompass technology, politics, economics and aesthetics. In formulating its theories, it drew on nineteenth-century thinkers, especially the British design reformers Pugin, Ruskin and the protagonists of the Arts and Crafts movement. By the inter-war years it had transformed those early thoughts almost beyond recognition in the light of the demands of modernity. The modernists exalted, in highly rhetorical terms, the wonders of the new technology, of the new architecture and design, and of the new way of life that, they believed, flowed naturally from these elements.

Architectural modernism set out to control not only the material chaos and fragmentation that resulted from the process of modernisation but also the alienation of modern man (women were rarely discused in this context) as he grappled with modernity in all its guises. From the outset the social and the architectural were, for the modernists, intrinsically linked. Together they defined the 'problem', the solution for which was envisaged as creating a material order which would not only inject a level of rationality and purpose into everyday life but would also, in the words of Mies van de Rohe 'establish new values'.[3] To these ends, the modernist architects wrote articles and books, lectured, proposed buildings (and even built some), and talked and argued endlessly among themselves about the best strategies to be adopted. Their work and words, spreading over at least two generations, broke down into three main phases – protomodernism which lasted between 1890 and the outbreak of the First World War; high modernism which was in evidence between 1918 and the late 1920s; and disseminated modernism which took its influence, as much a style as an ideal, into the international arena in the years leading up to the outbreak of the Second World War. However, its influence didn't stop there, as yet another, even more democratised and culturally influential, phase of modernism came into being after 1945.

The movement was a global one, emerging simultaneously in a number of western industrialised countries. Its early stirrings in the USA and Britain were quickly taken up by Germany, Belgium and Austria where it took on new strengths. The Art Nouveau movement of the turn of the century – a pan-European and American movement in essence (with strong nationalist tendencies within it) which was concerned to locate a new ahistorical style for modernity – existed at its inception serving to consolidate some of its preoccupations, especially those concerned with architectural structure. From its base in the Germanic countries in the early century architectural modernism moved across to Holland and the USSR, aligning itself, in the latter instance, with the socialist revolution taking place there. By the 1920s, however, it was in France and Germany that the theoretical foundations of high modernism were laid down. Following that heroic decade, it was transformed into a stylistic and ideological movement which influenced progressive architecture and design in, among other countries, the USA, Great Britain, Sweden, Denmark and Italy. During its lifetime it attracted many people who committed their ideas to numerous texts – evidence of its ambitions if not of its achievements. Given the chronological and geographical spread of architectural and design modernism it is not surprising that the movement was characterised, indeed like all the other forms of modernism, by its internal inconsistencies and contradictions as much as by the shared beliefs of its protagonists. Nonetheless, the impact of the dramatic volte-face it presented, in theory if not in reality, was both sudden and deeply felt.

Under modernism's influence so complete was the proposed breach with the past that by the inter-war years the material world of the late nineteenth century had been irrevocably transformed. That transformation was effected by a shared commitment to a number of broad themes, all of which centred upon the renewal of the architectural language on the basis of a vocabulary which was inspired by, and considered appropriate for, the new democratic, technological society. Unlike the rational household movement, initiated by and participated in by women as a way of achieving greater freedom and equality with men, the rationalisation of the fabric of the house itself, and of the city in which it was situated, was proposed by members of a profession made up almost exclusively of men, and adhering to a completely masculine value-system.

Rooted in the desire for a total urban transformation, within which changes to the family dwelling would play a necessary part, the predominant model for that renewed dwelling was, like that of the rational household, the modern factory rather than the domestic haven. Furthermore, the values which underpinned that ideal were linked with the public sphere: the repeated emphasis upon rationalisation, standardisation, objectivity and functionality which ran through modernist propaganda from the turn of the century onwards was evidence of the movement's essentially masculine perspective. It was a perspective which was to reinforce the growing marginalisation of feminine values within material culture, and, by implication, within culture as a whole.

Through the institutions which adopted and promoted its views, and through the vast numbers of mass-produced goods which eventually came under its sway, modernism had, by the middle years of this century, become a powerful cultural force. Its influence was felt across a wide spectrum of material culture, in large public housing projects, in household furnishings and interiors, and in a range of domestic equipment. More importantly, perhaps, the values embraced by architectural modernism informed the criteria which have been consistently applied to the influential 'establishment' judgments about the material environment, from buildings to tea-pots, throughout this century. The concept of 'good design', a term used widely to separate the chaff from the wheat where material goods are concerned, was entirely dependent upon its laws. The effect of modernism's eventual cultural supremacy was to displace even further those alternative values – values which were linked with the symbolic role of goods in establishing women's socio-cultural and personal identities – which, through the nineteenth century, had come to constitute an important aspect of their culture. Once again that displacement was represented by a denial of the centrality of feminine taste, and all that went with it in social, cultural, economic and political life. That denial was built on the earlier one contained within nineteenth-century design reform, but now it moved into an international arena and across social boundaries.

Modernism's radical programme was overtly directed not at gender, but at class. In line with socialist principles it advocated a classless society and looked to mass production as a source of the democratisation of material goods that would help bring that society about. 'We must never forget,' wrote the French architect Riuox de Maillou, 'that we are a democracy, that we live in a century oriented ever more towards democracy, and that there can be no art if there is no society to enjoy it, to want it, and by wanting it, to allow it to be produced.'[4] This sentiment was reiterated in the late 1920s by the members of the *Congrès Internationaux d'Architecture Moderne* which was formed in Switzerland:

Rationalization and standardization . . . expect from the consumer a revision of his demands in the direction of a readjustment to the new conditions of social life. Such a revision will be manifested in the reduction of certain individual needs henceforth devoid of real justification; the benefits of this reduction will foster the maximum satisfaction of the needs of the greatest number, which are at present restricted.[5]

The principles underpinning mass production could, they believed, result in a process of democratisation, providing the beneficiaries, in the face of their 'real needs', denied their individual wants and desires. Fundamental to the modernists' vision was a hypothetical notion of a collective society: from the outset, the new standardised architecture and design presupposed a standardised society with standardised needs. Nowhere was this more evident than in the way in which several of its protagonists defined the functional bases of the new dwelling. For Le Corbusier, for example, a house was, essentially, a shelter against heat, cold, rain, thieves and the inquisitive. A receptacle for light and sun. A certain number of cells appropriated to cooking, work and personal life [while the number of rooms needed were] one for cooking one for eating. One for work, one to wash yourself in and one for sleep.[6]

The reduction to these functional base-lines of existence served to standardise the needs of the user and to eliminate personal idiosyncrasies and taste. Nowhere was there a space for display, social interaction, or any other form of psychological fulfilment of a stereotypically feminine kind. The German architect, theorist and pedagogue, Walter Gropius's 'townsman' was a similarly standardised, masculine being for whom 'the decisive consideration in the choice of a dwelling is utility'.[7] Hannes

Meyer, Gropius's successor at the Bauhaus school in Dessau, Germany, was even more rigorous about the standardised requirements of architecture and town-planning – 'The demands we make on life today are all of the same nature depending upon social stratification. The surest sign of true community is the satisfaction of the same needs by the same means' – demonstrating, perhaps, the most totalitarian face of modernism.[8] It extended also to the mass-produced consumer goods that were to have a presence in the modern home, among them, 'the folding chair, roll top desk, light bulb, bath

Henry Ford's Highland Park Factory, 1913. Illustrated here is the moment at which the body of the 'Model T' Ford automobile finally met the chassis. Ford's ideas about production, based on the principles of rationalisation and standardisation, were an important influence upon modernist architectural and design theory. (Ford Motor Company)

tub and portable gramophone [which were] typical standard products manufactured internationally and showing a uniform design'.[9] Although operating at the extreme end of modernism

Meyer's ideas revealed the extent to which individualism was banished, along with the aesthetic function of the architectural interior and its furnishings. Thus was eradicated, it was proposed, if only by implication, the housewife's role as the 'beautifier of the home'. Feminine taste had no part to play in this new picture of things.

The rejection of individualism and its replacement by collectivism, and the determining of the logic of consumption by rationalised mass production, were aspects of modernist theory developed in reaction to the inherited and despised nineteenth-century bourgeois culture. These propositions directly undermined the role of feminine culture which had increasingly become linked with the ideas of taste, desire and consumption as the nineteenth century drew to an end. The subordination of these forces to those of rationality and production placed an overt emphasis on modernism's commitment to the public, masculine sphere, in which it discovered all the principles necessary for its programme of reform.

A dislike of bourgeois culture and the feminised domestic aesthetic so closely linked with it ran through the modernist of the period, uniting many of its different faces. There may have been no common solutions but there was, at least, a common enemy. This shared conviction emerged from a number of texts, among them that of Maillou, who located bourgeois taste in the 'Louis-Phillippe era'.[10] The Austrian writer and architect, Adolf Loos, one of the key spokesmen of early modernism, was equally damning about the bourgeois interior,

and so the domination by the upholsterer began; it was a reign of terror that we can still all feel in our bones. Velvet and silk, Makart bouquets, dust, suffocating air and lack of light, portières, carpets and 'arrangements' – thank God, we are done with all that now.'[11]

Many other modernists shared Loos's sentiments. However, it was in the words of the French architect, Le Corbusier, writing in the 1920s, that the hatred of the bourgeoisie could be found at its most vehement. In *The Decorative Art of Today* he referred to the 'bourgeois king' with his 'bric-a-brac mind', an overt reference to the middle-class interior.[12] He was particularly disparaging about 'windows hung with lace curtains' and 'walls papered with damask',[13] both associated with the middle-class parlour.

For almost three decades the idea of bourgeois taste, linked with that of display, and, by implication, the aesthetic of feminine domesticity, provided an image against which modernist architects could react. Their programme of reform was rooted in an attempt to counter that image and to renew the language of material culture such that it could be cleansed of all associations with it. In the course of formulating that new language they were absolutely clear-sighted about what they were rejecting – all of it linked in some way with the idea of domestic display and feminine taste. Fashion and novelty were repeatedly singled out for disapproval, as signs of a decadent culture. Loos was characteristically adamant in his rejection: 'Fashion! What an appalling word!'[14] while the German architect Hans Poelzig was equally dismayed by the fact that 'we are still chasing after fashionable manners that after a short time, having been vulgarized by a series of imitators, become the object of contempt'.[15] He contrasted this with what he called 'real architecture . . . the product of intense thought by artistic considerations'.[16] Nearly three decades later the German architect and furniture designer, Marcel Breuer, a student and subsequently a highly influential teacher at the Bauhaus, reiterated the same belief: 'We have tired of everything in architecture which is a matter of fashion; we find all intentionally new forms wearisome, and all those based on personal predilections or tendencies equally pointless'.[17]

Fashion, most modernists agreed, was superficial and, above all, unsatisfying in falling short of the ideal to which they all aspired, embodied in the neo-Platonic idea of universal form. Purity, universality, simplicity, geometry and standardisation were linked, in modernist rhetoric, in their ability to transcend the ephemeral and confront the essence. 'We did not base our teaching on any preconceived ideas of form,' explained Gropius, 'but sought the vital spark of life's ever-changing forms . . . [A] 'Bauhaus style would have been a confession of failure and a return to that very stagnation and devitalizing inertia which I had called it into being to combat'.[18] The idea of vitality contrasted with inertia, of activity opposed to passivity, emerged over and over again, suggesting, paradoxically, that it was change, renewal – the very essence of fashion – which the modernists sought, motivated by fear of sameness. Ideologically, however, the idea of fashion was linked inextricably with the old bourgeois value system within which display and social aspiration had played such an important part.

Novelty, closely allied to fashion, was also inextricably linked to that 'old' culture and the modernists were keen to show their disapproval of that false notion. 'The ideas inherent in our movement are too serious for us to indulge in frivolous dalliance with changing fashions and novelty for its own sake,' wrote the German Hermann Muthesius,[19] the chief importer of British Arts and Crafts ideas into his country, while Gropius also rejected what he called 'transient novelties'.[20] But it was the idea of ornament which roused the strongest feelings amongst modernist architects, as they strived to renew the language of architecture, and thus to control, rather than be controlled by, the culture it found itself within. Without doubt, the most influential text was Adolf Loos' essay of 1908, provocatively titled 'Ornament and Crime'. Loos' ideas – themselves influenced by those of Chicago architect Louis Sullivan, who had written in 1892 that 'ornament is mentally a luxury not a necessity'[21] – were to influence all the key modernist protagonists of the 1920s. In 1898 Loos also embraced Sullivan's ideas about women's 'natural' inferiority claiming that, 'the woman has fallen behind sharply in her development in recent centuries'.[22] By the time he came to write 'Ornament and Crime', however, in which he made his famous claim that 'the path of culture is synonymous with the separation of the ornamental from the functional', it was non-European 'primitive man', another inferior in the evolutionary hierarchy, rather than woman, who was singled out as being responsible for this 'regressive' behaviour. 'The Papuan covers everything within his reach with decoration, from his face and body down to his bow and rowing boat,' he wrote.[23]

Loos introduced his ideas within a framework of Darwinian evolutionary theory which defined man's progress as a move away from the world of nature towards culture. And with culture came the rejection of ornament. Le Corbusier revealed his dependence upon Loos when he described decoration as,

baubles, charming entertainment for a savage ... it seems justified to affirm: the more cultivated a people becomes, the more decoration disappears. (Surely it was Loos who put it so neatly.)[24]

Contained within these words, if only obliquely was the assumption that 'savages' and women were both inferior to 'civilised' man and that their shared dependence upon nature and decoration was a sign of their shared evolutionary inferiority.

The outcry against ornament ran as a *leitmotif* through modernist writing and practice. The Russian artist Naum Gabo and Antoine Pevsner were adamant that,

We reject decorative colour as a painterly element in three-dimensional construction. We demand that the concrete material shall be employed as a painterly element.

We reject the decorative line. We demand of every line in the work of art that it shall serve solely to define the inner directions of force in the body to be portrayed.[25]

The German architect Hugo Häring proclaimed seven years later that,

We now consider it uncultivated to apply Pallas Athena to the bottom of a bowl; we regard it tasteless to fashion vessels in the shape of heads of animals and use their interior as containers; we no longer make table legs look like lion's feet.[26]

No naturalistic ornament, and no decorative application of colour or line were permitted in modernist architecture and design. Both implied a denial of function, a denial of the inherited Arts and Craft principle of 'truth' to materials, a denial of purity and of the essential universality of the object. Above all, decoration and ornamentation were part of bourgeois culture, that root of all decadence in architecture and design. As Gropius explained, 'that is why the movement must be purged from within if its original aims are to be saved from the strait-jacket of materialism and false slogans inspired by plagiarism or misconception'.[27]

The sense of outrage and moral panic which underpinned his and others' reactions drove them to propose extreme solutions in their search for purification. In the process of formulating those solutions, they undermined and repressed, however unwittingly, feminine culture as it was defined stereotypically at that time.

The feminine aesthetic which had helped define woman's self-image and identity in the nineteenth century had been crystallised in the Cult of Domesticity, in particular through the creation of domestic display. The domestic interior, and above all the feminine spaces of the parlour or drawing room and bedroom or boudoir, played an important role in this process. One of modernist architecture's key propositions was a total redefinition of the nature and significance of the inte-rior of architectural structures, the domestic dwelling among them. They eradicated the idea of gendered spaces in the home and instead opened up the interior to became an extension of the exterior. Gone was the idea of enclosed, womb-like fixed spaces with their rigid symbolic and ritualistic meanings and in their place was a more flexible set of possibilities linked to functions of a much more utilitarian nature.

The transformation of the interior was discussed, as were so many other aspects of the modernist building, in formal rather than symbolic terms, that is, with regard to mass and space rather than meaning. The American architect Frank Lloyd Wright was among the first to radicalise the interior. 'The sense of interior space', he wrote

'as a reality in organic architecture co-ordinates with the enlarged means of modern materials. The building is now found in this sense of interior space; the enclosure is no longer found in terms of mere roof or wall but as 'screened' space. This reality is modern.'[28]

Gropius reiterated this idea of the disappearance of the wall.[29] Now a non-structural element given the new uses of steel, concrete and glass in architectural construction, the wall no longer acted as the same psychological barrier that it had less than a century earlier. The modernist house was conceived as a much more open space with utility determining the uses of its components. With this new sense of openness came a redefinition of the spaces that existed in the domestic dwelling. Sharp distinctions, it was proposed, should be eroded. While specific room functions continued to exist, the equipment within the spaces was to become less indicative of social ritual and more utilitarian in nature. Le Corbusier, for example, recommended storing as much as possible behind screens and shutters, thus eliminating any kind of display:

'Hence there is no longer any cabinet-makers' furniture in the house ... The reduction of furniture to the state of pigeon-holes which, if necessary, form the wall itself, can also be obtained by basic methods of construction in reinforced concrete.'[30]

He also advocated the use of office furniture in the domestic setting as well as a range of standard items which could be obtained from the local store, among them doors, windows, radiators, light-bulbs and wash-basins. The architect's task was to supervise the equipping of the house in such a way that no further subsequent 'arranging' was necessary on the part of the future inhabitants. While the addition of a few personal items, such as books and paintings, were permitted, the inhabitants' role was to perform the activities that had been anticipated for them in the functional zoning of the house. No longer was there a need, it was implied, for any Ruskin-style 'arranging' on the part of the housewife. Her role as a creator of social display and exerciser of taste in the domestic context was rendered, as a result, entirely redundant.

These ideas were put into action most effectively in Le Corbusier's *Pavillon de L 'Esprit Nouveau*, designed for the 1925 *Exposition des Arts Decoratifs* in Paris. In this project he aimed to 'solve once and for all both the problem of furniture and that of the aesthetic content of the home'.[31] One of the pavilion's most prominent features was the sense of continuum between the inside and the outside such that the distinction between them was rendered ambiguous. This was emphasised by his leaving a tree on the site which was allowed to penetrate a hole cut into the building. Later, with his collaborator in furniture design, Charlotte Perriand, whom he described as 'our expert in domestic interior design'[32] he developed these ideas further. In stripping the house of its 'clutter', as he called it, he was aiming to create a meditative environment, encouraging contemplation – 'And perhaps we will take pleasure in contemplation, during this hour of rest, this hour of relaxation at home'.[33] What he failed to suggest, however, was a new role for women now that the 'beautifier of the home' was, in his eyes, relegated to the past.

By the 1920s, women had entered the public sphere to a significant extent, both as paid workers and consumers. Feminine taste continued to play its role, catered to by the 'spectacle' provided by department stores. Le Corbusier was not unaware of this and he extended his critique of bourgeois culture to include the department store and its contents, targeting women and salesgirls as the guilty parties. He blamed 'the display in shops and department stores' for encouraging 'iconolatry'[34] – the (false) worship of icons – and referred to what he evocatively called 'our boudoir-bazaars full of trinkets',[35] thereby reinforcing the link between feminine domesticity and the aesthetic of the marketplace. His most vehement attack on woman and consumption, however, was contained in this chant:

Decoration on all castings (iron, copper, bronze, tine etc).
Decoration on all fabrics (curtains, furnishings, fashions).
Decoration on all white linen (table cloths, underwear, bed linen).
Decoration on all papers.
Decoration on all pottery and porcelain.
Decoration on all glassware.
Decoration in all departments! decoration, decoration: yes indeed, in all departments; the department store became the 'ladies' joy'! [36]

The Ladies' Joy (Le Bonheur des Dames) was the title of a novel by Emile Zola from the previous century. In recalling it, Le Corbusier was evoking the whole gamut of exhilarating experiences for women participating in the public activity of shopping, which Zola had so evocatively described.

Le Corbusier reserved his strongest condemnation for the shopgirl herself, that newly arrived female worker whose role it was to spread the culture of consumption that he so despised. Elaborating his dislike of surface decoration, he admitted, sardonically, that it could be 'as charming, as gay, and as shop-girl-like as you would want', continuing, less ambiguously, to describe, 'The pretty little shepherdess shop-girl in her flowery cretonne dress, as fresh as spring seems, in a bazaar such as this, like a sickening apparition from the show cases of the costume department in the ethnographic museum'.[37]

Although it was the context, rather then the girl herself, which he was blaming for this show of tastelessness there was, nonetheless, a sense in which Le Corbusier held her responsible for complicity with it. Indeed, for a number of decades girls working for the retail trade had been viewed with moral ambivalence. Living independently of their families and partici-pating in city life in ways in which, hitherto, only female pros-titutes had been able to, the respectability or otherwise of these new female workers had been a subject of much discussion. In questioning her role in matters of taste Le Corbusier was simply adding a new dimension to that moral debate. Women, claimed Le Corbusier, were also responsible for the decline in the decorative arts. He wrote in a manner which recalled the words and moralising tone of Charles Eastlake,

So young ladies became crazy about decorative art – poker-work, metal-work, embroidery. Girls' boarding schools made room for periods of applied Art and the History in their timetables . . . At this point it looked as if decorative art would founder among young ladies, had not the exponents of the decorative ensemble wished to show, in making their name and establishing their profession, that male abilities were indispensable in this field: considerations of ensemble, organisation, sense of unity, balance, proportion, har-mony.[38]

This open condemnation of female amateurism and praise of male professionalism revealed his belief in the idea of two gendered systems of aesthetics, the masculine being naturally superior to the feminine.

While it was he who articulated the principles of high modernism and became probably the most internationally influential of the movement's protagonists, Le Corbusier cannot be charged with the sole responsibility of bringing about a masculinisation of architecture and design at this time. The disapproval of domestic display, of ornament, of historicism, of fashion and novelty and of bourgeois culture in general was widespread. Collectively, the modernist architects voiced and demonstrated their disapproval in such a way that trivialised and marginalised feminine culture as it had developed in the nineteenth century, a result not simply of their shared negative feelings but also of their modernist articulations, rooted exclusively in masculine culture and the masculine sphere. Nowhere was this more obvious than in the formulation of what came to be called 'The Machine Aesthetic'. Although mass production and the factory were never really more than a source of metaphorical inspiration for modernist architecture and design, they also served to bring to the modernists' attention ideas about standardization, universality and democratization which became so central to their thoughts. For many of them the engineer became a hero. 'The essence of what these people are doing,' wrote the Dutch architect and designer Henry van de Velde, 'is reason and their means is calculation. It is their employment of reason and calculation that can lead to the purest and most certain beauty.'[39] Here was a way out of, what was for them , the cul-de-sac of intuition – a set of mathematical rules which could lead to a new aesthetic. Many others followed Van de Velde's line of reasoning, putting their faith in the pure logic of engineering science. As Hans Poelzig explained,

It is left to the engineer to calculate and design a unity between load and support, the right measurements for the parts of the structure consisting of various materials. The architect all too often seeks his salvation in purely decorative constructions that have to be imposed on the fabric of the building and spoil its organic clarity.[40]

In the engineer, the factory and the rules of mass production was seen as escape from the bottomless pit of taste. Found there were a set of principles and rules, based upon reason and organisation, which could provide sure footholds. Countless fallacies were attached to this belief, but on a metaphorical level, it worked and interest in geometry, objectivity and what came to be called the theory of 'functionalism' derived directly from it. Le Corbusier was articulating the thoughts of many of his fellow architects when he wrote that,

Geometry is the means with which we have provided ourselves for looking around us and expressing ourselves ... geometry is the basis ... It is also the material foundation for symbols signifying perfection, the divine. It brings us the lofty satisfaction of mathematics.[41]

Objectivity underpinned the work and ideas of the architects and designers linked with the Dutch De Stijl group. Its key spokesman, Theo Van Doesburg, explained why: 'In order to create something new, we need a method, that is to say, an objective system. If we discover the same qualities things in different things, we have found an objective scale.'[42]

The modernists believed themselves to be following the logic of science and its offshoots into the worlds of technological progress and mechanised mass production. Not only did the American factory and its production system fascinate them and provide a model for them, it also produced standardised goods and materials for them to use. As if by magic, the logic of the production system was translated, in their eyes, into the geometrical appearance of the goods produced and they were exaltant in their admiration for them. The automobiles, the items of plumbing and bathroom equipment, the filing cabinets, the pieces of office furniture, the electric light-bulbs and the 'everyday drinking glasses and bottles of various shapes'[43] constituted the modernists' 'type-forms'. These were simple modern goods untainted by the aesthetic thumb-print of social display – the naive, innocent products of the engineer, not the decorative artist.

The theory of functionalism lay at the heart of the modernist architectural project. In its simplest form it required that the internal structure and utilitarian function of a building or object should determine its nature and appearance. This became a rule of thumb for designers and architects, a strategy to prevent them being distracted by the 'thrills' of the marketplace and of ensuring that the psychological and symbolic roles of the object were kept to a minimum. 'The shape of an object', wrote Hugo Haring in 1927, 'is determined by the forms arising out of its purpose',[44] reiterating Loos's statement of nearly three decades earlier that, 'The beauty of a useful object only exists in relation to its purpose.'[45] Gropius expressed the same sentiment in relation to work at the Bauhaus school,

An object is defined by its nature. In order, then, to design it to function correctly – a container, a chair, or a house – one must study its nature; for it must serve its purpose perfectly, that is, it must fulfil its function usefully, be durable, economical and 'beautiful'.[46]

Only after a number of rationally-conceived criteria were fulfilled could the idea of beauty enter into the picture.

While the idea of functionalism seemed a simple one, its execution was not always straightforward and the idea of 'looking functional' very often replaced that of 'being functional'. Inevitably, what was emerging was a new style which mirrored, rather than determined, a new way of life. It was a style which prioritised all those values linked with masculine culture and which pushed to one side those that could be thought of as feminine. In attempting to formulate an architectural and design theory which would move beyond cultural difference – a kind of Esperanto which would communicate on the basis of the universal language in which it was expressed – modernist architecture and design were risking alienating one half of the population – women. Intended to eliminate class and geographically-related cultural differences, it overlooked the fact that it was formulated in terms which only related, and which therefore were only easily and directly communicable, to one half of the society at which it was aimed.

Modernist buildings and designs, were destined for the urban environment. Le Corbusier's interest in town planning was a direct response to his own experience of modernity. 'The increasing disorder in our towns,' he wrote 'is offensive: their decay damages our self-esteem and injuries our dignity .. They are not worthy of the age. They are no longer worthy of us'.[47] This was reinforced by his feelings about modern Paris in particular, the urban space within which, several decades earlier, the 'flaneur', Charles Baudelaire had envolved his own poetic responses to the effects of modernity on city life.

At dusk, at six o'clock on the Champs Elysees, everything suddenly went mad. After the vacuum, the traffic furiously started up again. Then each day increased this turmoil further. You go out and the moment you are out of the door, with no transition, you are confronting death: the cars are racing past.[48]

The desire to bring a sense of order into urban existence underpinned the modernist architectural project in its many guises. One strategy was to introduce functional zoning which separated pedestrian walkways from the traffic. Siting their reforms in the urban context inevitably reinforced modernism's fundamental distance from feminine culture. This was compounded by the definition of the architectural interior, and indeed of the furniture within it, as an articulation of space which existed within a yet larger spatial system, that of the town or city. This was at odds with the much more personalised, enclosed definition of the interior which had been women's most recent experience of it. For them, the material model for the interior had been that of fashionable dress rather than the city. A symbol of personal and social identity, an extension of the body and of a gendered self, and a marker of social positioning, their relationship with fashionable dress had taught middle-class women how to use material culture to their own ends. In the nineteenth century this relationship had been extended to the domestic interior which became a site for social display and self-identification. In emphasising the urban context of the house and thereby minimising its inward orientation, modernist architects were, in effect, denying women that relationship.

Elizabeth Wilson has explained that women's experience of the city differed in essence from that of men.[49] The modernists' desire to create order in the city threatened to destroy the very characteristics that women, through their participation in consumption, commerce, leisure and the spectacle of the city, enjoyed in urban life. 'The utilitarian plans of experts whose goal was social engineering' were the main enemy of women's relationship with the city.[50] By rationalising the city and emphasising its functions rather than its meanings, modernists were minimising its role for women.

The rational reform movements, which focused on hygiene and household and which were displacing the role of feminine taste within the domestic environment, were embraced enthusiastically by the architectural modernists and used by them to further their cause. In defining the aims of the German *Werkbund*, a body set up to help encourage high standards in the design of German's mass-production goods, Herman Muthesius drew an analogy between form and cleanliness – 'form is a higher spiritual need to the same degree that cleanliness is a higher bodily need'.[51] In the equation of cleanliness with good form the spiritual and the bodily were merged. The bathroom made a frequent entry into modernist rhetoric as a key site for cleanliness, hygiene, modern technology and modern design. Loos was the first to isolate it, eulogising the advanced level of bathroom equipment in the USA, while Le Corbusier inherited the same obsession:

Demand a bathroom looking south, one of the largest rooms in the house or flat, the old drawing-room for instance. One wall to be entirely glazed, opening if possible on to a balcony for sun baths; the most up-to-date fittings with a shower-bath and gymnastic appliances.[52]

The idea of bodily cleansing becomes a metaphor for cultural cleansing within modernist architecture and it found its most obvious aesthetic expression in the dominance of the colour white. Le Corbusier waxed lyrical over the benefits of whitewash,

Every citizen is required to replace his hangings, his damasks, his wall-papers, his stencils, with a plain coat of white ripolin. His home is made clean. There are no more dirty, dark corners. Everything is shown as it is. Then comes inner cleanliness ... once you have put ripolin on your walls you will be master of yourself.[53]

Control achieved through a coat of white paint.

The most direct link between the application of scientific management in the home and the architectural and design modern movement came through the influence of Christine Frederick's translated writings. Rationalised housework inspired a number of modernist architects to translate the ideas involved into material form. One of modernist architecture's most significant achievements in the area of housing, a scheme built in Frankfurt between 1925 and 1930 by the architects Ernst May, Adolf Meyer and Ferdinand Kramer, had kitchens designed by Grete Schüette-Lihotsky, which were influenced directly by Frederick's guidelines.

Systematic housekeeping and modernist architecture aligned themselves in the shared aim of rationalising both the house *and* what was going on inside it in order to transform the way in which its inhabitants lived. Into an arena which had hitherto housed feminine values, themselves formed in part by the nature and role of that material environment, they were implanting an ideal rooted in masculine values. By attempting to transform both the physical nature and the function of that environment the modernists were proposing a transformation of women's role and value-system. Neither the rational household movement nor architectural modernism provided any ideas or suggestions as to how that transformation could, or should, take place, however. Within both movements the traditional sexual division of labour in the home was never questioned. Only the American material feminists had proposed architectural changes based on revised ideas about gender roles and their ideas were either unknown to the modernists or, if known, ignored.

Architectural modernism implied an end to the rule of women's tastes in the domestic arena and a clean wipe of the slate such that their influence was eradicated once and for all. In their place it substituted the controlling hand of the professional (male) architect and designer, working in tune with modernity, defined in masculine terms, and with a renewed architectural language which aimed to minimise the possibility of a resurgence of feminine values in the formation of the material environment. Design, defined as a professional and controlling activity, was to replace taste, defined as an amateur and essentially passive set of responses. In that cultural take-over bid, masculine values were to replace the feminine in the domestic interior.

In terms of buildings built and consumer goods designed architectural modernism remained a minority movement. Nonetheless it entered mainstream culture in a number of subtle ways, providing an ideological framework for much architectural and design theory and practice since that time. Most of the architectural and design educational institutions established in this century developed curricula based on modernist principles; the industrial design profession embraced its ideals; and many museums collected modern mass-produced work, selected according to criteria rooted in modernism. This has resulted in the formation of a design canon to which many objects have been judged either to be of 'good' or of 'bad' design. The leading design reform bodies of this century – among them Germany's *Werkbund*; Sweden's *Svenska Sjlödforeningen*; Britain's Design and Industries Association and its Council of Industrial Design – also adopted modernist principles in their efforts to raise standards in design. In addition, many of this century's design propagandists, working with the printed word and through other mass media, have embraced modernism and worked towards spreading its ideals as widely as possible.

In these, and many other ways besides, the ideals underpinning architectural and design modernism have filtered into the public consciousness. Most professional practice has been judged by its standards and has stood or fallen according to its terms of reference. Its hierarchy of values have subtly invaded the world of amateur aesthetic choices as well. Inevitably, given its gender bias, it has not served women well except when they have decided to join its ranks and adopt its values as their own in an attempt to liberate themselves and others.

Where the world of commerce, and the system of values which have guided *its* successes, is concerned, however, quite a different picture emerges, a picture in which gender cultures were not so easily ranked. When modernism had to confront the 'real', rather than the idealised world of mass production, and its twin, mass consumption, the compromises that had to be forged brought feminine culture back into the frame once again.

CHAPTER SIX

'The Selling Value of Art':

Women and the Moderne

'Modernism constituted itself through a conscious strategy of exclusion, an anxiety of contamination by its other, an increasingly consuming and engulfing mass culture.'
— Andreas Huyssen[1]

In his account of the tussle between modernism and mass culture Huyssen recognised the gendered characteristics in the two opponents. While he saw modernism, gendered as masculine, as 'objective . . . and in control of [its] . . . aesthetic means', mass culture, in contrast, was characterised as 'subjective, emotional and passive'.[2] Characterised by its dependence upon a set of stereotypically masculine values, modernism was confronted by the feminine values associated with mass consumer culture. In their idealised masculine formulation, architectural and design modernism rapidly reacted by transforming themselves into a set of stylistic and ideologic imperatives. Great Britain, the USA, the Scandinavian countries and Italy were among the countries which responded to its call. Nowhere in its purest incarnation, did it take a strong hold. Mediated through advertising, popular films and consumer goods, however, it made its presence known in a variety of modified forms.

The strongest modifying force on high modernism was feminine culture. The links which women had made, and continued to make in this period, with domesticity, consumption and commerce — indeed, their participation in a world in which comfort, display, fashion, visual spectacle, images, intuitive responses, desire and object symbolism were uppermost —

resulted in the emergence of a set of feminine forces which exerted a strong influence on culture as a whole . In their journey from culture to commerce architectural and design modernism were forced to comfort these forces head on.

One of the ways in which feminine culture came to influence design was through its alliance with mass consumption. With mass production, defined by Henry Ford and emulated by many of the producers of the new technological consumer goods, well in place by this time consumption became increasingly controlled by advertisers, marketing men and designers, whose tasks were to stimulate desire on the part of potential consumers. To do so, they had to enter into the unconscious thoughts and motivations of those consumers in order both to understand and accommodate the value system which impelled them to consume. These values then had to be injected into the definition of the product and its accompanying promotional material. The strategies which were evolved were such that the ideals of modernism were necessarily compromised and modified.

The first encounter between the idealism of modern architecture and design and the pragmatism of feminine commercial culture occurred at the end of the nineteenth century with the emergence of the Art Nouveau movement in France. This first international, modern style, manifested in a wide range of architectural, interior, and decorative arts projects, touched the world of women in a number of different ways. Janus-like, it looked in two directions at the same time, to the elitist world of the past and the democratised society of the future. Rooted in a commitment to the eighteenth-century ideal of woman as both embodiment and creator of beauty,[3] it also embraced the contemporary commercial world of mass consumerism. Its links with an elitist model of luxurious, aristocratic culture – the decorative 'style moderne' of the period of Louis XV, personified in the elegance and grace of Marie Antoinette and Madame de Pompadour – were frequently evoked. At the same time, its contemporary orientation was towards the 'new world' of the mass marketplace. Both of these worlds stood outside the framework of high modernism as it came to be defined. And both were linked to a feminine culture which resisted the reductive, mechanistic logic of that essentially masculine movement. Although these two worlds pulled in two quite different directions, they both refused the pull of standardisation and social homogenisation that lay at the heart of the modernist project.

The influence of the rococo style in decorative arts and interiors on the formation of French Art Nouveau was enormous. The latter leaned heavily upon the former's stylistic dependence on the organic, curvilinear lines and forms of nature; its aristocratic ties to luxury and artisanal manufacture; its commitment to the aesthetically unified interior, the 'organic ensemble' and to the unity of the arts in general; its belief in the importance of beauty and elegance as manifested in the decorative arts; its emphasis on the important of the private, domestic sphere; its devotion to a life-style defined by pleasure, leisure and sensuousness; and to the central role played by women, both as makers and as sources of inspiration. While the modernists followed William Morris's idea of social revolution as a means of overthrowing the bourgeoisie, the desire to reintroduce the rococo into French culture represented an alternative strategy for undermining the power of the middle-classes in favour of the old aristocracy rather than the empowered proletariat.[4]

Above all, the rococo had valued and prioritised women's tastes, as manifested in the domestic sphere, such that they had played a central role within visual culture. The attempts at the turn of the century by members of the French Central Union of Decorative Arts to reinstate the idea of feminine domesticity at the heart of decorative arts production signified a desire to refeminise that sphere of culture. They did not, however, consider women worthy, or capable, of participating in the world of painting, nor did they question the 'separation of the spheres' or recognize the importance of the 'new woman' in this period.[5] But their policies did serve to position feminine taste in the centre of the picture in terms of production and consumption, thus implying mainstream cultural approval of what had hitherto been called 'female accomplishments' and, by extension, recognition of those items of domestic use and display which women now bought rather than made. An 1892 exhibition, organised by the Union and entitled 'An Exhibition of the Arts of Woman' contained objects made and used by women, among them 'furniture, leather work, basket weaving, cutlery, jewellery, feathers, artificial flowers, lace, embroidery, clothing and apparel accessories'.[6] Women's production and consumption were seen as part of the same creative act.

Although the Union encouraged women to avoid department store goods and to work directly with artisans, the Art Nouveau movement aligned itself closely with commercial culture – in particular with advertising – demonstrating yet another face of its affiliation with feminine culture. A contemporary commentator, George Avenal coined the phrase 'the democratization of luxury' which characterised the way in which all department stores promoted their goods and services.[7] At the 1900 exhibition in Paris, the major showcase for the Art Nouveau style, the large department stores made their presences felt through widely-distributed promotional material, while in America the studio of the Art Nouveau glass artist, Louis Comfort Tiffany, produced an opalescent glass dome for the Marshall Field store in Chicago in 1902.[8] The work of the French Art Nouveau poster artist, Jules Cheret, had an enormous influence on American dry goods poster design,[9] and even the colours which played such an important role in department store display were inspired by the American dancer, Löie Fuller, who was linked closely to Art Nouveau and who 'ushered into existence new prismatic blends of tints in gauzes, artificial flowers, plumes and ribbons'.[10]

In the early decades of this century the links with the eighteenth century remained strong in the development of the modern French decorative arts. Committed to social elitism, luxury objects, craft manufacture and feminine culture, the movement was much derided by the arch-modernist, Le Corbusier. As with Art Nouveau, however, there was a direct line from these elitist manifestations to mass culture through their links with consumer culture. The Art Deco movement, so called after the Exhibition of Decorative Arts held in Paris in 1925, straddled these cultures, extending the example of

Art Nouveau and moving, in the inter-war years, into the mass environment through the medium not only of exhibitions but also of mass market films. Like Art Nouveau, Art Deco was a modern decorative movement, or style, rooted in the idea of artisanal manufacture but conscious, also, of the need to respond to industrial production, and committed to *objets de luxe* as it looked to the 'golden age' of the eighteenth century.

In the period 1900–1930, in emulation of Germany and the achievements of the *Werkbund*, France looked to the reform of its decorative arts as part of a bid for international supremacy and consolidation of a strong national identity in the international marketplace. However, unlike Germany, which had a collective vision of society and a democratised, standardised model of design, France's self-identity was linked with the concepts of 'taste' and 'elegance', suggesting the pre-eminence of individuality, fashion, novelty and, above all, a close relationship between the worlds of the decorative and the fine arts. Nowhere was this more in evidence than in the work of the early fashion *haute couturiers*, Worth, Doucet and Poiret among them, who made elitist claims for their creations, but who also sought wide audiences for their innovative designs. Poiret, one of the first French fashion designers to link fashion with modern art, made his impact in America through elaborate shows at department stores, among them Wanamakers and Macy's in New York.[11] His 'Atelier Martine' was set up to extend his ideas, formulated in the context of fashion, into the realm of interior decoration, and he joined the other French *ensembliers* – men such as Francis Jourdain, Emile-Jacques Ruhlmann, Paul Iribe and, a little later, the firm of Süe and Mare – in providing tasteful, unified decorative interiors, often with little more than lip-service to eighteenth-century taste.

The Art Deco movement also played an important part in the 'democratization of luxury'. Once again, the department stores were important agents in this process. Maurice Dufrène, furniture designer and director of the design department of the Galeries Lafayette department store in the 1920s, explained the role they had to play,

The large stores clearly do not create fashion on their own, but they disseminate it, they make it accessible to the general public, and they can now promote furniture, decoration fabrics and objects in the same way as they have promoted dress – as 'novelty' and 'fashion'.[12]

Three other key Parisian department stores – Printemps, Bon Marché and Magasins du Louvre – also created design departments at this time, keen to capitalise upon the new, popular interest in modern interior decoration. They were directed by key protagonists in the Art Deco movement and their successes in this venture led them to be given prime locations in the French section of the 1925 exhibition in which to construct their pavilions and promote their wares. The story of Art Deco was one of democratisation and internationalisation. The 'moderne' style as it came to be called, characterised by its rich decoration, its hints of luxury and exotica, and its aggressive modernity, mixed with allusions to both the near and distant past, was an early inspiration to many architects and designers in Europe and the USA in the 1920s and 30s. The work that resulted was primarily commercial in nature. Factories, hotels, office blocks, department stores and cinemas emerged in the 'moderne' style, as did vast numbers of interiors, including those of the new transatlantic liners. In addition, a plethora of decorative and utility goods, conceived in a wide range of materials from exotic woods to the new plastics, adopted the new style in a bid to enter the world of modernity.

A distinctly feminine version of the modern, Art Deco drew consciously on the decorative tradition; it acknowledged the commercial framework of material culture and, above all, it understood, and defined itself in terms of the process of consumption and the role of object symbolism. It presented an image of modernity which was as much about dreams and fantasy as it was about the realities of living in the first half of the twentieth century. It appealed to consumers internationally, and was central to the transformation of the modern from an elite to a democratised base, a shift which helped construct a bridge between masculine and feminine cultures. The artefacts that responded to the pull of Art Deco tended to be confined to the traditional areas of architecture,

'Art Deco' dressing table items, 1930s. Representing the first truly popular modern style the geometric forms of Art Deco were linked with feminine culture in a number of ways, providing a significant means through which women could encounter modernity.

interior design and what had formerly been called the decorative or the applied arts, in short, artefacts with a basis in craft manufacture, many of which had strong feminine associations. Furniture, domestic textiles, plastic dressing tables sets, cigarette cases, glass perfume bottles, vases, and jewellery, all

surrendered to the Art Deco stylistic onslaught. Goods from the more masculine world of technology took a little longer to be convinced of its attractions. By the 1930s, however, automobiles, office machines and domestic appliances had found their own feminised popular aesthetic in the style known as 'streamlined moderne', 'streamform' or, most commonly 'streamlining'. Displaying a high level of gender ambivalence, these usually dark-coloured, monochrome, seemingly seamless, organically-shaped objects with their chromed steel highlights, or 'speed whiskers', evoked simultaneously a masculine world of advanced technology and aesthetic minimalism and a feminine one of symbolism, sensuousness and fantasy.

Although the visual results looked rather different, the cultural formulation of this aesthetic revealed a continuity with the 'democratisation of luxury' which had underpinned the emergence of Art Nouveau and Art Deco. These modern French 'traditions' crossed the Atlantic, rapidly finding their equivalents in the strongly consumerist climate of post-war America. Just as American department stores had emulated many of the selling techniques of their Parisian counterparts at the turn of the century, so now American commercial culture looked to French practices for inspiration. This was particularly evident in the new interest in modern store design which swept the large American cities in the 1920s, as the cultural historian

Neil Harris has explained,

Shopping architecture in the major cities [emerged] as American retailers tried to incorporate some of the possibilities of modernism, as they had been evidenced at the great 1925 exposition des arts decoratifs in Paris ... It is only in comparatively recent years that merchants have been brought to realise that art has a selling value.[13]

Several of the men who were to become the most widely publicised and successful of the American industrial designers of the inter-war years cut their teeth on store design, thus confirming its central role in the commercialisation of art. Walter Dorwin Teague, the elder statesman of that generation, created a new store for the Eastman Kodak company in New York City[14] which, with its wood-panelled walls and chrome trim, had strong Parisian overtones, while Donald Deskey, another member of the same pioneering group, designed the Franklin Simon department store's first modern windows, using corrugated and galvanised iron, copper and bronze.[15] He went on to do the same for the Saks department store on Fifth Avenue while Norman Bel Geddes, the *enfant terrible* of that generation of designers, dressed the windows of the Franklin Simon store with a series of stark, highly dramatic displays of clothing which owed much to European avant-garde stage design and window-dressing techniques.

The idea of display moved out of bourgeois culture and the home and into the public sphere of consumer culture with selling as its primary end. Now professional and almost exclusively male 'commercial artists', rather than housewives, controlled its language and meanings. In the words of Frederick Kiesler, a European emigré designer who worked on a number of store projects in America in the 1920s, 'The store window is a silent loud speaker and not a dead storage. Its language appeals to everybody and has proved to be the most successful Esperanto for promoting merchandise.'[16]

The universal appeal of the visual image proved a vital means of communication in a consumer culture in which the eye was proving itself supreme. Visually trained individuals, knowledgeable about new forms of visualisation which would

attract and stimulate desire, were needed to create the necessary images. As Kiesler explained, 'Contemporary art
reached the masses through the store'.[17] In order to ensure that
the masses would like what they saw, the creators of store
displays combined their knowledge of modern art with that of
popular imagery. To this end the display manager 'is the first
to read dozens of periodicals, he overlooks no important
theater opening, he neglects no important film or exhibition.
He must be able to absorb information like a sponge.'[18]

Acting as filters for popular imagery derived from the most
directly taste-forming areas of the mass media and combining
this with more avant-garde, European-derived imagery,
American designers carried on the process, initiated across the
Atlantic, of feminising mass-produced material culture. It did
this by emphasising those aspects of visual culture which were
more traditionally linked with feminine, rather than masculine, cultural values. The environment in which women's
consumption took place was becoming more and more attuned,
aesthetically, to their culture, as, indeed, were the mass-
produced goods on offer in the marketplace.

However, it was in advertising, rather than product design,
that America took its first steps in bringing art into contact
with commerce. Although advertising grew out of the need for
mass-production industry to sell its goods and the advertising
profession was almost exclusively male, it realised that for the
goods they were promoting to succeed in the marketplace, it
had to understand and appeal to the taste of consumers, who
were predominantly women.

The word picture that served to collapse the class audience into the
mass audience was female in gender. The consumer, whether, class
or mass (but intrinsically mass) was a 'she'. As one advertisement in
Printer's Ink succinctly put it 'The proper study of mankind is man
. . . but the proper study of markets is woman'.[19]

Advertisements were one of the key means through which
the idea of modernity was communicated to a mass audience,
largely of women. A combination of factors served to make
advertising an essential facet of modern commercial life:

the technological and economic exigencies of rationalised, standardised mass production and corporate capitalism; socio-cultural and demographic changes which led to the invention and mass manufacture of many new goods; the creation of new branded goods which had emerged with the industriali-sation of the home;[20] and the formation of large manufacturing corporations in the USA. Ads formed a bridge between the masculine culture that had engendered them and the feminine culture at which they were directed. Along with department stores, advertising played a key role in bringing women face-to-face with modernity in all its manifestations. In its role of providing a middle-ground between production and consumption, it had to tread a strategic middle path which crossed from one to the other. Thus, while it was focused increasingly on women, it retained one foot in the world of production, a foot which, although increasingly disguised, was fundamental to its *raison d'etre*. Advertising served to trans-late masculine culture into a language which women could understand and a number of strategies were devised to make this possible. Selling the benefits of a product, for example, replaced selling the product itself or its brand name. This represented a 'shift from the "factory viewpoint"' to a concern with 'the mental processes of the consumer',[21] accompanied by a parallel shift from a dependence on copy to imagery which would appeal more to what was generally believed to be the 'greater emotionality' of women.[22]

The thinking behind American advertising in the inter-war years was essentially 'feminine'. It sought to penetrate women's psychological make-up and stimulate desire by fixing on images and ideals of femininity which it believed would relate to women's lives as they would have liked to be living them. A key strategy in advertising's effort to embrace the world of the feminine was to accept the Veblenesque idea of upward emulation and to invite women of all classes to partici-pate in the world of luxury, expressed for the most part, by the presence of beauty in the goods it promoted. Luxury democratised was a paradox; it was advertising's job to resolve, or rather, to conceal this. Luxury suggested uniqueness, craftmanship and individuality and brought with it the level of refinement, tradition, and comfort that was still an important part of women's culture as stereotypically perceived. These had to be offset, nonetheless, by an element of novelty. Advertisements promised to meet all these requirements. One obvious means of injecting 'novelty' into goods was to promote their fashionable looks. Colour was a relatively simple way of making sure that something was the 'flavour of the month' and, from the mid–1920s onwards, an emphasis on colour featured in a wide range of advertisements from Cannon and Martex towels to Parker pens and Hoosier kitchen cabinets. As the decade progressed, it was clear that 'beauty' had become, in the words of the advertiser and commentator Elmo Calkins, a very important 'selling tool'.[23]

Goods themselves were also beginning to look 'stylish'. Many of the young industrial designers had done their apprenticeships in the worlds of advertising and retailing and knew how to appeal to consumer's wants and desires. George Sakier, Lurelle Guild and Norman Bel Geddes had all been art directors at some time in their early careers while Walter Dorwin Teague, trained as a typographer and lithographer, had worked for the Calkins and Holden advertising agency in his early days in New York. Raymond Loewy had been a freelance advertising illustrator, as had John Vassos. Unlike their more purist modernist European counterparts, whose roots were in the architectural profession and for whom mass production was an abstract ideal rather an everyday reality, the American industrial designers embraced a modernism which addressed technological and economic modernity head on. Their was a modernism which had its being in the paradoxical relationship between mass manufacturing and sales. Their task was to straddle the gulf created by the separation of the spheres, to evolve an open language which could bridge the value systems of both. Advertising and product design set out to create a single image which concealed all the contradictions implied in this ambition, to make a seamless join between the gendered worlds of production and consumption.

It was the streamlined automobiles, refrigerators, food-mixers, irons and pieces of office machinery rolling off the American production lines from the late 1920s onwards that

Cash Register, manufactured by the National Cash Register Company, 1930s. The American Industrial designer Walter Dorwin Teague's redesign for this product, which replaced the surface decoration of its antecedents with a sleek, streamlined profile, was part of the visual modernisation of the world of consumption. (Walter Dorwin Teague Associates)

best expressed this ironing out of contradictions and paradoxes. Streamlining brought together the minimal aesthetic of European modernism and progressivism with a modernised vision of beauty, luxury and comfort – concepts which linked it with feminine culture as it had been constructed nearly a century earlier. As such, it played a key role within twentieth-century gender politics. The main stimulus to

injecting beauty into the consumer machines that had dominated American mass manufacturing since the turn of the
century was economic in nature. A set of industrial, economic,
social and demographic circumstances had caused a rapid
increase in consumption in the years following the First World
War. However, by the late 1920s, that graph of consumption
was in decline and market saturation threatened to destroy a
number of the large-scale manufacturers. At the same time,
female consumer power was enhanced: women had more
money to spend, fewer children, more mobility and – with the
advent of electrical domestic appliances – more time in which
to shop. In the climate of intense competitiveness that characterised the late 1920s it was logical that manufacturers, in their
increasingly desperate attempts to sell their goods with the
assistance of marketing men, advertisers and designers, should
target women: thus their open acknowledgment of the need
for a 'beauty' or fashion element in goods. While this had long
been the case in traditional goods categorised as 'decorative' or
'applied' arts, in the products of the new technological industries the emphasis had been placed on their utilitarian, rather
than on their aesthetic characteristics. Many goods, intended
for use by the servant and kept out of the areas of the house
allocated for display, carried the hallmarks of plain engineering
rather than aesthetic discussions. Only a few – sewing
machines, electric fires, suction sweepers, and toasters, among
them – which had penetrated the public areas of the house,
bore traces of fashionable rococo or Art Nouveau decoration,
transforming them into aesthetically acceptable additions to
the parlour or dining-room. These aesthetic modifications had
been essentially superficial in nature. Other goods were
overtly archaic in design so as to appear familiar and unthreat-
ening: coffee-makers, for example, resembled traditional
samovars. Cabriole legs and paw feet had been common
features on other early domestic appliances, injecting a level of
'furniturisation' into these otherwise unfamiliar domestic
machines.

Early appliances were characterised by this aesthetic diversity. Prior to the 1920s, appliance manufacturers, many of
them small in scale, had adopted a pragmatic approach towards

the question of style, adapting their products according to the symbolic requirements of the consumers and environments for which they were intended. Within Fordist mass production as it was formulated when the 'Model T' went into production at the Highland Park factory in 1913, however, this flexible approach was no longer practicable, given the level of rationalisation necessary to make its production formula viable. In Henry Ford's famous phrase, Ford customers could have their car in any colour 'as long as it is black'.[24] Product standardisation, as a result, became increasingly the norm.

Ironically, the feminisation of technological consumer goods was initiated through that most symbolically masculine of objects, the American automobile. Advertisements for many goods – and indeed the goods themselves – had already responded to the challenge of colour, injected to put a level of 'added value' into consumer products which no longer appealed simply on the basis of performance, price, or their hygiene-enhancing of labour-saving qualities alone. By the mid–1920s one message, appealing, perhaps, to the consumer's rational judgement, would be stressed in the advertising copy while the product's appearance would be sending out quite a different one, intended, perhaps, to evoke a more emotional response. By the end of the decade, products increasingly spoke for themselves, articulating a sophisticated symbolic language of form and decoration which appealed to the purchaser's subconscious in a number of different but simultaneous ways.

Following nearly a decade in which the mass-produced, standardised automobile had been 'a drab, dreary machine devoid of decoration to relieve the vast expanses of metal',[25] in 1923 General Motors introduced colour in its Chevrolet Superior model, an innovation made possible by a new form of nitrocellulose lacquer, called Duco, which could carry more pigment than the enamel used hitherto. This small, but enormously significant decision, marked the moment at which American automobile design, rapidly followed by product design in general, acknowledged the need to recognise beauty as well as utility. Soon colour was joined by a consideration of line and form as well, and cheap, mass-produced automobiles began to emulate the expensive, carriage-built, luxury cars which had recognized the laws of elegance and finish much earlier than their mass-market equivalents. The text of an advertisement for the 'Model A' – Ford's first car to recognise the imperatives of style – made clear the new preoccupation with what was commonly called the 'through-line' of the streamlined automobile:

You will take real pride in the smart style and fresh new beauty of the Ford just as you will find an ever-growing satisfaction in its alert capable performance. From the new deep radiator to the tip of the curving rear fender, there is an unbroken sweep of line – a flowing grace of contour and harmony of color heretofore thought possible only in an expensive automobile. Craftsmanship has been put into mass production.[26]

The new approach was rapidly adopted by all the key manufacturers such that, by the early 1930s 'style' had become a prerequisite of automobile manufacture and consumption. The implications were widespread, both in terms of the organisation of production and in the meaning of automobiles within American mass culture.

This introduction of beauty into a hitherto standardised utility object was accompanied by product diversification and rapid style change. Once again General Motors, with the assistance of Harley Earl, head of its Art and Color section from 1927 onwards, led the way in injecting principles, long in operation in the fashion industry, into the world of automobile manufacture. The idea of feminine fashionability which had been transferred, in the previous century, from women's dress to the domestic interior, was now extended into a new arena, one much more overtly masculine in nature. The links between 'parlour-culture' and the transformations that were occurring in automobile manufacture were not lost on those involved. In 1912 Walter Chrysler had exclaimed, 'What is the use of finishing up the hidden parts of a chassis as if you were going to put it in the parlor?'[27] Just over a decade later it seemed as if that was exactly the intention of the automobile manufacturers for 'the automobile was part of the domestic refuge of consumption and people wanted it to be as beautiful as anything in their parlors.'[28]

The aesthetic of streamlining, with its emphasis upon the creation of a visual whole and upon concealing the complex mechanisms within – a strategy which also, perhaps, concealed the harsh realities, monotony, alienation and fragmentation in the sphere of production – was comparable to that of the Victorian parlour.[29] With its abundance of textiles used to create continuity and flow, and to disguise the separateness of its component parts, the parlour was also in the business of 'concealing'. Although steel had replaced chintz and lace, the desire to lay a smooth layer over disjointed elements, to impose an impression of visual unity, and to eradicate inherent contradictions, was similar in both instances.

Although this imposition of the parlour aesthetic resulted in a feminisation of the automobile this did not mean the provision of a new culturally valued space for women through a rehab-ilitation of feminine taste. Although women were now using automobiles more widely, primarily in their capacities as consumers and mothers – 'while men buy cars, women choose them', remarked a contemporary commentator [30] – its femin-isation benefitted men rather then women. The gendered ideology of the separate spheres meant that men could not admit to their need for beauty, novelty, spontaneity and irra-tionality. Increasingly, the cultural historian David Gartman has argued, mass consumption acted as a compensation to the working class for selling their labour to the mass manufactur-ing corporations. According to him, involvement in 'commod-ity consumption' was not a passive but an active phenomenon, based on the real needs of the human spirit. These needs were met by the injection of 'feminine' features into products which played a key role in leisure activities. From the mid–1920s onwards, according to Gartman's thesis, the automobile was 'feminised' primarily in order to ameliorate the lives of working-class men. This is not to say that this didn't go some way towards improving the lot of women as well.

The design of electrical appliances followed hard on the heels of the automobile, responding to the same 'will to style'. Hitherto, the three visual alternatives for these goods, depending upon their destinations in the world of consumption and use – aesthetic archaism, the 'engineered look', and fashionable surface elaboration – were now replaced by the dominant modern appliance aesthetic of the inter-war years, streamlining. Although it was American-born and bred, streamlining had much in common with the 'French taste' that had influenced the earlier 'Deco Moderne' style as well as with avant-garde modernism.[31] The art historian Terry Smith has written

Loewy's Model 66 (gestetner duplicator) rises off its grained plywood cabinet in forms stepped like those of Paul T. Frankl's famous 1930 skyscraper bookcase. The graining, two-toning, and the contrasts of chromium silver handles with the darker body are all Art Deco devices. The 'restraint' of the rising forms, their planar surfaces, and the rounding-off of the cabinet and main form derive from a more purist modernism.[32]

This claim for a high European modernist heritage for streamlining was reinforced by the industrial designers themselves who sought this cultural validation. Simul-taneously, however, the new refrigerators, vacuum-cleaners, food-mixers and ovens represented an incursion of modernism into the feminine sphere, albeit primarily into the kitchen rather than the parlour. The arrival of these smooth, unified white mono-liths signified a number of things simultaneously: like the automobiles they followed, their aesthetic was a feminised version of modernism inasmuch as they rejected 'honesty' in favour of disguise and concealment; they displayed a prefer-ence for natural, organic shapes over rectilinear forms (insofar as pressed steel could be pushed in this direction); they espoused surface decoration in the form of chrome details; they appealed to the eye rather than to the mind; and above all, they evoked desire. In addition, they rejected universality in favour of stylistic obsolescence, as Raymond Loewy's series of 'Coldspot' refrigerators for Sears Roebuck in the 1930s so clearly demonstrated. Beauty and novelty combined in these objects to provide a modern, kitchen-based equivalent of the Victorian parlour.

However, the opportunities for women's direct intervention in influencing the appearance of these domestic machines were minimal. In spite of their gestures towards 'feminine taste' these products were still essentially standardised, mass-produced factory-made goods, designed by men, albeit on the basis of decisions which recognised the importance of feminine consumption. Their essential standardisation was offset only by symbolic references to luxury and individualism. Like the department stores and advertising before them, these goods straddled and concealed the contradiction implicit in the idea of the 'democratisation of luxury', presenting women with a fixed, compromised aesthetic formula which resisted any form of negotiation.

Streamlining was responsible, nonetheless, for the domestification of the modern machine. This had an enormous impact upon the home and upon women's lives within it. On the one hand, the vast majority of these machines, especially the large-scale ones, were coated in white enamel, making them, in effect, the domestic equivalent of the Model 'T' Ford. The call to order, the homogeneity and the rationalisation symbolised by this aesthetic standardisation was enhanced by its strong associations with cleanliness and hygiene. In addition, their much-vaunted labour-saving and 'easy-to-clean' qualities pushed them even further into the camp of the 'rational consumer'. On the other hand, through their sensuous curves and dramatic chrome details, they evoked a world in which fantasy and desire could be achieved. They straddled the worlds of masculine and feminine culture through an essentially androgynous aesthetic which allowed both sexes a space. Most significantly, perhaps, like the department stores and advertising before them, they both encouraged women to encounter the world of modernity, and provided lasting material evidence of that encounter.

So strong was the impact of modern design in the kitchen that inevitably the living-room was pulled towards it as well. An ideal of the modern living-room entered American culture, heavily influenced by mass circulation film and magazines. In her novel centering on the lives of four Vassar graduates in New York in the 1930s Mary McCarthy provided a caricature of just such a self-consciously modern environment:

Kay had been showing the apartment to everyone who hadn't seen it. Two rooms, plus dinette and kitchen, plus a foyer, plus Kay's pride and joy, a darling little dressing room, so compact, with closets and cupboards and bureau drawers built in. Pure white walls and woodwork ... The latest models of stove, sink, and ice-box ... Every stick of furniture was the latest thing: blond Swedish chairs and folding table ... in the dinette ... ; in the living-room a bright-red modern couch and armchairs to match, a love-seat covered in grey-and-white mattress ticking, steel standing lamps, a coffee-table that was just a sheet of glass that Harold had had cut at the glazier's and mounted on steel legs ... There were no rugs yet and instead of curtains, only white Venetian blinds at the windows. Instead of flowers, they had ivy growing in white pots.[33]

A combination of European avant-gardism, indigenous American streamlining and 'do-it-yourself' modernism charac-terised this fashionable interior. The use of the word 'instead' on two occasions revealed the extent to which it was presented as an alternative to the Victorian interior, a kind of invisible shadow which still haunted this unequivocally modern space in the form of the absent curtains and the abandoned flowers.

The reality of most women's domestic spaces was, however, less rigorous than this. In those areas where they could still exercise their tastes, women adopted a range of responses to the image of modernity that was presented to them and which it was up to them to negotiate on their own terms.

CHAPTER SEVEN

'We are All Creators':

Women and Conservative Modernism

'We must gather round us the things we love and following our preferences live in modern "period" rooms or in houses where works of different ages and countries make friends.' –
Margaret Bulley[1]

Streamlining provided a ready-made symbolic language which expressed women's first encounter with progressive modernity. Through an identification with their own culture, packaged and re-presented to them, women were given the possibility of forming a new relationship with the technologically-oriented, forward-looking face of the modern world. What it did not provide, however, was those equally vital conservative components of feminine culture, the ideas of comfort and tradition, and the sense of the home as refuge from the world of manufacturing and commerce. Given the continued existence of the separate spheres in both Britain and the USA, and the need for large numbers of women to continue in the roles as homemakers and mothers, those components were still a fundamental requirement.[2]

The image of women in the home, with a renewed emphasis upon a conservative model of domesticity, was promoted through the mass media – women's magazines, household manuals, novels, films and newspapers – with the result that it became embedded as an ideal across class lines with inter-war society. And the particular model of domesticity it resembled was that of Victorian society nearly a century earlier. The image of the Perfect Lady – 'the angelic wife and mother . . .

firmly based in the home: she was isolated from the outside world of industry and squalor and represented the warmth and refuge of the hearth'[3] – re-emerged (if indeed she had ever gone away) in the inter-war years as a vital component of the new post-war social order. In England the hidden agenda was no longer the Victorian need for stability in the face of potential disorder but rather the more practical one of a dwindling population and the need to swell its numbers. Women's domesticity mitigated against their role in the workplace and there was much antagonism to married women joining the ranks of the workforce. In Britain, the marriage bar operated in a number of professions, preventing many women from working in a paid capacity outside the home. And the ideological pressures upon women were such that the progressive model of modernity, even in its feminised version as represented by the new technological consumer goods, could not fulfil all of women's symbolic requirements. Indeed, within women's aesthetic practice in this period, there was a significant level of resistance to the model of modernity that they were being asked to negotiate.

In their various capacities as designers, consumers, craftspeople and home-makers, women negotiated modernism and the moderne in a variety of ways. Many of them responded by developing their own brand of what has been called 'conservative modernism'. The literary historian, Alison Light, has written,

Janus-faced, it could simultaneously look backwards and forwards; it could accommodate the past in new forms of the present; it was a deferral on modernity and yet it also demanded a different sort of conservatism from that which had gone before.[4]

Alison Light located 'conservative modernism' in the writings of a group of 'middle-brow', middle-class women novelists of the period – Ivy Compton-Burnett, Agatha Christie, Jan Struther and Daphne du Maurier – writers who were considered by most literary critics to exist outside the canon of 'good literature'. The parallels between these writings and feminine taste as it was manifested in material culture in this period was both strong and significant. Marginalised from the establishment canon of 'good design', and considered both trivial and 'tasteless' by many cultural critics, one face of women's interwar material culture – the face that they made themselves – was as far removed from the world of progressive high culture as a murder mystery by Agatha Christie.

In this period women, both as professionals and amateurs, expressed their tastes in a variety of ways. Their work crossed a spectrum from an acceptance of what modernism had to offer and an attempt to align themselves with its programme to a total rejection, whether conscious or otherwise, of that model of aesthetic and ideological practice. Inevitably, the bulk of their work resided somewhere in the middle blending modernist ideals with those of feminine domesticity, resulting in artefacts and interior settings which would have been at home in a Daphne du Maurier novel.

A commitment to modernism underpinned a significant amount of the work of those women, relatively few in number, who joined the new profession of 'designers for industry'. To date, most attention has focused on the tiny handful of professional female aesthetic practitioners who aligned themselves to the ideals and forms of European architectural and design modernism by working alongside its heroes: prominent among them were the French designer, Charlotte Perriand, who collaborated with Le Corbusier on his furniture; the German designer, Lilly Reich, who joined the German architect Mies van der Rohe on a number of architectural projects; and the Irish designer, Eileen Gray who worked in Paris in the 1920s alongside that city's avant-garde architects and designers. Their professional careers were all rooted in interior design, furniture design and the decorative arts, those areas of professional practice which were linked most directly with women's traditional role and sphere. Their origins notwithstanding, their liaison with modernism was complete and uncompromised, although recognition of this fact has been long in coming.

A considerable number of female students attended the Bauhaus school in Weimar and subsequently in Dessau (they constituted a quarter of the first intake in 1919),[5] although, in spite of Gropius's claim that he was interested in producing anonymous (by implication, non-gendered) designers for industry, many of the Bauhaus women – 19 out of the total of 50 in 1929: for instance[6] – were associated with the textile workshop led by Gunta Stölzl, thus perpetuating the traditional idea of gendered aesthetic production. A contemporary commentator, Helene Nonne-Schmidt, explained this in essential terms,

The ability of women to become absorbed in detail and her interest in experimental 'play' with surfaces suit her for this work. In addition her feeling for colours finds reign for expression in the multitude of possible nuances.[7]

The implication was that women were to be excluded indefinitely from participating in formal experimentation.

Grete Marks was a Bauhaus student who *did* work with form in her capacity as a ceramic designer. However, when she arrived in Britain in the 1930s she was given less of a hero's welcome than the three male ex-Bauhaus modernists – Gropius, Marcel Breuer and Laszlo Moholy-Nagy – who arrived in the same decade.[8] Grete Marks's story was typical of those female designers who embraced modernism for ideological reasons but who found that it was hard to get work and make a living as a result. On one level, this was simply a reflection of the general situation of women wanting to work in the professional sphere in the 1930s, both in Britain and the USA, where any woman working was seen to be keeping a man out of a job. On another level, it reflected the conservatism of the bulk of manufacturing industry, especially in Britain, which had an eye on the market and felt that it had its finger on the pulse of feminine taste, perceived as essentially conservative in nature. The small number of women working in design, especially where it was linked to industry, was explained by a number of other factors as well. C.R. Richards observed in the USA in 1922 that:

No women designers were found in any of the establishments visited. The explanation is probably that designers are often required to supervise the production of furniture in the factory. The requirements of travel and visiting buyers are also met more readily by a man than a woman.[9]

Design, quite simply was not perceived as part of the feminine sphere. The American industrial designer Henry Dreyfuss reinforced this cultural prejudice when he explained that the strengths of the male designer were that 'he has an understanding of merchandising, how things are made, distributed and displayed'.[10] Had he completed the object cycle and included the concepts of 'consumption' and 'use' in his list, women's contribution to the design process would have been clear. Significantly, however, he stopped short, thereby eliminating women from that process altogether.

By aligning themselves with the architectural and design avant-garde, and thus participating in the masculine sphere, female modernists were seeking to negate the stereotypical feminine aesthetic inherited from the previous century and, by implication, their involvement with the concept of middle-class domesticity that had underpinned it. They saw this as a means of achieving cultural emancipation and gender equality. Their strategy paralleled exactly that of those feminists who believed that female emancipation should be based on women's participation in political and public life on equal terms with men. Inevitably, the implementation of this strategy involved denying conventional femininity and adopting a masculine stance. So persuasive and so dominant was modernist ideology that a number of women, especially those who went through the architectural and design educational system, were pulled into its orbit, seeing there an opportunity to escape the aesthetic tyranny of stereotypical feminine taste. Even resonances of Ruskin and his vehement dismissal of feminine culture were heard in the words of one English modernist architect, Sadie Speight, as she described what she believed to be the proper way of designing glass artefacts: 'The special quality of glass is its transparency. When used for wine in particular, this transparency should not be destroyed by elaborate cutting or tinting.'[11]

Yet again, cut crystal was being singled out and outlawed on the grounds of its 'untruth', only now the sentiments were being expressed by a woman. Through the course of the nineteenth and twentieth centuries the glittering, shimmering surfaces of cut glass had been isolated as a recurrent symbol of middle-class excess, a major obstacle to the path of 'true' modernist values. As one American household manual from the early twentieth-century had explained, 'One need never mourn that she [the housewife] cannot afford cut glass vases for flowers, as they and their cheap imitation are among the most unsuitable of holders'.[12] The ripples of Ruskin's rhetoric had spread a long way.

Some female architects were undoubtedly attracted to modernism because they identified it with improved conditions for women.[13] Certainly it promised better housing, schools, hospitals, nurseries and labour-saving kitchens. However, these much-needed social advances were conceived in terms which prioritised masculine over feminine values, utility over beauty, collectivism over individualism. As such, they went only some of the way towards fulfilling women's needs.

Although female modernists aspired to move beyond the 'feminine', their work frequently told a different story. Whether influenced by their closeness to the marketplace, or by values which were simply 'in their blood stream', many of them produced designs which had decidedly 'feminine' qualities to them. Grete Marks's ceramics, for instance, included examples with stylised, curvilinear plant and flower motifs on their surfaces – which would have caused uproar at the Bauhaus – while the women associated with the Viennese craft workshops (known as the *Wiener Werkstätte*) in the years following the First World War also 'softened', or feminised, the more rigorous modernist forms that they had inherited from their masters, among them Josef Hoffmann and Koloman Moser. Isabelle Anscombe has written,

The women who now developed the Wiener Werkstätte's post-war designs were intimately familiar with their market and appreciated the appeal of a smart handbag or pretty scarf, concentrating on what would sell rather than on creating prototypes for furniture.[14]

As a result of their orientation towards the world of consumption and 'desire', their work, which drew on folk art, was seen as lacking in sophistication when attempts were made to export it to the USA in the 1920s.[15] Women's knowledge of the values of the marketplace made them ideally suited to become designers for industry, just as many advertising agencies employed women because they understood the tastes of their own gender. Ironically, however, the strong ideologically-based anti-commercialism of modernism mitigated against this collusion with commerce, resulting in an under-valuing of those products which were a result of women designers working closely with the tastes of consumers.

For this reason, as well as all the other familiar prejudices against women in the professional workplace, many women designers have been 'hidden from history'. While manufacturers might have seen, and often did see, advantages in employing female designers, the strength of the modernist ideology which underpinned the very idea of design as a cultural institution rendered manufacturers powerless to defend their goods as anything other than the results of commercial pragmatism.

The aesthetic language of domesticity and consumption was visible in many of women's design achievements in the period, partly due to the fact that the media in which so many women worked, whether through choice or necessity, were closely related either to the domestic environment, especially those areas linked with display and ritual, or to bodily adornment. The fashion editor of *The Queen* listed women's seven key motivations as, 'mother love, personal vanity, the home-making instinct, acquisitiveness, art or craftsmanship, romance or amusement, intellectual hungers.'[16] Women's design strengths in the areas of interiors, furniture, pottery and glass, jewellery and metalwork, textiles and dress reinforced the idea that where aesthetic practice was concerned, 'personal vanity' and 'home-making' were indeed, high on the list of priorities, if only stereotypically. It was a stereotypical picture, however, which directly influenced women's participation in professional design for industry. Although by the 1930s, women designers had encountered modernism in some way or another, their work was often much more 'moderne' in appearance and was frequently inspired by the aesthetic of domesticity, albeit a modernised version of it. Thus colour, pattern, and surface decoration – usually stylised and often floral in nature – characterised much of their work. In Britain, for example, the ceramic designs of Susie Cooper, Clarice Cliff and Dame Laura Knight and the textile designs of Joyce Clissold, Marion Dorn and Margaret Calkins James all conformed to this picture to a greater or lesser degree.

The most stereotypically feminine design work was produced by professional female designers for the domestic interior. In Britain in the 1930s this work was influenced less by European architectural modernism than by that of the interior decorators who had held sway in the USA since the early years of the century when a sharp distinction had emerged between the concepts of 'interior design' and 'interior decoration'. While the former was rooted in the programme of modernism and took architecture as its starting point, the latter was part of a continuous decorative tradition which went back to at least the eighteenth century and remained embedded in that overtly feminine world of luxury and elitism.

Since the last decades of the nineteenth century interior decoration had been one of the ways in which wealthy women could apply their home-making skills – their 'feminine accomplishments' – to the world of work. While a few female decorators, among them the sisters Agnes and Rhoda Barrett, had followed this path in England in the 1880s, it was in America that the route had been pursued most enthusiastically, a result of fewer restrictions on women entering certain professions. In 1897 the novelist Edith Wharton, with the architect Ogden Codman, had published a book on the subject of interior decoration. Their tone was the familiar one of reform and of vehement anti-Victorianism; they rejected all forms of excessive display, among them heavy curtains, pianos, knick-knacks, the 'inevitable jardinière' and 'that modern futility, the silver-table'.[17] They also abhorred novelty for the sake of novelty – 'No sooner was it known that beautiful furniture was made in the time of Marie-Antoinette that an epidemic of supposed 'Marie-Antoinette" rooms breaks out over the whole country.'[18] In its place they proposed a more common-sense approach towards decorating which respected 'fitness of proportion' and 'the harmony of all the decorative processes'. Their programme for the interior was less one of rampant rationalisation and severe functionalism than a moderate one of aesthetic reform to be achieved by removing all that was superfluous; by simplifying the interior to enhance its inherent beauty; to increase lightness and delicacy and the appeal to the 'fastidious eye';[19] and by applying common sense rather than scientific rigour. Technology did not have a role to play here; wax candles were preferred to gas and electrical lighting because of the soft light they gave forth. Old objects were preferred to brash new ones, as they felt that 'there is an intrinsic value in almost all old bibelots'.[20] Above all, they advocated the application of these decorative principles to the rooms of the wealthy in the hopes that the new 'taste' would filter through to other levels of society and bring about a general level of reform. In 1890s America, at the height of the 'Gilded Age', there were plenty such clients waiting to have their interiors transformed in this way.

Wharton and Codman's sensibility and their notion of elegant, uncluttered beauty undoubtedly influenced the work of the interior decorator Elsie de Wolfe who sympathised with many of their preferences and, like them, sought 'Simplicity, Suitability and Proportion' in her interiors.[21] She too wanted to stamp out heavy Victorianism but to replace it with a new, softer, overtly feminine domestic aesthetic characterised by a use of chintz and a palette of pale colours, among them 'old rose, gray, ivory and pale blue'.[22] In the ideas of Elsie de Wolfe, the qualities of feminine beauty which derived from the female body – grace, elegance, delicacy and softness – were being transferred to the domestic sphere such that the house became an extension of the idealised beautiful woman. A level of sensuousness and pleasure accompanied this transference with the result that the aesthetic of the interior attained an unprecedented level of femininity at this time.

De Wolfe's main source of inspiration was eighteenth-century France. She derived her highly influential idea of using trellis work in the interior, for example, from an eighteenth-century text by Jacques François Blondel. Above all,

William McGregor Paxton, 'The Front Parlour' 1913. This image provides evidence that the highly feminine interior and dress style associated with "French Taste" which had been so popular in the USA in the 1870s and 1880s, was still visible in the early years of the twentieth-century. (The Saint Louis Art Museum, Cora E. Ludwig bequest, by exchange and Edward Mallinckrodt Sr. bequest, by exchange)

she was committed to the presence of flowers in any and every interior, explaining that 'any home must be cold without them'.[23] Like the modernists who came after her, Elsie de Wolfe was keen to let in light and air, and to this end she made extensive use of white paint and muslin for curtains. Her working model derived, however, from the past rather than from the contemporary world of technology. Antiques also played an important part in her otherwise decidedly contemporary environments, reinforcing her commitment to defining the present in terms of the past. Like the French *ensembliers* who also looked back to the world of Louis XV, Elsie de Wolfe was working within a well-established decorative tradition which had strongly feminine associations. In so doing, she formulated a model of aesthetic domesticity which was subsequently emulated by many women, at all social levels, in various different ways. Whether through the inclusion of a vase of flowers on a dining table or sideboard, the use of white paint on walls, the presence of flowery chintz curtains, or the positioning of a treasured family heirloom on a mantlepiece, the tradition that she had unlocked and renewed was one which both respected the past and which could, like Alison Light's conservative modernists, build a bridge with the present. As such, it appealed enormously to women in the inter-war years as they searched for a means of crossing that bridge.

The society interior decorators of the 1930s in the USA and Britain provided a model of aristocratic taste which middle-class women could aspire to and, in their own eyes, at least, emulate. In Britain, Syrie Maugham and Lady Sibyl Colefax carried on the work which had been initiated by the Americans before them, aided in their tasks by the flower arranger Constance Spry. As all things Victorian had become blighted – linked in everyone's minds with a world that had led to, and disappeared with, the First World War – it was to earlier days that the middle classes now looked in their search for continuity and aesthetic inspiration. The elegance and grace of the eighteenth century, as interpreted by the interior decorators, provided just the right balance of historical reference and commitment to the present, an acceptable combination of archaism and modernity.

In addition to the female modern architects and designers, the interior decorators, and the decorative artists (many of who worked in humble, unacknowledged roles in workshops and factories), women also participated in craft manufacture in these years. The ideological roots for this face of their activity lay in the Arts and Crafts movement of the second half of the nineteenth century in which women had played a significant part, at first as a source of visual inspiration and subsequently as makers.[24] At the outset this was restricted to wives and families of the chief protagonists but it expanded in the early years of this century to include large numbers of middle-class women who had been visually trained as well as 'impoverished gentlewomen';[25] and 'working-class and agricultural labouring-class women employed in the revival of traditional rural crafts'.[26] Like its masculine equivalent, it spread from Britain to America where it found its most significant outlet in ceramic production, notably, at the Rookwood Pottery in Cincinatti, run by Maria Longworth Nichols.

In Britain the Arts and Crafts women were linked predominantly with textiles, especially embroidery and lace-making; book-binding; and the fabrication of jewellery and metalwork.[27] These had all developed out of traditional 'female accomplishments' and provided no threat to the established sexual division of labour. Whether or not this work increased women's subordination to men, or provided them with a space within which to be creative, by the inter-war years the idea of the middle-class female craftsperson, reviving traditional craft skills in a rural setting, was well established. The lives and work of the potter Katherine Pleydell Bouverie; the textile-printing team of Dorothy Larcher and Phyllis Barron; and the weaver Ethel Mairet, all bore witness to this.

Another level of craft activity also existed, linked ideologically to this world but essentially amateur in nature. Handicraft was generally perceived as a form of leisure activity. Skills were taught at evening classes and through the network of Women's Institutes which covered the country. The end products, among them raffia weaving and pâpier-maché work, tended to be positioned at the bottom end of the aesthetic hierarchy. As the design historian Pat Kirkham has explained, work of that nature 'solicits a range of pejorative responses formerly directed at embroidery and other "women's crafts"'.[28] The ideological extension of the idea of craft to what were essentially domestic skills – among them, in the words of W.R. Lethaby, 'laying the table nicely'[29] –

contained within it the potential to rehabilitate what had traditionally been seen as women's work and to render it the equivalent of men's labour. The judgment, however, that it was a
leisure activity rather than work, coupled with mainstream
culture's derogatory response to its artefacts, had the reverse
effect, trivialising and marginalising it even further from the
cultural 'centre'. The increasingly problematic notion of
'taste', which was becoming more and more overtly linked
with the feminine sphere, raised its head once again in this
context. Masculine culture could neither understand nor, more
importantly, value, the symbolic and aesthetic role that images
such as 'the crinoline lady'[30] – a much-loved subject inspired
by countless Victorian embroideries which re-emerged in the
inter-war years in a number of guises, including knitted tea-
pot warmers and nightdress cases – played within women's
culture. It was the subject, in fact, of many heated debates
between the Women's Institutes and the Design and Industries
Association.[31] However well-made such artefacts may have
been, they could never have entered the masculine canon of
'good design' objects, so rooted were they in the world of
women's domesticity and feminine taste.

A company called Dryad Handicrafts based in Leicester, was
highly influential at this time, providing as it did both handicraft materials and educational instruction.[32] In spite of its
good intentions of re-injecting a level of 'making' into peoples
lives, it never once questioned, and therefore by default
reinforced the gendering of different craft activities; 'women's
work' moved further and further away from serious consideration. The stereotypical femininity contained in its 'Leaflet no.
124', for example, entitled *More Felt Flowers*, with its buds of
vivid '"Margate rock", pink', did little to reverse this.[33] 'Leaflet
no. 92', which contained instructions on how to do netting,
may have seemed more neutral in gender terms but this
impression was immediately negated by the accompanying
advice on how the results could be turned into a shopping
bag.[34]

Women's aesthetic practice covered the areas of consumption and home-making inasmuch as it involved the exercising
of taste and creative decision-making. Often, indeed, it

involved 'making' proper as, for example, in the activities of arranging flowers or icing cakes. What has been called 'house-craft',[35] a field within which consumption played an increas-ingly important role, was still the main focus for feminine taste and the reason why it was at worst ignored, and at best trivialised, by mainstream culture. Linked as it was with the idea of leisure and with unpaid work, it was not valued in the same way as work which was seen as 'wealth-creating'. This was in spite of the fact that production without consumption would have resulted in the creation of very little wealth indeed.

Women also negotiated modernism in the course of their home-making and consumption in the inter-war years. Just as they had in their professional capacity as designers, so as amateurs they manifested a variety of responses to it: at one end, embracing what it had to offer, at the other, refusing it and taking refuge in historicism. By this period in Britain and the USA, most middle-class and increasingly many working-class women straddled the spectrum of modern to traditional in the activity of furnishing and running their homes. This varied according to the location of the home, whether urban, suburban or rural; to the age of the women concerned; to the home-maker's access to different forms of taste-making and to the goods themselves; and, of course, to individual preferences. Household manuals presented a picture characterised by a tension between the present and the past. Unlike advertising and establishment propaganda, they adopted a pragmatic rather than a rhetorical tone, presenting a picture of what could be realised 'on the ground'.

Many manuals promoted the idea of the labour-saving home, setting out to persuade women that the project of ratio-nalising and organising their households would lead to greater freedom. Indeed, this face of modernity, packaged in the modernist style, filled the pages of countless advice books. The pioneering work of Christine Frederick and Lillian Gilbreth reached a wide international audience in the 1930s, filtering into the ideas and beliefs of many women's consumer organi-sations, among them, the Electrical Association for Women in England. Founded in 1924, the EAW was a splinter group of the Women's Engineering Society; it included no questions relating to aesthetics on its highly practical and overtly feminist agenda. In spite of this, the group influenced a number of design decisions: 'In 1927 a discussion about electric cookers was organised by sending a questionnaire to all the branches; 11 types of cooker then on the market were investigated. Replies commented upon the need for more runners for shelves [for] removable enamel linings with moulded corners.'[36] And 'Five years later, in the pamphlet "The Design and Performance of Domestic Electrical Appliances" the EAW published recommendations that all cookers should have rounded corners'.[37]

When the group built a show house in Bristol in 1935 it chose a modernist design with a flat roof, attached garage, and large metal-framed windows.[38] Practicality had shifted, almost unbeknownst to them, into the realm of aesthetics. In opting for an architectural idiom which most closely symbolised their own preoccupations, the EAW was openly supporting architectural modernism. More significantly, however, the house was 'servantless' and it was most probably this, rather than the 'cultural capital' offered by modernism which, in the final analysis, encouraged them, and many other women besides, to consider the practical benefits of abandoning display and embracing a much simpler, more modern style in their domestic environments. The gradual demise of the servant from the end of the last century, and accelerating in the post-war period – a phenomenon even more accelerated in the USA[39] – was undoubtedly the key factor in many middle-class housewives' decision to abandon Victorian clutter and take on board the new minimalism.

English Suburbia, 1930s. The inhabitants of the new suburban, owner-occupied houses of the 1930s combined the conservative taste of the floral curtains at their windows, with a desire to participate in the modern world of electrical domestic appliances which could be delivered to their doors. (Electrolux Limited)

Evidence of that new minimalism, accompanied by an inter-est both in scientific management and in ideas relating to health and hygiene in the home, filled the household manuals which appeared on the book-shop shelves in their dozens right through this period. An American book of 1913 advocated the inclusion of 'concrete furniture which can be flushed clean every morning with the hose'[40], although it was cautious about letting rationalism take over completely:

Many are the sins committed in the name of sanitation and fire-proofing. Lace curtains and other draperies are banished, carpets and carpeting give way to rugs or even tiles and linoleum, wallpapers are eliminated, and we are urged by some architects to make our houses resemble hospitals as closely as possible.[41]

The voice of common sense and conservatism could clearly be heard balancing the rational extremism of household engineering.

In the years leading up to the First World War the manuals reflected a general move towards simplification in household furnishings and environments under the influence of the Arts and Crafts Movement and the ideas of the interior decorators. A burning need to erase all signs of cluttered Victorianism manifested itself widely. Although the aspidistra, the what-not and, sometimes, the piano were thrown out, the symbolism of feminine domesticity remained in place. New forms, new decorations, and new arrangements emerged to combine the requirements of display, novelty and comfort. As ever, beauty was uppermost in the mind of the housewife. In another American book of 1913 housewives were advised on flower-arranging, but now they were exhorted to abandon the fancy displays of their Victorian predecessors and to use only 'a few simple flowers, properly arranged'.[42] From the Japanese the author had learnt that 'flowers of the same kind should be grouped together, and that harmony and blending of colour are necessary to secure the most artistic effects'.[43] While the style may have changed, the symbolic function of flowers in the household had not.

Modernism entered the British and American inter-war

household in a number of guises. On one level, as we have seen, the ideas of Frederick and Gilbreth introduced the principle of rationalisation into home management. A British book of 1928, emphasized its importance: 'Where every unnecessary step means added fatigue, and every additional space an increased necessity for cleaning work, passages and hallways are to be avoided.'[44] This interest reached a peak in the USA in the 1930s as the report from President Hoover's conference on *Home Building and Home Ownership* made clear: 'laboratory studies of separate household tasks indicate that the time and motions required can be considerably reduced.'[45]

On another level, aesthetic modernisation meant introducing light, making surfaces flush, emphasising verticality in room settings and generally simplifying the interior as a whole. Greater simplification brought with it the possibility of householders making their own furniture. One book proposed the construction, now that simple furniture was the order of the day, of a 'simple inexpensive bookcase which could easily be transported and set up in a student's room', the design for which involved 'key and screw fastenings'[46] and unadorned surfaces. It was even suggested that the amateur woodworker, perceived as male, might attempt a simple Morris chair once he became confident. Fifteen years later, a British publication explained that such work was now possible 'due to the greater simplicity of furniture design now ruling. Except for a light bead, or a modest medallion, much of the furniture sold today is devoid of "frills". That this is not less pleasing than that of a generation ago is attributable to the fact that the design is better'.[47] This suggests that the new style, rooted in modernist idealism, had been significantly democratised.

By the 1930s unadorned furniture could be found gracing the living- and dining-rooms in the pages of many manuals on both sides of the Atlantic. A British publication from the middle of the decade illustrated a living-room made up of undecorated boxy armchairs, a small, low bookcase in the modern style and a coffee-table which looked like a carpenter's tool box, so basic was its design.[48] The author of an American publication commented on 'The message of Modernism' in words that might have been written by Le Corbusier:

The designers of our homes and their furnishings are interpreting the Spirit of our Times, rather than those invoking the ghosts of a dead past. Gothic – Italian Renaissance – Tudor – Jacobean – Louis Quinze – each of those great furnishing styles expressed the Spirit of its Time but they will not do for us today. We live in a new and faster tempo. Our habits, viewpoints and ideals are changed. This is often described as a complex, speed-mad age; a sort of Irish stew of shams, jazz, extravagance, hurry and nervous breakdowns.[49]

The illustrations told a more ambivalent story, however. While one modern bedroom came complete with a desk with a typewriter on it, undoubtedly aimed at the new professional woman,[50] another interior boasted draped, lacy and tasselled curtains and wallpaper, decorated with motifs of swags of fabric and baskets of flowers in the style of Elsie de Wolfe.[51]

What emerged from many of these manuals was the wide variety of stylistic choices, crossing the spectrum from modern to traditional, available to the inter-war home-maker.

Inevitably, preferences varied in different places. While British suburbia favoured the 'Tudorbethan' style, a 'cosy cottage look' which distinguished owner-occupied houses from their Neo-Georgian local authority equivalents, the American suburbanites leant strongly on the Colonial or Early American idiom, incorporating family heirlooms which had been relegated to the attic. The widespread interest in historical style, more visible in the living-room and dining-room than in the kitchen and bathroom, stimulated a huge trade in reproduction furniture, much to the dismay of the modernists. In the USA the Grand Rapids furniture manufacturers, and in England the High Wycombe firms, devoted most of their production to 'repros' in an attempt to meet the stylistic requirements of the majority of consumers.

While, on one level, embracing the past could be seen as simply another form of stylistic novelty, on another, for women, it also represented a means of retaining continuity with their cultural roots. The parlour and drawing-room had been transformed into the living-room or sitting-room, a much more informal family room, but it retained many of the same symbolic functions as it had had in the Victorian home.

Above all, it remained for women the key site for the expression of taste, providing an opportunity for display and social positioning; for the creation of comfort, both physical and visual, for the family; for retaining a link with the past; and, increasingly, in these days of diminished home production, for creativity, self-expression, and individualisation.

The suburbs continued to play a special role in encouraging the continuity of feminine taste as manifested within the domestic ideal. Both the USA and Britain saw a rapid expansion of suburbanisation in the inter-war years and with it, a new class of home-makers. Indeed Alison Light located her literary brand of conservative modernism in suburbia. It was also the home of conservative modernist visual taste. Nowhere was the continuation of the domestic feminine aesthetic more visible than in the act of flower-arranging which required a high level of creative intervention. Plenty of advice was on hand to help the housewife achieve the best possible results. In Britain Mrs Beeton was particularly helpful on the subject of table decorations, advocating the use of 'floating flower bowls' which were 'wide shallow bowls of coloured glass or pottery . . . only a little water is placed in the bowls, and the flowers, having had their stalks cut off quite short, are floated on the water. A brightly coloured bird, dragonfly or butterfly may be fastened to the edge of the bowl, and will greatly add to the effect.'[52] *The Housewife's Book* suggested the use of 'illuminated flowers [which] are sold in sets complete with silver leaves; the petals are of organdie and small decoration lamps form the centres'.[53] Children's birthday parties called for a high level of table display, as did 'help-yourself' suppers, providing yet more opportunities for the housewife to exercise her aesthetic discrimination.

While the excesses of draped fabric used in the Victorian parlour were much derided, an American book of 1936 made it clear that attention still needed to be devoted to this area, outlining the role they still played in the domestic setting, especially in those rooms with a 'period' feel to them. 'Strict period rooms', the author explained, are nowadays rare, outside of museums, but the spirit in which they were long ago conceived lives on; and so long as there continue to be thousands who are "Colonial minded" or who incline by temperament to surroundings in the Georgian, Directoire, or other historic modes, it is safe to conclude that, as with wall coverings and carpets, the supply of appropriate fabrics will be maintained.[54]

In the true spirit of 'conservative modernism', in one interior she even proposed the inclusion of a Venetian blind with a curtain draped across it!

Decorating was for the most part, still in the hands of the professional painter and decorator. An English text from 1932, aimed at the trainee decorator, was unambiguous about the mood that the trade wished to impart in what it still called the 'drawing room':

It is par excellence the ladies' room, and in its decoration we may cultivate a certain femininity of style, without weakness, in pretty contrast to the more masculine treatment accorded to the dining-room. Here, too, we have less rough wear and tear than in any room in the house. The presence of nic-nacs and bric-a-brac tends to more care in cleaning.[55]

The author could have been talking about a mid-Victorian parlour were it not for the fact that he prefaced his description with an account of the room which was decidedly modern in its use – 'a room used for work music, dancing and other recreations, giving unlimited scope for the absence of conventionalism'.[56] The inhabitants would have undoubtedly danced to music from a gramophone rather than a piano by this date.

The similarities in atmosphere, if not in stylistic detail, between the Victorian parlour and the inter-war living-room were dramatic. Housewives were encouraged to engage in a level of display as part of their duties and to think about comfort and gentility in their homes. The living-room provided a site for display, suggested by the, albeit now highly edited, continued presence of knick-knacks adorning all available surfaces. An English book of the late 1930s included a section on how to clean bronze ornaments, plaster figures and glass decanters, implying their continued importance within the domestic setting.[57] Employing her visual discrimination in the many aesthetic decisions involved in home-making was clearly a duty of the inter-war housewife. Although guided more heavily than ever before by manuals, magazines, exhibitions, 'movies' and goods themselves, this did not totally displace the level of individual creativity needed to fulfil this duty. Given the increasing influence of mass production, the ubiquitous presence of the mass media, and the hegemonic nature of modernism, both as a style and an ideology, women might well have lost confidence in their tastes, had they even had the opportunity to develop them. The manuals suggest that this was not the case. The sheer diversity of the possibilities meant that, in the end, women were on their own, even in deciding which guide to follow. No one dominant style emerged from their pages and women clearly had a range of options from which to make their own selections.

As in the earlier period, feminine taste had its ardent critics located within an increasingly wide range of cultural spheres. Now they included women themselves; notable among them were Ellen Richards and Christine Frederick, who considered display and pleasurable consumption to reflect all that was wrong with women's lives. Other critics[58] abhorred the effects of mass production but failed to see that in their home-making and consumption many women were resisting, or at least subverting, its pull. In many areas of their domestic lives, women were struggling to retain a level of autonomy and individuality in a culture which valued less and less the sphere within which they pursued their goals. The breaking-up of older communities throughout this period undoubtedly caused many housewives to form their tastes as isolated individuals rather than as social beings. This made them more vulnerable to the potential manipulation of advertising, marketing and, increasingly, design, intent upon dictating women's lifestyles and creating their tastes for them. At the same time, however, feminine taste and women's role as consumers lubricated the system of production and consumption. Increasingly, demand influenced supply, not the other way round. Why else would Henry Ford have closed down his factory for a year and why else were psychologists brought in to assist advertisers? In the years following the Second World War, when the notion of taste came to the fore once again, providing a key battleground for vital issues raised by sexual politics, the influence of consumption upon production was to become even more obvious.

PART THREE

Modernity and Femininity, 1940 – 1970

CHAPTER EIGHT

'The Happy Housewife':
Domesticity Renewed

'One of the key patterns is that of "good taste" in personal appearance, house furnishings, cultural things like literature and music. To a large and perhaps increasing extent the more humanistic and cultural traditions and amenities of life are carried on by women ... These things are of a high intrinsic importance in the scale of values of our culture.'

– Talcott Parsons[1]

The words of Talcott Parsons, the American sociologist whose views on the centrality of the nuclear family to contemporary life were so influential in the two decades following the Second World War, suggested an important, and, potentially at least, highly satisfying role for women. However, in evoking such an optimistic picture, they are at radical odds, with the dominant image of women's lives handed down to us by feminist accounts. From the writings of, among others, Betty Friedan, whose picture of contemporary suburban life for women was characterised by anxiety, depression and an utter lack of fulfilment or purpose, we have inherited an idea about women's lives in the 1950s and early '60s which is marked by a sense of their deep oppression.[2] Indeed, the prevailing image is one of darkness preceding the dawn of opportunity that came with the wakening of women's own awareness of their condition in the late '60s and early '70s. Somewhere between Parson's vision and that of the protagonists of the Women's Liberation Movement lies a reality that needs to be looked at again if we are to discover whether or not feminine culture, expressed through the material and aesthetic manifestations of feminine values and tastes, provided a source of 'life-enhancement' for women at that time.

Above all, the two decades after the war, both in Britain and the USA, bore witness to a re-energised domestification of women, rooted in a set of ideals of which some were familiar and others were new. This much-publicised and much-justified new chapter in the domestification of women was, as ever, part of a wider picture which related to a vision of society as a whole. In both Britain and America fear of a declining population re-emphasized women's role within family life. Fresh from their war-time experiences in the paid labour force and their undoubted frustrations at having to juggle family life and work, post-war housewives were encouraged to abandon the latter and devote themselves entirely to their households.

The images of domesticity and femininity were deeply intertwined in the period in much the same way as they had been in the nineteenth century. The same need for social stability underpinned their alliance and, once again, the home was seen as a refuge from the moral anarchy of the market-place. The family as a site for human values was becoming increasingly central. 'Women's traditional role,' Elizabeth Wilson has explained, 'as a stabilizing and civilizing force – the ideology of the Victorians – was made a lynchpin of consensus now that women were citizens.'[3] In their enfranchised, newly-educated and, as was generally assumed, totally liberated capacities, women, it was believed, could now relaxedly apply their knowledge to maintaining the domestic sphere and bringing up children. Armed with the skills of household management, new labour-saving appliances, new affluence and consumption possibilities, and with the help of expert professional academics in the fields of sociology, psychology and psychoanalysis,[4] keeping house and bringing up children was no longer considered a drudgery but rather a combination of pleasures and a set of professional tasks and challenges. With unfulfilling work seemingly banished for ever, the housewife could concentrate on becoming a nurturant, a beautifier and a consumer, roles which were seen to reflect women's essential differences from men.

But this idealised picture was destroyed by the almost

The housewife can 'look her best' when acting as her own cook

An illustration from 'The Happy Home', 1950s. By the post-war years the 'laboratory kitchen' of the early century had been replaced by a family living area which combined the new domestic machines with signs of decorative display borrowed from the living-room. In turn the 'housewife-worker' was transformed into a glamorous wife, mother and hostess.

complete disappearance of domestic servants by this time. Middle-class housewives now had more work to do.[5] Although the 'domesticated male' was a term more frequently used by the mid–1950s, his assistance was restricted to evenings and weekends, often manifested only in entertaining the children, mowing the law or washing the car. Household work was still undertaken by housewives and although appliances and convenience foods reduced some aspects of that labour, time spent in housework was not reduced.[6] The increased level of expectation where household decoration and maintenance was concerned; new standards of childcare; the emergence of new tasks, such as chauffeuring children hither and thither which arose from the new geography of suburban life; and the enhanced pressures on consumption, created by increased affluence and the availability of greater numbers of goods, combined to ensure that a post-war housewife's life was never an idle one.

The fact that middle-class women now had to do their own housework served to erode the distinction that had existed between themselves and working-class wives. In addition, the growing affluence of the working-class family and its desire to participate in the culture of consumption resulted, as a contemporary journalist described, in a general 'embourgeoisement' of the population,

Nowadays it is quite literally true that the solicitor's wife with three children and no mother's help in Wimbledon has a life which, so far as claims upon her time are concerned, is no different from that enjoyed by a steel-workers's wife with the same size family is Middlesbrough. Each has the same modern equipment in her kitchen and vacuum-cleaner cupboard.'[7]

Apparent both in Britain and in the USA, this change resulted in an increasing homogenisation of the market such that both regional and class variations became less marked and it assisted the mass manufacturing industry in being able to standardise its products and to emphasise the role of gender over that of class in the formation of distinct taste cultures. Manufacturers were quick to exploit this market segmentation

and 'gendered' many of their products accordingly. The principle of social homogenisation was part of 'the ideological enterprise which was to unite the classes and to identify the interests of the working class with the national interest'.[8] This
related also to the energetic efforts of many bodies, both public
and private, to educate consumers into an understanding of the
principles of 'good taste' – yet another attempt to give everybody middle-class status, thus creating a consensus and
enhancing social stability, as well as making the process of
production and consumption as efficient and streamlined as
possible.

The idea of the sexual division of labour which justified
feminine domesticity in the 1950s was rooted in a fundamental belief, still informed by Darwinian ideas, in the difference
between men and women. By this time, however, the ideas of
Sigmund Freud also exerted a strong influence, particularly
with respect to the differences between masculinity and femininity; according to Freud, these differences were determined
by the different developmental paths taken by boys and girls
in the first five years of their lives. The question of gender
difference and distinct roles was fundamental to a commitment to the nuclear family, which in turn meant social stability. That stability was threatened by a masculinity crisis: men
returning from the stimulus of their wartime lives to
mundane jobs in offices and factories felt themselves to be
leading fragmented, anonymous lives. This sense of alienation
and degradation threw men back into the home in search of
consolation in family life, only to find there what has been
called the 'megalomaniac mom'.[7]

A complex scenario has been depicted of women having their
energies dissipated by sexual activity with their husbands such
that they became more passive, masochistic and 'giving' in their
relationship with their family members, thereby restoring
masculinity to their husbands, avoiding feminising their sons,
and providing an 'appropriate' image of femininity for their
daughters. The threat in the post-war years of the combination
of 'feminised men' who now performed a domestic role,
however limited, and of the 'masculinised women', the post-war
descendant of the 'New Woman', who had had unprecedented

The Ideal Home Exhibition, 1954. The modern domestic ideal, as represented by electrical appliances, was central to post-war British culture. The newly-married Queen Elizabeth, seen here looking longingly at a dishwasher, provided a role-model for many young housewives of the period. (Thorn EMI)

access to the world of men during the war years, brought about a sudden reversion to highly stereotypical models of femininity and masculinity in an attempt to reverse what was seen as a worrying trend. These models, promoted through a wide range of propaganda material and mass media outlets, attained a ubiquitous presence in the post-war environment. On one level, many women were probably willing to abandon their gender image of the war years and to search for a glamorous antidote to that overtly masculine, rational, and utility-inspired image. On another level, the model of the happy housewife, content to please her husband and sacrifice herself for her children, was thrust at her from all directions.

Perhaps most dominant of all the themes to characterise the new post-war domesticity was that of 'togetherness'. Women were encouraged to be friends and companions to their husbands; major purchases were to be planned jointly; and beautifying and improving the home was to be undertaken together. The 'do-it-yourself' movement was to be engaged in by both partners, as the covers of the magazine of that name indicated, although, of course, there were clearly gendered tasks within it. While it was up to the husband to fix the plumbing and the electrics, the wife would make the curtains, and while the husband went up the ladder to paint the ceiling, her role was to support it at its base, a perfect metaphor for the relationship between the sexes. Thus, while togetherness might have meant sharing, it also served to refine and enhance, rather than to diminish, the sexual division of labour within the home itself.

Together these factors gave rise to the concept of 'frilly' femininity which pervaded the media at this time, especially in the USA. Providing housewives with a model of femininity linked to their stereotypical role as carriers and creators of beauty, and now much more overtly than ever before to notions of feminine sexuality, the media also wanted to encourage women to spend their new-found wealth upon the clothes and cosmetics that went with that image. But, now no longer part of a close community where dressing up was an aspect of public social display, the suburban housewife was being encouraged to dress up for her husband alone. Equally, however, there was also the strong possibility that she was doing it for herself and for her female peers in the community, establishing a self-identity of an unambiguously gendered and assertively modern self. In a discussion of the stiletto heel, for example, it has been pointed out that this archetypically 'feminine' object can be seen to have communicated several messages.[10] As well as an overtly feminine object, designed to enhance gender differences at a time when the roles of men and women were highly polarised, it could also be seen as playing a vital role within women's need to be 'up-to-date', a visible sign that they had entered the world of modernity, as well as rejecting the utilitarian character of wartime clothing. The essentially paradoxical notion of the 'glamourous house-wife' can be seen as one way in which women took domesticity on board, but simultaneously rejected it from within, the impracticality of the stiletto heel and the full skirts acting as signs of open resistance. 'Stiletto-wearing in the fifties,' the design historian Lee Wright has written, 'was part of a broader discussion of how to express the "new woman" – one who was not content with pre-war values and traditional roles. In this sense it could be seen as progressive rather than retro-gressive.'[11] Accepting an image of stereotypical femininity could be seen, from this perspective, as a form of resistance rather than one of compliance, perhaps a more effective way of challenging the dominance of male culture than by emu-lating it.

While women may not have been the passive consumers of pre-packaged femininity so frequently described, the climate of the post-war years made it difficult for them to create collective identities for themselves. Whereas the role that Victorian middle-class women had performed, as purveyors and creators of beauty in the home, had been seen as an essen-tial one in the climate of expanding industrialisation, their 1950s equivalents received no such approbation. Lacking the cohesive social, religious and political framework of their predecessors, theirs was a much more private effort. The only outwardly recognised rewards were those of achieving the demanded level of femininity, of being desired by their husbands, of bringing up their children in the required manner and of beautifying their homes effectively. These achieve-ments were only ever acknowledged privately; and were recognised publically only in a negative sense – by the fact that the status quo was not threatened if women undertook their role effectively. Inevitably, the idea of women working outside the home was looked upon with enormous disapproval in this period. Working mothers were blamed for the rise of juvenile delinquency, among other things. Ironically, also, given the increased income of working mothers, women's magazines, which depended upon income from selling space to advertisers, did not support the idea of women working because they thought they wouldn't have time to do so much shopping.[12]

However, the complex ideological underpinning of the notion of feminine domesticity that dominated the fifteen years following the Second Word War began to crumble as women themselves began to demonstrate their profound dissatisfaction with living in its grip. The sequence of events outlined by the Women's Liberation Movement in its account of women's oppression in that period has now become mythologised.[13] In September 1960 an article entitled 'Why Young Mothers Feel Trapped' appeared in the American women's magazine, *Redbook*. Fifty thousand women responded to it. In the same year a television programme entitled 'The Trapped Housewife' was broadcast on CBS and this was followed by countless

articles on the same theme in numerous women's magazines in the following months. Subsequently many women started going out to work because 'they needed the money and they were "going nuts".'[14] Whatever the real reasons for women entering the workplace in expanding numbers in the early 1960s, the image of feminine domesticity was transformed dramatically and the passive housewife was replaced by images of the single girl and of the much more masculine and efficiency-oriented career, or simply working, woman.

As has been said, while a strongly negative picture of women's culture in the 1950s dominates most accounts, in sharp contrast, a few provide a picture of joyful affluence and pleasure in consumption. The design historian Thomas Hine has written that 'there was ebullience in this grand display of appetite,'[15] a much more optimistic picture of the materialism which others have been quick to dismiss as decadent, illusory and a sign of 'false consciousness'. This optimism was rooted in the idea that the possession and display of material goods moved beyond mere materialism into a level of symbolism which was expressed actively by consumers, both through the purchase of goods and through the functions that such goods performed in women's everyday lives. Where women and feminine culture were concerned, this related to the exercise of taste which, in turn, represented an important aspect of their engagement with culture in general and a potential arena for resistance – whether conscious or not, acknowledged or not – to whatever oppression they may have been experiencing.

The oppressive culture that Friedan and others described was located in suburbia, the site, as we have seen, of many women's encounters with a feminised model of modernity and of the failure of masculine architectural and design theories to take a hold. It seemed, at first sight – if the simplified houses and goods, the uses of new materials, and the engagement with light and space that characterised the new housing of the 1940s and 1950s were anything to go by – that architectural and design modernism was making a second attempt to infiltrate that bastion of feminine culture. A closer look, however, reveals a much more subtle, and in gender terms, more complex situation. Both in the USA and in Britain, the post-war years saw large numbers of young women getting married and having families early. There were acute housing shortages in both countries for such families and temporary solutions were made possible by new methods of pre-fabrication. However, a more permanent American solution to the housing problem was provided by William J. Levitt, a developer who, through his company Levitt and Sons, constructed from 1947 onwards vast numbers of simple, standardised dwellings in hitherto undeveloped areas of land. In its first four years the company built 17,450 houses in Levittown, Long Island.[16] 'By 1950,' the architectural historian Gwendolyn Wright has explained, 'the company's factory was producing one four-room house every sixteen minutes.'[17] From there Levitt moved on to Pennsylvania and New Jersey, constructing even larger suburban developments in these new areas. The Levitt house has been described as 'the model-T equivalent of the rose-covered cottage – or Cape Coddage, as someone has called ... it is meant to look like the Little Home of One's Own that was a subsidiary myth of the American

Dream, long before Charlie Chaplin put it into *Modern Times*.'[18] It certainly brought a model of standardised dwelling into American suburbia which owed a debt to the work of the modernist Frank Lloyd Wright for a number of its features, among them the use of a three-way fireplace in the centre of an open plan.[19] A more accurate analogy, however, would have been with a General Motors' automobile which shared its chassis with other models but which, with the addition of colour, upholstery and other styling details, aspired to an ideal of craft-manufactured uniqueness, individuality and luxury. While the early houses were as alike as peas in a pod, that is until they were occupied and its owners set about personalising and individualising them, the later ones came in a variety of styles, ranging from the very popular ranch house to Cape Cod and Colonial styles. Other American suburbs even included a version of the English Tudor style while split level housing became widespread after the mid–1950s.

Styles and personalised details varied enormously within the constraints of the basic concept – a one-storey cottage with gently sloping roofs and large picture windows, with a kitchen at the front to allow the living area to look out over the back. Modernity and tradition were blended in almost every instance. Even the historical pastiches were realised in modern materials by modern means and were essentially modernised evocations of a traditional concept rather than faithful reproductions. Modernity and tradition sat side by side in American suburbia in the 1950s and, indeed, often merged into one and the same. The contemporary adventure of moving into the unknown paralleled and recalled that of the American pioneers who had made the land their own and forged their own identities, and those of their families, in the process. In a spirit which was nostalgic, romantic and progressive at the same time, America's new suburbanites called on their predecessors to validate their own adventure. 'The suburban ranches,' the cultural historian Russell Lynes has written, 'are often a quarter of an acre or less, and the view from the picture window is of another picture window. The pervasive Western spirit of the open range and the barbeque, of sunshine and leisure is nonetheless nationwide.'[20]

While some of this romanticism was provided by the nature of the building itself, much of it was created by the furnishing, decorations and embellishments that were selected by the occupants, especially the housewife. Through the tasks of consumption and home-making, her role was to create a bridge between the past and the present; to unite fashion, novelty and the spirit of the new with those of comfort, stability and the spirit of the past. As ever, this was a complex role which demanded a high level of knowledge, skills, creativity and intuition. The aim of the exercise was one of combining shared with individual values and of selecting goods and decorations which, in conjunction with each other, could express the symbolism required to turn a house into a home. While, as in the Victorian era, the idea of social aspiration was part of what was to be symbolised, it was less significant in this predominantly single-class context where there was no social ladder to climb. The only way to improve one's social status was to move to another suburb. In 1950s American suburbia, the chief task of the housewife was to create a sense of belonging.

The women whose role it was to domesticate these new dwellings straddled a subtle path between the new and the old, as indeed they had done for over a century. The main difference now was that, post-Depression and post-war, and with the new affluence of the 1950s, many of them were in a position to start from scratch for the first time and to furnish and embellish their homes without the weight of past possessions hanging heavily upon them. There existed for many women from the new American middle-class an unprecedented opportunity to express themselves – and there is plenty of evidence to suggest that they grasped it with open arms.

In Britain a similar housing shortage in the early post-war years and the same pattern of young women marrying and having children at a young age existed. New housing came in the form of the government-funded New Towns which took young families from the slums of the inner cities into 'green sites'.[21] Later in the decade, private developers built extensive estates of simple, modern-style housing outside the cities. The model for these developments was that of the 'garden city' which was characterized by the concept of rural-inspired 'picturesque planning', a much more ordered approach than that adopted across the Atlantic.[22]

The American suburban houses had incorporated a number of radically modern features in their plans. They were all, in essence, 'open-plan' in which either there was an open living area which combined living and dining in one space, or dining was integrated into a large kitchen area. The idea of keeping one room for display, to be used only on special occasions, was eliminated and openness, in line with the notion of together-ness, underpinned the dominant ideological picture of family life at this time. The lack of privacy for individual members of the family, other than in their bedrooms, was seen as a means of encouraging increased interaction between them, thought to be a vital ingredient of the nurturing of children.

Open-planning was also visible in the otherwise less radical British housing of the 1950s. The living and dining areas were frequently combined, although often with folding doors between them, to suggest the possibility of privacy even if it was never actually needed. However, the ideals of the architects who planned the houses were frequently at odds with the way in which their inhabitants embellished and used them.[23] Not only did women feel uncomfortable about having (in emulation of the Levitt house-plan) their kitchen at the front of the house – positioned there to make them feel part of the community as they went about their daily tasks – it had the reverse effect of making them feel utterly isolated and shut off from the world. They also insisted on introducing net curtains into their new, open light and open spaces and polishing their furniture in the way that their mothers and grandmothers had done before them. The architects had not anticipated, and clearly had no understanding of the impor-tance that privacy, pride of ownership, and tradition played in these women's lives, offsetting, complementing and indeed combining with their pleasure in the new and the modern. There were, for the New Town housewives, no contradictions in what were seen by the architects, steeped in modernist ideology, as tasteless compromises.

There was space for resistance in women's role as home-makers and as beautifiers of the domestic environment. While

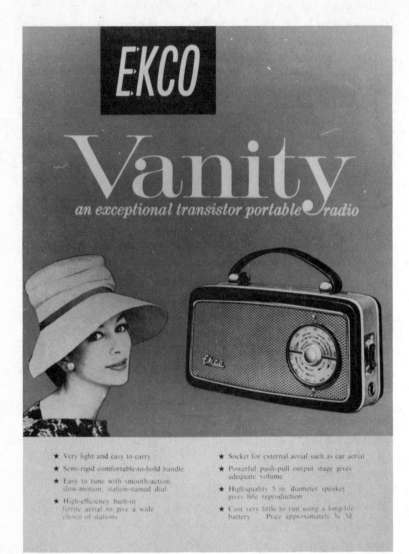

Cover of sales brochure for Ecko 'Vanity' portable radio, 1950s. Increasingly in the post-war years goods were targeted at gendered markets. The 'Vanity' radio was designed to resemble a lady's handbag and, in the process, was transformed from a piece of equipment into a fashion accessoory. (Reproduced by courtesy of Southend Museum Service)

they may have lost the parlour, much of their privacy from the rest of the family, and a strong community around them to support and validate their work they nevertheless found ways of negotiating the modernity that confronted them in ways which eased their transition, and that of their families. The absence of the parlour may have meant a diminution of display space in the 1950s home, but this was compensated for by the emergence of a range of new, essentially modern items of furniture which enabled the housewife to show off her knick-knacks to her full satisfaction. To make up for the lack of divisions between rooms, for example, room dividers and open shelving systems appeared on the market. These had their origins in avant-garde modernist ideas but once they had found their way into suburbia, they were used to very different ends. Within modernism, storage furniture had been a means of rationalising the interior, removing traditional bulky items such as wardrobes and clutter from it. As the designer George Nelson explained,

The old idea of the living-room never included a closet. Nor was storage space considered essential. There might be a table with two or three drawers in it which would be jammed with playing cards, seed catalogues, letters, cancelled cheques and dozens of other odds and ends ... the living-room in the modern house invariably has one or several cabinets filled with shelves, drawers and compartments.[24]

These storage cabinets, most of them low level and often mounted on spindly legs, and sometimes with compartments to house gramophones and records as well as everything else, quickly became ubiquitous items of furniture replacing the small side-tables and desk of the Victorian interior. Rather than removing clutter, however, they provided an ideal surface for display and were frequently embellished with family photographs, vases of flowers, or increasingly, houseplants, and countless small ornaments, among them gifts and holiday souvenirs. Household manuals of the 1950s all continued to offer advice on flower arranging, the role of colour and integration into the general decorative environment being considered crucial. 'Colours should be chosen with regard to the background,' advised a British publication of 1951,

'Some rooms will take almost any colour, but in others it is necessary to guard against a clash of colours, eg. scarlet and pink. Flowers
can sometimes be matched with a small object in the room, eg. a
cushion cover, and another idea is to put the least patch of yellow
into mixed vases; this lightens up the general tone and emphasises
the other colours'.[25]

Ruskin's housewife who spent her time 'arranging' things in the domestic environment was still alive and well in the 1950s and determined not to succumb to the minimalist, functional requirements of the modern style.

Room dividers and bookcases, whether built-in or freestanding – interestingly the modernists allowed the latter to be included as they felt that the presence of books in an interior was an indicator of the intellectual standing of the inhabitants – were equally welcomed by the housewife as opportunities for display, as were the top surfaces of pelmets and the ubiquitous cocktail bar, used more frequently for this purpose, most probably, than for social functions.[26] When kitchens and dining rooms were combined, shelved partitions appeared there as well, bringing display into a hitherto generally neglected area. A British publication from the mid–1950s depicted a woman cooking with her back to just such a partition which was festooned with potted plants, a cut-glass decanter and a variety of small glass vases and decorative kitchen artefacts.[27] Advice books for housewives generally tended to underplay the need for display, however. The British journalist Molly Harrison explained that, 'Gone are the days when women were content to surround themselves with all manner of elaborate ornaments which not only made work, but whose main purpose was ostentation, to show other people how wealthy and important their owners were.'[28] While this may well have been the case, given the increasing privatisation of the home, the role of display as a form of self-identification for the housewife was clearly still an important one. The reasons put forward against display were the well-worn ones of health and efficiency to which was added the need for leisure time to spend with the children and on voluntary work in the community.

Not all 1950s homes were overtly modern in their choice of furnishings. Some mixed old and new while others favoured reproduction furniture which was in plentiful supply. In Britain it came in a variety of styles – from Elizabethan to Queen Anne to Chippendale – while in the USA there was an even wider breadth of choice from Early American to French Provincial. 'In 1957,' according to Thomas Hine, 'one average-sized manufacturer offered twenty different styles of standard sofas, three styles of sectionals, eighteen styles of love-seats and thirty-nine upholstered chairs, each available in seventeen different qualities of fabric, each available in a dozen or more colors or patterns.'[29] It was in their choices of colours and patterns, perhaps, that the 1950s housewife had the greatest aesthetic responsibility and outlet for creativity and personal expression. Whereas modernism had favoured a restricted palette of colours in the domestic interior, 'official' culture now embraced colour and pattern in a much more open manner – primarily because they could now be approached scientifically. 'Scientists,' Molly Harrison explained, 'know that colour has a tremendous influence on the daily lives of everyone; that people are cheered or depressed, rested or fatigued by various colour combinations.'[30] Rooted in behavioural psychology, a scientific rationale for the use of colour in the home now made it possible to align it to the rational programme of modernism.

Modern pattern could equally be achieved by scientific means, as the work of the Festival Pattern Group, established in Britain in 1951, made clear.[31] Their work with organisms viewed through microscopes resulted in a whole new set of modern decorative possibilities which rapidly found their way on to curtains and into the shapes of coffee tables. A whole new language of colour and pattern was made available to the modern housewife who used it, as she always had, intuitively and creatively, relishing the possibilities and happy to have some of the guilt removed from her task of aestheticising the domestic interior. In the process, she continued to make the bridges between the past and the future, between tradition and modernity, that had long been part of her household duties. The soft, sensuous nature of much modern pattern, and the richness and variety of the new colours – made available by technological advances, and (particularly in the USA) influenced by colour television, the 'movies', advertisements and printed publications – all served to enhance the feminine nature of the modern home and, like the stiletto heel, to reinforce the housewife's sense of her gendered self, albeit one expressed in an essentially stereotypical aesthetic vocabulary.

Increasingly the post-war housewife found ways in which to locate her femininity, defined stereotypically, within the material culture of domesticity as it was formulated by the dominant ideology of the day. She did this primarily through accepting rather than rejecting the image of femininity on offer and utilising it to her own ends. She could take from the new manifestations of modernism what she wanted and transform or subvert what she did not want. This freedom to exercise her tastes was expressed through the processes of consumption and home-based 'amateur' production.

While the idea that women were the key consumers had been widely understood in the pre-war years, especially in the USA, this was now discussed even more openly. Mary Grieve, the editor of *Woman* magazine, explained that,

American home economy had long been based on the sure knowledge that it was the woman who spent the money on consumer goods, including consumer durables. The vast and profitable women's magazines in the States were founded and prospered on that fact. But Britain was a man's world and still is in decisive matters. So it took our tycoons longer to believe that it is Mrs Jones, not Mr Jones, who chooses the goods that go into their home and down their throats.[32]

In this period of increased general affluence and wide availability of consumer goods, the links between the home and marketplace were stronger than ever and women provided the key link between the two. While they may not have been the main earners they were certainly the key spenders and there was plenty of advice on hand in the form of books, exhibitions, advertising, magazines and even television programmes, to help them undertake their task. Consumption fell into two general camps – rational consumption which was seen as part of housework, and which needed to be reduced through efficiency measures, and leisure consumption which was linked to fashionableness and pleasure. Inevitably, there were significant overlaps between them. The new self-service supermarkets played music while women shopped for food and basic household items, suggesting that this was a similarly pleasurable social occasion to a day out at the department store where women might meet for lunch. The pre-war idea of the 'shopping day-out' continued into this period, as the economist Gertrude Williams explained,

Thousands of women in the suburbs and small country towns look forward enormously to the weekly or fortnightly visit to the nearest big town where they can do all their shopping, have their hair dressed, and meet their friends for meals in much more glamorous surroundings than one offered by the little shops near their homes.[33]

The middle-class housewife played by Celia Johnson in David Lean's memorable film *Brief Encounter* was just one such woman, combining a trip to town with a visit to the cinema, a chance to change her library book, and a romantic interlude which, although unfulfilled and full of pain, provided a level of fantasy in an otherwise routine, suburban life. The day in town was linked with desire, release and pleasure, fulfilling the same role that shopping had done for the Victorian middle-class housewife. However, by the 1950s, with the disappearance of servants, the enormous increase in factory production and processing, and the diminution of home-based production, shopping was also a form of time-consuming drudgery. The construction of huge shopping malls, and, in Britain, traffic-free shopping precincts, were intended to contain and facilitate the shopping experience and make it a local rather than an urban one. But like the suburbs themselves, they also contributed to housewives' isolation.

The picture of consumption projected in the media which emphasised the pleasure of possession rather than the work involved in acquiring goods, was one of material abundance and joy. It did not fit with the prevalent image of the self-denying housewife, and it served, therefore, to provide an alternative to the highly instrumental picture of the housewife presented by the rationalists. Consumption – one aspect of it, at least – provided a form of compensation for the oppressive nature of suburban life by providing a form of pleasure and of escape and by offering another model to that of the housewife giving herself body and soul to her family.

In spite of the fact that most of the goods and services required by the household were acquired, ready-made, outside the home, it was not until the 1960s, when the number of working women increased significantly that the concept of women's 'house-craft' or aesthetic production in the home, faded almost entirely from view. In the 1950s it was still going strong andit undoubtedly provided a form of creativity and therapeutic release for many women. Knitting, crochet work, flower-arranging, baking cakes and making children's clothes were all forms of necessary work *and* sources of pleasure and women's magazines and advice books encouraged and helped women to involve themselves in such activities. The idea of 'female accomplishments' underpinned these practices, proving that house-making was not yet entirely a de-skilled activity. A British publication from 1946 provided assistance on home baking with some sophisticated suggestions about cake decorating: 'don't be too conventional with your iced cakes. Make your own holly and mistletoe sprays or show Continental gaiety and dash off a snowscape in the modern manner.'[34] As in every other area in this decade, a modern artistic idiom for traditional practices was available and it was left to women to bridge the gap. In the area of dressmaking, for example, it was suggested that 'a shabby blouse could be made gay with a collar and a panel of lace'.[35] The lack of detailed instructions accompanying this suggestion implied that the housewives being addressed still had the skills with which to realize it. The emphasis on 'make do and mend' which characterised the immediate post-war years was transformed subsequently into more exotic projects. Knitting and sewing for the family remained popular right through the 1950s and the complex patterns in magazines made few allowances for women who lacked the required level of skill with which to follow them. A copy of *Woman's Weekly*, for example, included instructions for a woman's cardigan and matching hat in a complex rib pattern, and details of how to acquire a paper pattern for a 'ballerina party dress for a special occasion' to be made in printed taffeta or brocade.[36] Patterns for children's dresses invariably involved smocking or embroidered motifs, examples of feminine skills which had clearly not yet died out.

The pervasive image of the isolated 1950s suburban housewife, suffering from neuroses and taking tranquillisers in order to be able to face the void of the day ahead was only part of a much bigger picture. Where the material culture of the home was concerned there were signs of resistance to the oppression that many women experienced. There were, in any case, a number of contradictions within the dominant ideology that allowed women some room for manoeuvre. There were clearly opportunities for pleasure and personal fulfilment in the lives that many women found themselves living. In contrast   to the pressures that came later, with women working and still bearing the brunt of the responsibility for home-making and child-rearing, women in the 1950s had a defined role which was relatively unambiguous. 'From a permanent position on the assembly line,' the women's historians Barbara Ehrenreich and Deirdre English have maintained, 'it does not look so terribly degraded to bake cookies for spoilt children.'[37] It was also an existence which was rooted in the morality of family life rather than in the amorality of the marketplace. While they may have lacked the shared religious beliefs that united society in the mid-nineteenth century, basic human values still underpinned life in the home at that time. As Ehrenreich and English have explained, 'The alternative to the suffocation of domesticity turns out to be the old rationalist nightmare, a world dominated by the Market, socially atomized, bereft of "human" values.'[38]

In many ways, the suburban housewife of the 1950s stood at the end of an evolution which had begun with the Victorian separation of the spheres. Her role was a similar one, although the tools with which she had to perform it came increasingly from outside her sphere and control. At the same time, however, women's alliance with the world of commerce and consumption were such that her control moved increasingly outside the private sphere, much to the annoyance of masculine culture which continued to negate the territory of women's expanding authority or, at least, to trivialise and marginalise it. It was the marginalisation, ultimately, of women's culture in the 1950s, rather than the absence of it that lay at the roots of Betty Friedan's 'problem without a name'. As fast as women discovered, embraced, began to feel at home with, and finally made their own, the stereotypical image of femininity that had been constructed for them through this century, so masculine culture systematically set out to undermine it. As a result, women turned away from it and began once again to emulate men and aspire to their condition. By the late 1960s and early 1970s this latter tendency had become dominant once more and, in parallel, modernism took a hold on the mass environment as never before.

Before that occurred, however, women had very nearly succeeded in harnessing mass-produced, technologically-advanced material culture to their own ends, with manufacturing and commerce bending over backwards to feminise their products in an attempt to win over the female consumer. As a result, the material culture of 1950s modernity was overridingly feminine.

CHAPTER NINE

'A Kind of Golden Age':

Goods and Femininity

'Blocked in their true realisation, American desires for autonomy and community were channeled into privatized, reified commodity consumption.'

– David Gartman[1]

The idea that private consumption was an inadequate form of compensation for what Americans had lost by moving to suburbia in the 1950s is a compelling one. 'The public image,' explained Betty Friedan, 'in the magazines and television commercials, is designed to sell washing machines, cake mixes, deodorants, rejuvenating face-creams, hair tints. But the power of that image ... comes from this: American women no longer know who they are. They are sorely in need of a new image to help them find their identity.'[2] Seen from this perspective, women were the lost, passive dupes of the media whose task it was to project an image with which they could identify, and, in so doing, perpetuate the system of corporate capitalism. Such thinking has a relentless logic to it and is in line with a broader belief that consumption was a passive activity, an albeit ultimately unsatisfying form of sexual and spiritual sublimation.[3] The idea that consumption held women captive has been reiterated through this century, forming a *leitmotif* in much feminist writing, suggesting an indissoluble bond between women's suppression and their role as consumers.

However, the symbolic relationship between women and the objects of their consumption provided a possibility of women becoming relatively free agents – not necessarily the creators of their goods but certainly their active selectors and, to an increasing extent, through their tastes and their growing positions of strength in the marketplace, forces influencing both the nature and the appearances of the goods in question. The increasingly overt aesthetic feminisation of goods in this period, manifested in an explosion of pink radios, coloured appliances and a preponderance of pattern and texture in the domestic interior, bore witness to the expanding power of the female consumer and, concomitantly, to the growing stature of feminine culture as a whole.

Simultaneously, however, as feminine taste came increasingly to constitute the central dynamic of the marketplace and to determine the visual character of the domestic environment, it found its critics once again lining up and getting ready to attack under the establishment banner of 'good design'. Just as it seemed to be acquiring an unprecedented autonomy and influence in everyday life, feminine taste found itself banished in the name of 'kitsch' or 'bad taste'. Its banishment was reinforced in the subsequent decade when it was youth, rather than women, whose values penetrated the world of establishment taste and reversed many of its tenets. Linked to a show of neo-modernism, young people rejected the 'middle-aged' values of their elders and demonstrated that it was possible to combine technocratic, progressive culture with 'fun' and style-consciousness. The housewife was relegated once more to the marginalised position that she had occupied in the early days of Fordist mass manufacture.

Before the power of youth culture had succeeded in undermining the authority of establishment taste, the 'housewife's aesthetic' enjoyed a short period of rehabilitation between the mid- and late–1950s. It was manifested not only in women's determination to perpetuate their role as homemakers in the traditional sense but also in their new-found love affair with modernity and in manufacturing industry's efforts to provide goods that appealed to their tastes. This may have looked like cynical manipulation, but also meant a wholesale re-evaluation of feminine culture in the marketplace, an acknowledgment of the power of the female consumer over the world of Fordist mass production, and the creation of a space in which women could come to terms, and identify themselves, with a feminised model of modernity.

The economic situation in America in the early 1950s resembled that of the late 1920s. The seller's market for consumer goods of the early post-war years, the result of a backlog of demand, was transformed into a highly competitive one by around 1953, such that the large manufacturing corporations were in search of a new strategy to keep their production lines flowing. Once again, the solution was intensified advertising and product styling. As in the '20s, this sequence of events coincided with a shift in the prevailing image and ideology of femininity. This time, however, it was characterised less by a masculinisation of that image – a result of the incursion of modernist values into the home in the form of the rational household movement – than with a re-feminised vision of modernity which looked back to its mid-Victorian equivalent, emphasizing gender difference. The femininity of the 1950s embraced the stereotypical picture of feminine beauty represented by softness, delicacy, elegance and grace, combined with the domestic ideal in which a desire for novelty merged with the more traditional notion of comfort. It was a picture which was both mirrored by, and embodied in, the material culture of the home.

This was especially apparent in the ideals that underpinned the decoration and furnishing of the living area. The 'contemporary' aesthetic, as it was called to differentiate it from first-generation modernism from which it nonetheless derived its essential tenets, was unashamedly 'of the moment' in its forward-looking search for space, light, gaiety, harmoniously unified interior settings, organic forms, bright colours, contemporary patterns and new materials. Unmitigatingly 'new', it was received with unbridled enthusiasm by women as part of their bid to participate in modernity. In Britain this feminine enthusiasm for the new household style was reinforced by the results of an exercise undertaken by the Design and Industries Association with an exhibition entitled 'Register Your Choice', held in 1953 at London's Charing Cross railway station. Two rooms were decorated, one with the 'best sellers' of the day – which were, not surprisingly, highly conservative in nature – and the other with items thought by the DIA to be of exemplary contemporary design. The organisation then asked people to indicate which room they preferred and to explain the reasons for their choices. Although the audience consisted for the most part of middle-class Londoners, the results revealed that whereas 59 per cent of the men questioned preferred the contemporary room, 61 per cent of the women liked it better. More of the latter group were under the age of 35 than above it. Reasons for preferring the contemporary (right-hand) interior – which included small, two-toned, winged chairs with wooden arms and splayed legs, a modern wall lamp, and one wall decorated in a Regency-style striped wallpaper, as opposed to the more traditional (left-hand) one – which contained an upholstered three-piece suite and a free-standing standard lamp with a fringed shade, were varied but clustered generally around a distinction which opposed novelty with comfort. An article in the DIA Yearbook in the same year explained,

Those who liked R tended to advance aesthetic reasons, but those who disliked it were more inclined to criticise it on practical grounds, [whereas] in L, those who liked it often said they could put their legs up. It was appreciated usually either as comfortable or cosy, or else homely, or restful, a family room where it would be possible to live or relax.[4]

Clearly the aesthetic home, the home in fashionable taste made beautiful by the hand of its pre-eminent beautifier, the housewife, was in the ascendant and the traditional home was becoming less appealing. Many middle-class women, the exercise suggested, had finally found a modern domestic aesthetic which could represent their unambiguous passage into modernity. One woman was probably speaking for many more when she declared herself 'an enthusiastic follower of the contemporary trend in furnishing and I can only hope that this room tops the poll with a very large majority.'[5]

The fact that this was an aesthetic borrowed from the postwar Scandinavian model of modernism which favoured craft skills over mass production, natural over synthetic materials, and light, nature-inspired, contemporary patterns and colours over monochrome minimalism, and which was rooted in essentially humanistic rather than mechanistic values, made it possible for women to identify with, and embrace, it unreservedly. Also, in its proportions, in many of its decorative details, its preoccupation with 'elegance', its commitment to the unified interior, this contemporary style recalled the eighteenth century. And above all, in its appeal to the senses with its soft pastel colours and sensuous textures rather than to the intellect, it was unashamedly 'feminine' in nature.

In search of a new modern identity through which they could demonstrate the fact of their 'belonging' somewhere, many women found in the contemporary style a ready-made language with which to express their optimism about the future. Importantly, it was a language which, although completely of its time, did not exclude the conventional requirements of the feminine domestic aesthetic, but simply changed the terms of reference in which they were articulated. It was an adaptable aesthetic, appealing across a range of tastes from the most avant-garde to the most conservative. An advertisment for a contemporary-style chair manufactured by a London-based company called Cintique, which aimed its goods at high street chain stores, depicted a tightly trousered modern young woman explaining that 'first I loved the wonderful colours; then the elegant styling. But most of all I loved the comfort.'[6] Novelty and comfort were not mutually exclusive – something women could identify with.

The way in which housewives appropriated the new domestic aesthetic did not necessarily conform to the expectations of those who had created and promoted it, namely the professional design profession and design reform establishment, however. Indeed, the gap between consumers and producers, and their differently gendered models of modernity, were such that while the former pushed the new possibilities of colour, pattern and modern form to their aesthetic limits, relishing this new-found freedom to express their participation in modern life, the latter stood back and judged their achievements in words which had an all-too-familiar ring to them. When members of the Council of Industrial Design expressed their predictable dismay at the way in which contemporary design was being interpreted by the public they were noting their disappointment at what they saw as a betrayal of their ideals.[7] 'They see the "contemporary style",' wrote the furniture designer Ernest Race, 'merely as a fashion.'[8] In the following year Gordon Russell, the director of the Council, created the category of what he called 'Imitations of Contemporary Furniture' in which 'all clichés will be seized on avidly and such features as tapered legs will be overplayed. In extreme cases they will be made of boards rather than wood of square section, giving a flimsy appearance when seen from one point of view and an unduly heavy one from another.'[9] This just shows how little the criteria of the British design establishment had evolved since the days of the Arts and Crafts movement, and reinforced the idea of a quality and taste hierarchy within the umbrella concept of 'contemporary' design.

Like Charles Eastlake before them, the design reformers of the post-war years also blamed the salesmen for what they perceived as the low level of public taste. 'High pressure salesmanship is seen,' wrote the journalist Dorothy Meade,' at its very worst in new, isolated housing estates where families depend mainly on mail order catalogues and travelling salesmen for their choice of furnishings.'[10] In one such housing estate, Hartcliffe outside Bristol, Meade discovered a cocktail cabinet in which the family kept its bread, irrefutable proof of its inability to make considered decisions about its furniture. Paul Reilly, the director of the Council from 1960, also condemned the highly-polished 'half-baked, eye-catching misrepresentation of originally good ideas that are everywhere coming to the fore in the gaudier windows of the cheap furniture emporia' which had 'cut into the bread and butter market'.[11] For the most part, these comments were class-based condemnations by middle-class intellectuals of the tastes of those whom they considered to be both their social and their cultural inferiors. At the same time, however, an awareness of the role of the female consumer also crept into their rhetoric. In a discussion about the way in which a young couple, about to be married, decided what furniture to purchase, Gordon Russell explained that while the girl was influenced either by her mother or by a salesman the boy simply wanted to please the girl: 'Under these conditions well-designed contemporary furniture does not get much of a look in.'[12]

The sheer quantity of writing on the vulgarization of contemporary furniture was an indicator of the extent to which its popularisation was gaining ground as the decade progressed. Whatever the response of masculine modernist culture to their tastes, large numbers of women, across a range of social classes, appropriated contemporary-style furnishings and decorations and made them their own in the 1950s. The transformation of modernist ideology into a fashionable style represented an expanding feminisation of culture in general. The growth of the 'do-it-yourself' movement and women's sustained production in home-making facilitated this appropriation, as did the expansion of market-led manufacturing and retailing. As Paul Reilly reluctantly admitted, 'Modern furniture now finds its way into homes which were formally the exclusive preserve of "the trade". And the trade has not been slow to spot this.'[13] The alliance between contemporary style and feminine culture meant that both were significantly transformed. This was the first time, however, that space had been built into a modern interior design movement to allow that transformation to occur on a significant scale. By the 1950s, women had both negotiated modernity on their own terms *and* found a modern domestic aesthetic with which they could represent their entry into that world.

The feminisation of the modern domestic living space affected the other rooms of the home as well. The bathroom in particular – the first room to have succumbed to the influence of rationalisation in the home half a century earlier – now abandoned that pull and joined the living room to become a centre of comfort, display and fashion. The kitchen also changed its character to become much more than the housewife's little laboratory tacked on to the back of the house. Indeed in the new suburban dwellings in the USA and Britain the kitchen/diner became an important living space for the 1950s family. In an *Evening News* article of 19 June 1957 a British journalist pinpointed the characteristics of this new hybrid, describing the kitchen of her 'dream home' as being, separated from the dining-area by only a 'room divider' unit, that also serves as a step-saving pass-through counter. I was lucky to find a unit which exactly matched my kitchen colour scheme down to the push-through drawers – one yellow, one grey. Kandya make this, also the yellow Formica-topped kitchen table with white-metal legs I fell for ... To sit down to a quick and handy breakfast as most of us do these days, I chose a matching slatted bench, yellow and grey alternating, and a small settle with a white metal frame upholstered in wipe-clean yellow plastic.[14]

The most striking new feature of 1950s kitchens was the introduction of colour and decoration and of other 'feminising' details such as potted plants and knick-knacks, hitherto reserved for the parlour. The new colour revolution, which dramatically transformed both the American and the British popular interior, closely resembled that which had preceded it in the 1920s when the General Motors automobile company, with its new approach to marketing, had taken over the market lead from Ford. Colour was re-introduced in response to the expansion of feminine consumption which demanded, or so it was perceived, an enhanced level of personalisation and aestheticisation in its products. By the 1950s the technological base for its introduction into mass manufacturing had expanded considerably as had the consumers' expectations of it.

Women's requirement for individualisation in interiors and products at this time grew from the need for self-identification in the face of increasing social homogenisation. This was especially obvious in the USA where the new tract housing was creating an image of 'sameness' for millions of families. So while colour found its first and most obvious outlet in the painted and papered surfaces of the structural elements of the home, introduced either by the 'do-it-yourselfer' or the hired decorator, it rapidly moved into moveable two- and three-dimensional items manufactured outside the home. Floor and kitchen surface coverings were joined by add-on details such as cupboard and door handles and, eventually, by household goods themselves, from dinner plates to refrigerators which abandoned their sanitary whiteness in favour of a richer palette.

If colour denoted beauty in modern living it was also a sign of fashion awareness and the presence of novelty in the home. Another long-term component of the housewife's task had been to act as a filter between the external world of fashion and the internal world of aesthetic domesticity. While in mid-Victorian Britain and the USA this had been an essential social requirement, marking a family's entry into middle-class status, in the suburban world of the 1950s it contributed to the construction of a personal identity for the housewife as part of the process of transforming public media messages into private meanings. Nothing was so easy to change as the colour scheme of an interior. Equally, the increasingly available and afford-able plastic materials used on floors and as curtaining could be used and discarded with growing rapidity. Even dinette chairs could be reupholstered at regular intervals with the new vinyl fabrics. Above all, colour united the components in an interior setting to create a harmonious whole, the ultimate of the aestheticised home in which beauty reigned over utility.

The 1950s saw a continuous sequence of new hues appear-ing on the horizon. 'In 1955,' the cultural critic Vance Packard has revealed, 'the consultants had forecast that pink would be the leading colour. In 1956 turquoise was the predicted leader. This year it was lemon yellow.'[15] Pastels and rich tertiaries, with highlights of gilt, reflected the image of soft femininity and exotica that characterised domesticity in that decade. Pinks, light greens, pale blues, greys, turquoise and soft yellows were especially popular. The Tupperware company's first range of containers produced in 1945 had come in 25 translucent frosted pastel shades while Raymond Loewy's refrigerator for the Frigidaire company of 1950 had an ice-blue interior and came complete with gold trim. By 1955 Frigidaire was offering models in Sherwood Green, Stratford Yellow and Snowy White. By 1960 it had expanded its range to offer six colours.

Praising the use of colour in the modern home, the American interior decorator Dan Cooper advised his readers to think of the blue of the sky and the cooling effects of 'white, gray and pale lemon yellow' in a hot climate.[16] Above all, colour was used by the housewife at this time in a sensorial rather than a scientific way, linked with emotions and moods rather than with measurable effects. A newly refurbished hotel in Florida – one of the holiday destinations for more and more suburban Americans at this time – was described in highly evocative terms: 'The entire concrete floor of each was covered with woolen carpet, some the crisp pink of a little girl's hair ribbon, some light blue, some a green almost the shade of water in the bay outside.'[17] These were hot weather colours, linked with ideas of leisure and visions of exotica. Transferred to the suburban home, they brought with them an image of outdoor living and of relaxation and informality that helped define the modern lifestyle of the mid-century. Pastel colours, with such evocative titles as 'lagoon blue', 'Bermuda pink' or 'sand yellow'[18] were among the strongest visual symbols in the 1950s home, redolent of escape and tranquillity. In fulfilling this escapist role, they performed a parallel function to the flowery wallpaper of the mid-Victorian home. Now, however, the imagery of escapism was less that of the rural past than of the contemporary vacation. Respite from work, whether the paid labour of the husband or the domestic drudgery of the servantless suburban housewife, had become the universal dream by that time and it was represented symbolically in the colours of the everyday domestic environment. Indeed, the American car designer for General Motors, Harley Earl, had likened stepping into an American automobile to 'going on a holiday', given the scale of the vehicle and the number of diverting accessories inside it.

Pink was the mostly obviously feminine colour of all those that appeared in the 1950s domestic interior. It made an appearance in a wide range of shades – from rose pink to salmon pink to 'shocking' pink – on automobiles, radios, refrigerators, 'Barbie' dolls and the luminous iced cakes at children's parties. Linked with the idea of female childhood, it represented the emphasis on distinctive gendering that underpinned 1950s society, ensuring that women were women and men were men. Gendering had to start at an early age and parents were the key role models. The use of pink in the home emphasised the essential femininity of girls and women and showed daughters that their mothers both understood this and

Sales brochure for Kenwood Food-Mixers, 1950s. In response to the need to 'aestheticize' the kitchen many manufacturers began to provide goods in a range of fashionable colours. In order to ring the changes the Kenwood food-mixer offered a choice of coloured plastic accessories which could be attached to a standardised metal base. (Thorn EMI)

wished them to recognize the distinctiveness of their gender as well. Indeed, many of the young suburban housewives were little more than girls themselves. In her depiction of the young women that emerged from contemporary women's magazines, Betty Friedan described them as, 'young and frivolous, almost childlike; fluffy and feminine; passive; gaily content in a world of bedroom kitchen, six, babies and home'.[19] Later she discussed a young housewife whose 'favourite possession is her four-poster spool bed with a pink taffeta canopy'.[20] Pinkness reinforced the idea that femininity was a fixed category in the lives of women from childhood onwards and by surrounding themselves with it women could constantly re-affirm their unambiguously gendered selves. However, according to one British adviser, there were dangers in using a particular shade of pink in certain situations! 'It is probably the association of pink with underclothes that makes it less desirable for us in its lighter shades for net curtains.'[21]

Pink also served to unite 1950s femininity with the past. Used in combination with gold, it instantly evoked the historical decorative idiom so beloved of Elsie de Wolfe, the eighteenth-century 'French taste' of Madame de Pompadour and Louis XV. Re-emerging in the 1950s interior on the surfaces of radios and refrigerators, these evocative colours recalled the feminine taste, craftsmanship and luxury that were part of that historical moment, reconfirming in the process the essential femininity of the domestic sphere. Pink and gold subsequently became linked with what was seen as the vulgarity of 1950s consumerism and of the exaggerated image of feminine sexuality, epitomised in the appearances, homes and possessions of the Hollywood filmstars of that period.

American automobiles responded to the same process of feminization as kitchen appliances – indeed, often leading the way – through their pioneering use of two-tone styling, abundant chrome trim, and visual references to jet fighter airplanes and rockets. The automobile manufacturers, reduced by the mid–1950s to 'The Big Three' – Ford, General Motors and Chrysler – because of the high investment needed in what were now two-yearly major body redesigns, experienced the same problem of market saturation in 1953. Once again, they looked to styling as a means of increasing their sales. Although the aestheticisation of the American automobile in the 1950s, resulting in the huge, low-bodied, winged machines resplendent with glittering chrome details, can be seen as one of the most clear-cut examples of the feminisation of material culture of that decade, women were still not their chief consumers.[22] There was, however, an expanding female market for cars as one advertisement made clear: 'She's Married – She's Happy – She drives a Mercury'.[23] Suburban living, shopping trips and chauffering children mean that many women had to drive. Equally, suburban living also meant that many men had to drive their automobiles on the new highways to get to work. It has been suggested that the automobile manufacturers pretended to be aiming their cars at women because men could still not yet admit to being attracted to such obviously non-utilitarian artefacts. Stereotypically, men were still perceived to be the rational consumers, if they consumed at all, while women had more intuitive responses. However, 'the dirty little secret' of 'automotive sales' according to Gartman, was that men made the major decisions'.[24]

While automobiles were widely bought and used by men, there was a sense in which women also had an increasing stake in automobile consumption if only in their capacity as passengers and occasional drivers. The fact that all three major manufacturers employed women designers in their styling studios to work on interior textiles and other interior details implied that feminine taste had a significant role to play both in production and consumption. The Mercury advertisement cited above referred to 'his and her' glove compartments and described the product as 'their car', suggesting that the concept of 'togetherness' extended outside the home and into the family automobile. In fact, the car became an extension of the living-space of the home and an extension of the female sphere. The bulky bodies of the 1950s American automobiles can be seen as containers of mobile living-rooms in which feminine culture and feminine taste held sway. Viewed from this angle, the automobile was an androgynous object appealing to both sexes in rather different ways. On one level, they were extraordinary exercises in form – pieces of mobile sculpture designed by men for men with female sexuality used as a selling tool – but they were also feminised, domesticised spaces fulfilling all the aesthetic and symbolic requirements of home life, albeit on the move. If the level of gender ambiguity in the design of automobiles in the 1950s was linked to the

question of who used and bought them, the gendering of
domestic appliances derived more from the priority given to
either their utilitarian or to their aesthetic and symbolic
features. By the 1950s, appliances had completed the process of
modern feminisation, or feminine modernisation begun in the
inter-war years. Streamlining was still the dominant formal
idiom and increasingly appliance curves were described with
such feminine epithets as 'graceful', 'sleek', and 'sensuously
styled'. An advertisement for an International Harvester
refrigerator from 1950 went so far as to describe its product as
being 'femineered'.[25]

In the 1950s, the kitchen took over from the boudoir and
the drawing room as the heart of the feminine home. The final
demise of the servant, along with the importance of 'togetherness in the home', turned the kitchen into a combined workplace and social centre for the family. This was made possible –
primarily in the USA, but also to an increasing extent in
Britain through its exposure to modern American living as
depicted in magazines and films – by new ideas about house-
planning, and enhanced by the availability of powered domestic appliances which combined utility and aesthetics. The
prime justification for the presence of these goods in the home
was still their role as labour-saving devices, an even greater
necessity now that the housewife worked alone and with
increasing demands upon her role as hostess, however informal entertaining was supposed to have become by that date.
The demands of food preparation were considerable. The new
small appliances, food mixers and processors among them,
created as much work as they saved in introducing the making
of food which had hitherto been reserved for the restaurant or
factory. To win the housewife round to the joys of 'mixing,
beating, mashing, whipping, and kneading', the British manufacturer Kenwood, offered its 'Chef', an all-purpose kitchen
machine, in a choice of colours for its nose cap, cover cap and
control switch.[26] In varying the colour of these small, easily
manufactured fittings – they came in 'sunshine yellow', green,
'gay red', blue and 'ultra-smart black' – rather than redesigning the main components of the machine, Kenwood was
demonstrating the lesson it had learnt from General Motors

and its subsidiary company, Frigidaire.

Kenwood was one of the few British companies to follow the American example in this area. It boasted, for example, that its small food-mixer, the 'Minor' was as beautiful as it was useful, explaining to the housewife that, 'You'll be nearly as thrilled with your Minor when it's not in use, as when you're using it, for its smart appearance would make anyone proud to own it'.[27] These were work tools which were meant to be seen as well as used, items of display helping to transform the kitchen. Their appeal was less a means of establishing social position than of evoking pride of ownership on the part of the housewife. Through that sense of pride would come, it was assumed, an enhanced sense of the commitment to, and satisfaction from, the role she had to perform.

The new plastics, many of which had been developed during the war years, also made an enormous contribution to the domestic landscape. In the form of small kitchen accessories, and, increasingly, as the '50s progressed, items of tableware, they performed the role of units of pure colour which could be arranged in the interior like paint marks on a canvas. They combined cheapness and diversity in a way that was entirely 'natural' to them. What's more, they succeeded in straddling the gap between what could be seen as the conflicting demands for utility and democratised luxury in the home. They were unbreakable, and therefore childproof, easy to clean, and yet capable at the same time of simulating more expensive, craft-based materials, among them leather, china, wood or even alabaster and jet.

Plastics' historical origins in the world of simulation, and their chameleon-like ability to adopt either a traditional or modern aesthetic, situated them outside the canon of modernist mat-erials. Lacking craft roots, they could have no essential 'truth'. In contrast, their essential 'dishonesty' cast them into a world without values, the world of the marketplace where anything was possible. Women's easy and willing assimilation of plastic into the home provided yet one more justification for the modernists' rejection of feminine domesticity.

Plastic's versatility was especially applicable to the new technological leisure products such as portable radios.

Motivated by the consumer boom of the 1950s and the problem of market saturation, radio manufacturers set out to try to sell families more than one set. Although this mitigated against the concept of togetherness, it was a response to the different needs of the members of the family. While the housewife could listen during the day, moving her set with her from room to room as she performed the household chores, the husband could listen to sport on his, while teenagers could listen to their favourite music programmes in the privacy of their own rooms. This perceived diversification of needs was met primarily by the appearance in the marketplace of plastic radios designed to appeal to the different user groups. Women's radios proliferated, boasting colours and forms deemed appropriate for that audience. Some emulated vanity cases and handbags, extending the gendering of personal items, which had gone on for years with fountain pens, watches, wallets, and cigarette lighters. In the process, radios were redefined as personalised luxury items rather than pieces of technological equipment.

By the late 1950s most of the rooms and many of the artefacts in the British and American popular home had been touched by the process of feminine modernisation. Increasingly, manufactured goods offered themselves in a range of options to be assimilated into a harmonious whole by the housewife, as components of the modern, feminised home, their meanings confirmed through her creative effort.

The huge investments in design changes – both fundamental and superficial in nature – made by manufacturers in this period suggested that the tastes of the female consumer played a significant part within the social, economic and cultural life of 1950s Britain and the USA. While Betty Friedan and others bemoaned the role that consumerism and 'excessive' materialism played in the dissatisfaction and ennui of the suburban housewife it was not consumption in itself that was responsible; rather it was the lack of social and cultural approbation for the material culture that represented women's negotiation of modernity. Women's relationship with the material culture of domesticity in the 1950s was considered to be both 'inauthentic' and damaging. This bringing together of women, material culture, and the prevailing aesthetic in a way which was, potentially at least, symbolically satisfying, proved too much for masculine culture to take.

By the end of the 1950s, the moment in which women and culture had all but merged had passed. It was youth, not women, who were to underpin the transformation in material culture that was about to take place. The youth 'revolution', which effected a significant shift in the ideological basis of mass-produced material culture and created a newly-affluent group of consumers to oil the wheels of mass production, adopted many of the strategies already long established within feminine culture. Fashion, novelty, the primacy of visual culture and of surface over form, and the subversive role of colour and decoration, were all harnessed as the means by which modernism was first taken to its formal limits and then brought to a level of crisis such that its criteria were, one by one, examined and found wanting. When, in 1967, Paul Reilly wrote despairingly that, 'we may have to learn to enjoy an entirely new palette for gaudy colours have long been associated with expendable ephemera', it was in response to youth's new-found dominance in the marketplace rather than to the demands of feminine taste.[28]

In the wake of Betty Friedan, radical feminism repudiated women's alliance with material culture and initiated instead a new programme of liberation in which women began to examine their consciousnesses as a means of challenging their oppression and of asserting their equality to men, once again, on masculine terms. For them the 1950s had been less a golden age than a return to the Dark Ages.

CHAPTER TEN

'The Anxiety of Contamination':

Highbrow Culture and the Problem of Taste

'In place of the nineteenth-century what-not we may have
substituted the more functional idea of what-for; for Ruskin's
and Downing's brand of aesthetic morality we have substituted
another brand more suitable to our industrial age. But I doubt
that taste has improved.'

— Russell Lynes[1]

In matters relating to taste there existed a strong sense
of continuity between the mid-nineteenth and the mid-
twentieth centuries. While the means of expression of the
prevailing aesthetic had undergone a substantial transformation, one 'brand' of 'aesthetic moralising' had simply been
replaced by another. Within that moralising, patriarchal and
masculinist assumptions and attitudes played as strong a role
as ever. However, whereas in the nineteenth century and
within early modernism the antagonism of design reformers
and protagonists to women's threatening tastes had been both
direct and overt, in the years after 1945 the attacks on 'bad
taste' and feminine culture were more oblique, more complex,
and, as a result, more subtly damaging.

The straightforward, moralising rhetoric of the likes of
Ruskin and Downing, and later Loos and Le Corbusier, had by
the 1950s, been superceded by a highly complex network of
ethically-based responses to popular taste as part of 'mass
culture'. Noting the remarkable and bewildering plurality of
the British 'campaign' against the levelling down effects of
mass culture, cultural critic and historian Dick Hebdige has

listed, 'Groups and individuals as apparently unrelated as the British Modern Design establishment, BBC staff members, *Picture Post* and music paper journalists, critical sociologists, 'independent' cultural critics like Orwell and Hoggart, a Frankfurt-trained Marxist like Marcuse, even an obsessive isolationist like Evelyn Waugh', among its activists.[2] What brought them together was their shared commitment to 'highbrow culture'. From the first half of the century both in Britain and the USA, many other such campaigners emerged from three main areas: the general arena of design reform, which kept up its proselytising through the continued efforts of government institutions, design professionals, and museums; the world of academia; and popular journalism and social commentary. Individuals from all these fields took a stance on the question of mass culture which they felt threatened to engulf and destroy the world of authentic, high culture. Within the academy, in particular, in which from the mid–1930s onwards the antagonism to mass culture had been widespread, there was a broad spectrum of responses, from left-wing cultural theorists and literary critics, who upheld the view that within capitalism the bourgeoisie controlled the means of cultural production, as it did all other forms of production, to the more conservative supporters of the 'superior qualities' of 'high culture'. Their investment in high culture, in what they believed to be 'a repository of quintessential human values' brought them all together.[3] While some cultural critics targeted taste specifically, others directed their attacks at the products of the mass media in general – among them popular film, literature, and music – and the industries which created them; yet others focused their attacks on the mechanisms and techniques employed by the media to disseminate their manipulative messages, among them marketing, advertising and commercially-oriented design. Their responses amounted to a general malaise about the cultural tendencies within modern society as a whole.

While gender was seldom, if ever, overtly linked to the problems of mass culture and popular taste it was implied, nonetheless, in the adoption of the masculinist modernist canon which informed the criteria of 'good practice' embraced by these critics of modern culture. In addition, a notion of femininity subtly underpinned the commercialised model of culture, with its direct appeal to the emotions and to the 'pleasure principle', which represented modernism's unacceptable 'other' in this context. In aligning themselves with modernist, avant-garde, high culture – seen as the antidote to the prevailing tendency towards 'kitsch', 'ersatz', 'inauthentic' culture or 'bad taste' – the campaigners were perpetuating the masculinist assumptions and prejudices which had lain just below the surface of the design reformers and early modernists before them.

By the Second World War taste cultures were less and less obviously determined by traditional notions of class. As Russell Lynes explained,

The consumers and makers of taste cannot be divided according to the conventional social strata. Good taste and bad taste, adventurous and timid taste, cannot be explained by wealth or education, by breeding or background. Each of these plays a part, but there is no such thing as upper-class taste and lower-class taste as there was once supposed to be. In recent years a new social structure has emerged in which taste and intellectual pretension and accomplishment plays a major role. What we see growing around us is a sort of social stratification in which the highbrows are the elite, the middlebrows are the bourgeoisie, and the lowbrows are hoi polloi.'[4]

The British exhibit at the Milan Triennale, 1954. Containing furniture designed by Robin Day this interior represented the ideal of 'good design' which the Design Establishment exhorted consumers to emulate. Even within this rigorously minimal setting, however, a potted plant is included to 'soften' the otherwise austere preferences of its creators. (Design Research Unit)

Taste and traditional class categories could no longer easily be aligned. This enabled other factors, such as gender, age, level of aspiration, and individual potential and achievement,

to enter the picture, in addition to the possibility of new defin-
itions of class being determined by taste rather than the other
way round. This new scenario emphasised the centrality of
taste to the dynamic of contemporary life and, by implication,
the importance of feminine culture to cultural values as a
whole. It also implied a much more complex and fluid picture
of taste formation than had hitherto been presented and
embued the concept of taste with an authority that it had
never enjoyed. Indeed taste, rather than class became *the*
marker of social and cultural distinction. Writing on this
subject in the 1970s, the sociologist, Herbert Gans believed the
idea of 'good taste' to be a preoccupation of a culture which
was characterised by the fact that its constituent members read
the *New Yorker* and 'bought more quiches than TV dinners'.[5]

The aesthetic moralising that continued to reverberate in
the post-war years was a confrontation between taste cultures,
each made up of representatives from different strata of society.[6] It was not simply a question of one social class condemning the tastes of its 'social inferiors'. Thus the taste culture,
dubbed 'highbrow' by Lynes,[7] which aligned itself with the
ideals of high culture, as represented by modernism, defined
itself in opposition to the culture characterised by tastes which
were formed through the agency of the mass media. In taste
cultural terms that latter group was predominantly made up of
'middle-brow' consumers, the group which, through their
preference for what Lynes called 'creature comforts' over
'intellectual uplift',[8] threatened the 'authentic' values of their
'cultural superiors'. By virtue of the 'passivity' of its
consumption; its emphasis upon comfort within domesticity;
its reliance upon the mass media for many of its objects of
consumption and their aesthetic language; dependence upon
stereotypes for its self-identification; and its acceptance of, and
indeed strong identification with, certain material goods, such
as streamlined products and plastic artefacts which stood
outside the modernist canon, 'feminine taste' was generally
perceived by highbrow culture as being essentially 'middle-
brow' in character.[9]

Links between mass culture and femininity were now well
established. From the last decades of the nineteenth-century

mass culture, formed by the twin forces of industrialization and democratisation, the 'universalisation of commodity production'[10] was perceived by supporters of high culture as feminine by virtue of what they believed to be women's 'natural' inferiority to men where aesthetic production was concerned. 'Mass culture,' Andreas Huyssen has written, 'is somehow associated with women while real authentic culture remains the prerogative of men'.[11] The role of world exhibitions and 'the elaborated staging of the commodity in the giant department stores' were, according to him, influences upon mass culture.[12] Both, as we have seen, also had a special relationship with feminine culture. The links between mass culture and the feminine were reinforced, Huyssen contended, by literary criticism and philosophy. It was Nietzsche who 'ascribed feminine characteristics to the masses', and who condemned Wagner because he 'had succumbed to the adoring women by transforming music into mere spectacle'.[13] Another witness brought in by Huyssen to give evidence was Gustave le Bon who, in his book *The Crowd* of 1895, described the newly emergent metropolitan masses as being 'distinguished by feminine characteristics'.[14] There was a sense in which women and mass culture had become indistinguishable one from the other. A kind of metaphorical transference had taken place: that which was feared and disapproved of by men, namely women daring to enter the public sphere, had come to stand for everything else that presented itself as a threat to the stability of bourgeois male culture.

By the inter-war years that sense of an overt feminisation of mass culture had disappeared, but it remained, nonetheless, nestling between the lines of writings by members of the Frankfurt School, in the works of Theodor Adorno and Max Horkheimer in particular. In their seminal text concerning the manipulative nature of mass culture within capitalism entitled *The Culture Industry: Enlightenment as Mass Deception*[15] Adorno and Horkheimer perpetuated the belief in mass culture as feminine, if only through their use of language: 'Mass culture in her mirror, is always the most beautiful in the land.'[16] Furthermore, while they reserved most of their criticism for popular film, music and literature, they also isolated the aesthetic of streamlining as a product of a culture industry which was manipulating its audience. For them also department stores and supermarkets were 'cemeteries of culture'.[17] While they may not have targeted women directly, they focused their attacks nonetheless on a set of highly feminised cultural forms. In singling out streamlining – among the first modern design languages applied to the goods of mass production industry to incorporate overtly feminine values – for attention, Adorno and Horkheimer were responding to what they saw as a threat to authentic culture which was, in essence, masculinist and modernist in nature.

The heart of the war on mass culture waged by Adorno and Horkheimer and others in the late 1930s in the USA was the fear of a loss of quality in cultural life, a dehumanisation which they believed to be the inevitable result of the standardizing, homogenising, and stereotyping effects of mass replication in the hands of monopoly capitalism. They had seen the 'levelling-down' effects of totalitarian culture under fascism and identified the same system operating in the world of American big business. The sense of 'pseudo-individuality' that was created by mass culture and the inauthentic 'built-in' reactions to its forms on the part of its passive consumers were, for them, strong reasons for an outright condemnation of it. In his famous article of 1939, 'Avant-garde and Kitsch',[18] the American art critic Clement Greenberg explained that kitsch spared the spectator any effort, providing him with instant pleasure in the same way as, for Adorno, commodities seduced consumers while offering them no ultimate sense of gratification.[19]

By the 1940s and '50s Huyssen's 'Great Divide' between the worlds of high and mass culture seemed unbridgeable and it became increasingly apparent that the growing alliance between women's culture and modernity, manifested in the enthusiastic appropriation of the new consumer goods aimed at modernising the domestic environment, was causing members of the masculine 'highbrow' élite to feel even more threatened. As a result, the moral backlash was intensified. Huyssen wrote, 'It was only in the 1940s and 1950s that the modernism gospel and the concomitant condemnation of kitsch became something like the equivalent of the one-party state in the realm of aesthetics.'[20] The intellectual critique of mass culture, now commonly equated with the notion of kitsch or 'bad taste', came from above and below simultaneously. While in the USA members of the Frankfurt School and others continued to rail against the evils of cultural homogeneity – Herbert Marcuse pinpointed its effects in the idea of the 'negro with a Cadillac', an ultimate sign, for him, of commodity democratisation[21] – in Britain academics such as Richard Hoggart[22] and Raymond Williams[23] wrote nostalgically about the authenticity of working-class culture, also in danger of erosion from the new standardization of cultural life. Middlebrow culture, lacking the vitality of low-brow culture and the human values of highbrow culture, became sandwiched in between, besieged from both sides.

There were very few signs of support for this 'inauthentic' middle layer, although one or two writers hinted at that possibility. David Riesman's The Lonely Crowd: A Study of the Changing American Character, published in 1950, is frequently cited as evidence of the anxiety and anomie experienced by modern man trapped within the material environment of mass society.[24] Riesman's aim was to provide a full picture of life in contemporary America with its strong commodity culture and increasing conformity. Like Christopher Lasch after him, he pinpointed what he defined as a level of 'narcissism' with the American character as it confronted the culture which enveloped it. In the midst of his unrelenting pessimism there was, however, a small ray of hope attached to what he called 'taste-exchanging'. Unlike the critics of the popular arts, Riesman noted a rise in the 'taste gradient' where movies, popular novels and magazines were concerned.[26] He was pleased to find 'how energetic and understanding are some of the comments of the amateur taste-exchangers who seem at first glance to be part of a very passive, uncreative audience' and he praised jazz for its high aesthetic standards.[27] The nub of his support for some aspects of the popular arts centred on the observation that just as mass production did not in the end produce standardised objects, but in fact a highly diversified range of goods, so the popular arts – admittedly the

Buick 'Roadmaster', 1951. In its campaign to improve the standards of the public's consumption choices the British Design Council earmarked the sensuous curves, decorative details and overt ostentation and 'uselessness' of American automobile styling as the epitome of 'bad taste'. (National Motor Museum Photographic Library)

exclusively masculine practices of jazz and hot-rodding – offered a level of individualisation and increased access to the high standards of élite culture.[28] Riesman's small crevice of optimism was built upon by the anthropolist Margaret Mead who criticised his book, claiming that ultimately he had

highlighted only negative sanctions: 'shame but not pride, guilt but not the sense of initiative, anxiety but not identity'.[29] Her comments implied a possible space in which feminine culture could be considered as a positive force.

These few tentative words were drowned later in the decade, however, by the wave of paranoid pessimism and moral outrage contained in the writings of journalist Vance Packard who, in three highly popular books, *The Hidden Persuaders* of 1957, *The Status Seekers* of 1959, and *The Waste-Makers* of 1960, laid bare for all to see the allegedly immoral workings of the advertising, marketing and design industries in their creation of 'artificial obsolescence' and false desires. While Packard was not particularly concerned with the aesthetic implications of this manipulation, he allied himself directly with the ethical framework of the neo-modernist project by voicing his concerns in such a way as to suggest that he had reason and commonsense on his side. He claimed, in essence, to be exposing the way in which psychology, psychoanalysis and the social sciences were being used by commerce as means of working with the consumer's unconscious mind. A sense of moral outrage and neo-puritanism were linked in Packard's writings with a characterisation of the 'housewife-consumer' as a passive dupe, responsible, it was implied, through her inaction for letting commerce have its wicked way. There was

no place here for pleasure or desire. The introduction of colour
into the world of kitchen appliances, for example, was seen
solely as a conspiracy on the part of manufacturing and
marketing to sell more goods and not at all as a response to a
desire on the consumer's part for a new meaning for an existing object. He totally ignored also the possibility of the appropriation of an object, such that its meaning might be modified
or even transformed by its entry into the world of use, or the
possibility of consumer resistance to the propositions put in
front of them.

Packard's commitment to the world of rational consumption
and to the utilitarian functionalism embodied in his question,
'How much can a toaster or sofa or carpet sweeper or sewing
machine be improved, really?'[30] linked him firmly with the
moral crusade of the neo-modernists and with those for whom
the feminisation of culture, a culture in which a dynamic
created by the exercise of taste-making and pleasure were
uppermost, was profoundly threatening. In denying the
importance of novelty, fashion, and style as markers both of
social positioning and of individual identity, and in employing
such highly rhetorical and moralistic language to communicate his deep-seated fear of a loss of control Packard was, in
effect, the mid-twentieth century equivalent of John Ruskin.
He used the examples of domestic appliances and automobiles
repeatedly in his treatises, seeing in them the victory of indulgence and hedonism over reason, morality and common sense.
They were symbols par excellence of the 'wasteful, compul-
sive' consumerism he saw all around him.[31] Indeed, streamlined cars and coloured refrigerators occupied centre-stage in
many of the key debates in the gender politics of taste both in
the USA and Britain in these years. Although conceived
within masculine culture, they had moved into feminine
culture as representatives of commerce's efforts to express its
values openly. They stood in defiant opposition to the universalising ambitions of the modernist project and reinforced the
polarisation of high and mass culture. Within the modernist
project of the early century the disciplines of architecture and
design had been closely linked, whereas by the post-war years,
they had moved into two separate arenas and were, for the

most part, represented and supported by different institutions. On both sides of the Atlantic modernist product design was promoted by the 'good design' movement, a reforming programme which set out to raise the level of public taste through the establishment of a design canon and the creation of a consensus of values. The streamlined automobiles and fridges posed powerful threats to highbrow culture's attempts to influence middlebrow taste.

In Britain, the Council of Industrial Design was the key institution upholding and promoting highbrow standards. In the USA, a similar role of paternalistic advisor and cultural mentor was performed by the Museum of Modern Art in New York. Linked with the idea of modern design in the 1930s,[32] the museum's director of the department of industrial design, Edgar Kaufmann Jr, established a series of annual exhibitions in 1949, in collaboration with the Merchandise Mart in Chicago, entitled 'Good Design'. Their aim was to encourage retail outlets to imbibe and learn to appreciate the modernist values that the museum supported and promoted.

Kaufmann's intention was to offset the inherently commercial interests of the retail trade with values which derived from the 'highbrow' cultural preoccupations such as good craftmanship, simplicity, quality and a beauty which was linked to function. 'We felt', he explained, in a discussion about an ashtray, 'that people who bought the ash-tray had something that deserved to be considered not only from the point of view of how well it sold, or how well it was advertised, but what it was like to live with – how useful it was, how beautiful and how sensibly priced'.[33] The criteria expounded by Kaufmann, rooted in modernist ideology, both moral and aesthetic, were consistent with those he had outlined four years earlier when he had answered his own question. 'What is Modern Design?' with a list of twelve characteristics, a list which could have been written by William Morris or Walter Gropius before him. Proclamations such as 'Modern design should express the purpose of an object, never making it seem to be what it is not',[34] 'Modern design should express the qualities and beauties of the materials used'[35] and 'Modern design should blend the expression of utility, materials and process into a visually satisfying whole'[36] had an all too familiar ring to them. What had changed was the enemy – no longer the cluttered Victorian parlour but the twin demons of streamlining and built-in-obsolesence.

Kaufmann's design canon comprised a range of domestic artefacts, among them furniture, ceramics and glass. Objects of transportation and domestic appliances were notable by their absence, with the exception of Raymond Loewy's Studebaker, one of the few minimally-decorated European-inspired American automobiles around at the time. For the most part, the Museum of Modern Art project stood in direct opposition to these garish manifestations of American mass culture. In 1948 Kaufmann had written a highly evocative article entitled 'Borax or the Chromium-plated Calf' in which he had explained that 'Streamlining is the Jazz of the drawing-board'. The analogy was close. Both were indigenously American phenomena; both were 'popular' in their appeal; both were far removed from their sources (negro music and aerodynamics); and finally both were highly commercialized and utilised the 'star' system.[37] Clearly, for Kaufmann streamlining signified what Hollywood film had meant to Adorno. His dislike of it was evident in his antipathetic description of streamlined goods characterised by their 'over-sized curves of transition' and their 'sullen, solid colours'.[38] A couple of years later he was equally unambiguous in his opposition to this commercial idiom in his description of

the widespread and superficial kind of design known as streamlining used to style nearly every object from automobiles to toasters. Its theme is the magic of speed, expressed in teardrop shapes, fairings and a curious ornament of parallel lines – sometimes called 'speed whiskers'. The continued misuse of these devices has spoiled them for most designers.[39]

If streamlined automobiles and domestic appliances, with their strong allegiances to feminine taste, were the *bêtes noires* of high cultural's masculinist design reform in their country of origin, they were even more so across the Atlantic. Transported to Britain, they not only threatened highbrow culture through their aggressively anti-modernist stance, they also became prime symbols of what Dick Hebdige has called the 'spectre of Americanisation'[40] which hovered over all the heated debates about mass culture in the post-war. For post-war British 'highbrows', American culture, manifested in advertising, pulp novels, popular music, television and Hollywood film, represented everything that was vulgar, tasteless and trivial in contemporary life. Explaining why American production methods were not seen as appropriate in the British context, Alec Davies, editor of *Design* magazine, wrote that,

British industries depend for their existence on our tradition for quality, which never existed in America because there has never been an aristocratic background to set such standards – but always an insatiable demand for goods, so that speed of production became the first priority in American industry.[41]

Davies' comments formed part of a wider response to American culture. Resentment of the USA's economic revival after the war and its dominant position in the world trade, of the huge debt that Britain owed to it, and irritation at the presence of American troops and their culture on British soil combined to create a strong anti-Americanism which found its outlet in a number of different forms. Primary among them was antag-onism to the new American-influenced 'life-style', disseminated increasingly through the mass media and represented by a number of material goods and stylistic idioms in the marketplace. Caricatured by the phrase 'the good life', it was a life-style which was characterised by a focus on consumption rather than production, on an alliance between commerce and culture, and on a high level of materialism and display. As such, it openly embraced feminine culture and prioritised its value system. In rejecting American mass cultural values, British highbrow culture was reasserting its allegiance with modernist, masculinist culture and thereby seeking to retain its hold over the sphere of everyday life.

Where goods were concerned, it was the Council of Industrial Design which took on the role of fighting the highbrow battle in post-war Britain. In its rigorous attempts to stem the flow of American products and practices, it was like a dog with a bone, gnawing on a few themes which it felt epitomised all that was wrong with American culture. High on this list were plastic products which threatened 'good British design' in a number of ways. First, the new materials had grown out of large-scale American manufacturing; second, they negated the principles of modernist form; and third, they came in garish colours. In an argument which was reminiscent of Clement Greenberg's earlier comments about mass culture being too 'easy'[42] Paul Reilly presented his objections to the plastics aesthetic,

The temptation to adorn a moulding, to imitate carving or to impress a stylistic cliché, such as the three parallel lines is certainly hard to resist when one considers the extreme ease of reproduction in plastics. It is in fact this very ease of processing which so often leads to trouble and to that reputation for tastelessness which clings to certain categories of plastic products, this ease of shaping, of giving a texture . . . and of colouring demands great discrimination on the part of a plastics manufacturer or designer. The temptation to exploit the spectrum is considerable and much damage had been done to plastics through gaudy, or worse still, sentimental colouring.[43]

In keeping with Ruskin's comments about cut-glass a century earlier Reilly looked to the process of making as a focus for his criticisms rather than to the meanings of the objects. As with cut-glass so with plastic products, it was their conspicuousness as objects of display that so offended their critic's sensibilities. However, to have admitted as much would have meant standing outside the Arts and Crafts philosophy of 'right-making' that informed their conscious appreciation of material goods. It would also have revealed the extent to which gender entered into their assumptions about the 'rightness' or otherwise of such goods.

The Council was equally vociferous about streamlining. From 1949, when it was first published, not a copy of *Design* magazine appeared without a negative comment about American automobiles or streamlined goods.

Such negative feelings appeared in other areas of highbrow culture as well: this is George Orwell's description of an American-style milk bar in *Coming Up for Air*: 'There's a kind of atmosphere about these places that gets me down. Everything slick and shiny and streamlined; mirrors, enamel and chromium plate whichever direction you look in. Everything spent on the decorations and nothing on the food.'[44] Streamlining connoted Americanness, commerce, superficiality and, the greatest threat of all, a life-style epitomised by modern feminine domesticity, even in automobiles, those mainstays of masculine culture. In a valiant attempt to defend it, the American industrial designer, Harold Van Doren, wrote an article in *Design* in October 1949, entitled 'Streamlining: Fad or Function' – the very title evoking the polarity between the feminine world of fashion and the masculine world of utility – in which he set out to justify it in terms of technological efficiency and industrial expediency: 'The truth is that much so-called streamlining is imposed on the designer by the necessity of obtaining low cost through high speed production.'[45] While even he couldn't justify automobile styling – 'let us skip the automobile: few thoughtful American designers really go along with the monstrous inflation of the current motor-car body' – he was adamant that the curved corners on refrigerators were the result of technological necessity rather than an example of consumer-orientated symbolism. 'It may therefore readily be seen', he concluded, 'that what appears to the unsophisticated eye as a preference for soft curves is the result of economical high-speed production methods, which kept prices of refrigerators moving steadily downwards as volume increased.'[46]

His voice proved to be one in a wilderness and the Council remained unconvinced by his arguments. The neo-modernist tenets which underpinned its notion of 'good design' remained in place through this period, informing the large body of propaganda material produced under its auspices. A series of books published in the late 1940s entitled 'The Things We See' addressed the 'common sense' values that the Council sought to promote, expressing them in terms that it hoped the public world understand. In *Indoors and Out* of 1947, for example, the author Alan Jarvis attempted to explain the difficult concept of visual taste by using it in the more familiar context of food: 'We know the childish impulse to gorge on sweets and we recognise at once a visual example of the same thing: a mature taste in either food or furnishings would be made sick by too much sweetness'.[47] We should eat bread, he continued, rather than cakes. Like Packard a decade later, Jarvis was motivated by a strong neo-puritanism and he exhorted the public to follow his example. The tone was, however, one of benevolent British paternalism, rather than American Cold War alarmism.

By the 1950s a consensus had emerged within British highbrow circles about a fundamental threat to human values. These values were, in essence, rooted in the period of the Enlightenment and had underpinned the progress and dominance of patriarchal culture through the previous two centuries. Feminine taste, by now a totally marginalised phenomenon which, through its alliance with commerce, was attempting to regain its former nineteenth-century position of cultural viability, was embedded in the threatening face of material culture and had, therefore, no hope of redemption. The stronger a commercial and mass culture force it became, the harder highbrow culture fought to undermine it. So important had taste become as a determining factor within economic and mass cultural life that women could not be left to control it. The solution was take it out of their hands, regender it, call it 'good design' and align it to high culture.

Although the dominant culture's struggle to defend its position was fought on the basis of gender, this was a largely hidden agenda. When change did come, helped along by the work of the Independent Group,[48] the victory was expressed in terms of age and class. Feminine pleasure had been superceded by youthful fun and working-class vitality, both of which manifested themselves in the transgressive aesthetic language of pop culture. Writing about Pop Art, Huyssen has expressed the view that it was still 'patriarchal, misogynist, and masculinist',[49] an opinion that could be extended to include pop culture in general. The youth revolution of the early 1960s dealt the death blow to highbrow culture that feminine taste had failed to do. The 'alternative' youth culture which emerged, complete with its array of symbolic consumer goods, although shocking and offensive to many, found a level of validation alongside mainstream culture through its strategy of publically-staged resistance. As a subculture, however large, it could define its own identity in direct opposition to that of the status quo. Women had never been able to achieve that subcultural status nor its visible resistance through the consumption and appropriation of goods. Women's culture was perceived as being 'complementary' rather than 'alternative' or oppositional, and their place in the domestific sphere rendered theirs a private rather than a public revolt.

As a consequence, although it was increasingly vital to the commercial system in the post-war years, feminine taste remained marginalised by dominant masculine culture through the establishment of a clear-cut polarity, epitomised in the dualisms of 'good design/bad design', 'good taste/bad taste' – or perhaps more accurately 'good design/bad taste' – within which feminine culture was always linked with the morally and aesthetically inferior category. As long as the ideological and aesthetic programme of modernism remained the main cultural rationale and means of expression for dominant masculine culture, feminine taste – however satisfying and important it may have been for women's lives, and however vital it became for economic growth – remained both illegitimate and marginal within cultural life as a whole. However, with the destabilising effects of pop culture upon mainstream modernism came a sudden fall from grace of that cultural monolith, such that by the end of the 1960s, there were signs that it had finally lost its hegemonic hold. With the subsequent strengthening of a 'post-modern' movement, the question was raised for the first time in this century of whether women's culture might finally find an alliance with a valued cultural programme and feminine taste become recognised as a legitimate force.

Conclusion:

Postmodernity, Postmodernism and Feminine Taste

'It is ... problematic to undertake the task of articulating women's experience, silenced as it has traditionally been in patriarchal culture, in the categories, concepts, and language available'

– Janet Wolff[1]

The trivialisation and downgrading of feminine taste that has taken place ever since women became exclusively linked with the domestic sphere has resulted in its marginalization within contemporary cultural life. Within the context of domesticity, which remains undervalued in comparison with paid labour, politics and technological innovation, women's aesthetic production in the private sphere is seen as little more than a form of light relief from those other, more serious and meaningful activities in the public sphere.

Part of the problem lies in the difficulty in describing women's aesthetic culture in terms of the patriarchal cultural status quo.[2] The language of modernism, rooted in the British design reform movement, excluded feminine taste from its self-definition through the formulation of a hierarchical, binary system of terms and concepts: thus 'private' was contrasted with, and valued less than, 'public'; 'fashionableness' with 'universal values'; 'surface ornamentation' with 'minimal form'; 'nature' with 'culture'; 'tradition' with 'modernity'; 'consumption' with 'production'; 'taste' with 'design'; and so on. The modernists evolved a language and a philosophy of 'modern design' – simply an alternative, more masculine term for what had previously been referred to as 'the aesthetic of everyday life – which denied the validity of all the characteristics linked with feminine culture. In so doing, they left no linguistic or philosophical space for feminine culture to compete with what rapidly became the dominant culture.

It has been suggested that women's communication operates on the level of the prelinguistic.[3] Their relationship with material objects, which themselves communicate outside the rules of formal language, is as a consequence, a potentially more direct and expressive one than that enjoyed by men. Children enter into language, it has been argued, at the same time as they enter into patriarchy. By implication, therefore, women's pre-linguistic relationship with artefactual culture has the potential to free them from patriarchy and allow them a liberating space. It is a space, however, from which they cannot communicate back to, or in any way challenge, mainstream culture, reached only through linguistic means.

The freedom that women have gained through their relationship with material culture is a politically powerless liberation – and indeed not even necessarily consciously recognized. While it sustains women within the framework of domesticity, allows them to form self and group identities, to express their social and cultural aspirations, to form social relationships, and to enter into the wider arena of women's culture, it cannot in itself overthrow patriarchy. In the public sphere, its impact has been felt only negatively through the sustained attack by the dominant masculine culture on the values underpinning feminine domesticity, especially as they relate to the functioning of the marketplace. However, within the evolution of industrial capitalism in this century, it has been women's taste values rather than men's cultural institutions which have effected the key transformations in commercial life, expressed in the aesthetic of goods and by changes in marketing strategies. The constant attempts by masculine culture in the arenas of design reform and academia to undermine that feminine culture, is a mark, ironically, of the latter's increasing influence.

As long as modernism remained the dominant cultural ideology feminine taste had no hope of being other than marginalised and undervalued culturally. But the apparent demise of modernism in the post-war years offered an opportunity for women's culture, and with it feminine taste, to rise up from its oppressed state and find a more public voice as well as approbation and validation in the new pluralistic culture.

The birth of postmodernism is highly contested and depends largely upon the discipline within which one is approaching it. Literary critics tend to locate its appearance in the 1950s, although some have claimed that its origins go back as far as the 1920s, within the epoque of modernism itself.[4] Regardless of the date of its origins, as a cultural critical relating to practice in the areas of architecture, design, dance, theatre, painting, music and film, postmodernism found its most common currency in the 1970s and 80s in the USA and Europe. As an umbrella concept, it embraced a number of contradictions, the most obvious being whether it constituted a new phase of modernism or a radical departure from that earlier movement. Whichever, postmodernism carried with it a number of implications for women's culture in general and for feminine taste in particular. Most obviously, it represented a crisis of credibility in the cultural authority, rooted in the rationalism and universalising principles of post-Enlightenment thought, which had dominated cultural practice throughout the twentieth century.[5] For the first time the unity and hegemonic nature of that dominant culture came under serious attack. Among the many reasons for this was the impact of mass, or popular, culture upon mainstream culture and the different set of cultural values now in the limelight.

Much has been written about the relationship between postmodernism and feminism and whether the former either was or was not a liberating agent for the latter.[6] Most agree that while the challenge to cultural authority opened up a space, the lack of a political agenda in postmodernism meant that it could not ultimately be harnessed by feminists seeking to overthrow hegemonic culture and to inject their own culture into the gap. Janet Wolff has welcomed its 'destabilizing' effects, explaining that 'the radical task of postmodernism is to deconstruct apparent truths, to dismantle dominant ideas and cultural forms, and to engage in the guerrilla tactics of undermining closed and hegemonic systems of thought. This, more than anything else, is the promise of postmodernism for feminist politics.'[7] She was less optimistic, however, about the possibility of this cultural shift actually helping to realize the ambitions of feminism since the inherent pluralism in the new non-authoritarian view of culture meant that any alternative to the mainstream was valid – as indeed was the mainstream itself one of the options on offer.[8]

Postmodernism's initial promise but ultimate inadequacy to represent women's interests was linked to the nature of its origins and its institutional allegiances. This was the case in one of postmodernism's strongest manifestations from the early 1970s onwards. In architecture and design the key cultural shift was effected not by an acknowledgment of women's culture but rather by the emergence of pop culture and the idea of the aesthetic expendability of the environment. This had grown out of a consideration of the life-style values of the expanding youth market of the 1960s. Postmodern architecture and design's most articulate and influential high cultural protagonists, among them Robert Venturi in the USA and Ettore Sottsass in Italy, evolved their aesthetic languages and cultural positions through negotiations with the rhetoric of pop culture. Armed with a new sensibility and language, they challenged the authority of an older cultural generation by replacing its basic vocabulary with its polar opposite – form with surface, minimalism with decoration, rationalism with intuition, universality with expendability. Finally they moved into a position which rejected the idea of binary oppositions altogether, embracing instead a more plural belief system. In Venturi's much-quoted words from his postmodernist manifesto *Complexity and Contradiction in Architecture* of 1966, he set the agenda for an architectural and design movement which was both anti- and postmodernist at the same time

I like elements which are hybrid rather than 'pure', compromising rather than 'clean', distorted rather than 'straightforward', ambiguous rather than 'articulated', perverse as well as impersonal, boring as well as 'interesting', conventional rather than 'designed', accommodating rather than excluding, redundant rather than simple, vestigial as well as innovating, inconsistent and equivocal rather than direct and clear. I am for messy vitality over obvious unity. I include the *non sequitur* and proclaim the duality ... I prefer 'both-and' to 'either-or', black and white, and sometimes gray, to black or white.[9]

He had evolved these ideas through an engagement with the 'pop' commercial world of Las Vegas, responding with pleasure to the instantaneity and aesthetic brashness of that temporary architectural environment.[10] While his was a high cultural appropriation of popular culture – a strategy much used by the contemporary pop artists on both sides of the Atlantic – it made no overt references to the feminine characteristics of the world he was embracing or of the feminine nature of the aesthetic values he was promoting. The alignment of high cultural postmodernism with the popular culture of the mass media could be seen as an alliance with feminine taste as it had come to be culturally stereotyped, but the pop movement defined itself in terms of a new set of aesthetic possibilities derived from an urban, technologically progressive, and aesthetically innovatory vision located in the public arena in which the 'fun' of youth, and all that flowed from it, had displaced the seriousness of mainstream culture. Although the result was an engagement with fashion, colour, decoration, symbolism, irrationality, spontaneity, and sensorial experiences – characteristics of the material world long associated with the value-system of the feminine sphere and women's pleasure – the pop project was not conceived or couched in terms of women's experience and their links with the aesthetic of commercial life. Instead, as it moved into mainstream culture, youth became the guardians of these anti-modern values, leaving women with even less to call their own. The only options available were either to operate on a level beyond taste – a modernist masculine strategy adopted by many of the protagonists of the women's movement through the 1970s – or to remain committed to feminine domesticity, and to accept cultural marginalisation. Thus it was age and not gender which provided the fundamental impulse for cultural change and the shift in sensibility that transformed modernism into postmodernism. While postmodernism's roots in the public, urban world of pop, rather than in the private, suburban sphere of feminine taste provided one barrier to its developing a rapport with women's culture, another lay in the continuing overtly masculine nature of the institutions that supported the new movement. Postmodernism's chief architectural and design practitioners were still professionalised men and the institutions that supported them – museums, manufacturing industry and the mass media – were all still essentially patriarchal in nature.

However, one of postmodernism's key ambitions was to eliminate the barrier that divided high from popular culture. While the movement's high cultural manifestations can be seen in many ways as sustaining the essentially masculine message of modernism in a renewed form, its impact on popular culture was more sympathetic to feminine taste and consequently to women's experience. Andreas Huyssen wrote 'I suspect that such merger attempts [between high and mass culture] occurred more or less simultaneously with the emergence of feminism and women as major forces in the arts, and with the concomitant re-evaluation of formerly devalued forms and genres of cultural expression (e.g., the decorative arts, autobiographic texts, letters etc).[11] The simultaneity of the emergence of postmodernism with women's changing political and cultural roles suggested to him the possibility of some kinds of active links between them, whether consciously perceived or not.

The idea also of cultural pluralism, of the importance of 'difference' between cultural groups and a commitment to a wide range of aesthetic possibilities rather than to a single monolithic style, invited designers in the late 1970s and 80s to reactivate the idea of gendered markets, not widespread since the late 1950s. By this time, many women had become part of the paid workforce, having as a consequence independent incomes. The idea of 'niche' markets meant that goods could be directed at a range of socially and culturally defined consumer groups, women belonging potentially to a number of them. In terms of goods, this more sophisticated form of gendering – albeit still based entirely on stereotypes – also took age, class and lifestyle into account. From cars to office furniture, from cameras to hi-fi systems, and in the USA, even to handguns – all were transformed into highly charged symbols aimed directly at specific cultural groups, several of them defined by gender. As ever, colour, shape and size were among the primary visual messengers of femininity and in the early 1980s postmodernism's use of historical quotation resulted in a spate of designs aimed at women which were highly reminiscent of the pastel-coloured goods directed at the 1950s housewife, exemplified by English designer James Dyson's innovatory pink vacuum cleaner. There was also an avalanche of Japanese high technology goods, from cameras to compact tape-players for the dressing table or the pocket, to woo women into participating in the technologically-based leisure revolution. The Japanese electronics giant Sharp produced a radio/tape cassette player, the curved edges of which recalled those of a 1950s refrigerator. It came in a range of shades, including pink and white, its openly nostalgic femininity associated with an epoque which had not yet witnessed the more complex picture of sexual identity of later decades.

The use of such strategies by designers can be viewed in a number of ways. These were clearly tactics aimed at increasing sales and can be seen, in that light, as a manipulative and exploitative means of offering women what they thought they wanted. Equally, this could be seen as men taking women's culture out of women's hands in order to feed it back to them in a pre-digested form, thereby denying them the opportunity for creativity. It was also a means of reinforcing stereotypes which bore little or no relation to the way in which women actually lived. Less negatively, however, this could also be seen as a celebration of femininity, giving it an equal footing with masculinity. In gendering objects, designers were acknowledging their cultural role and their dependence for meaning upon their users. In contrast to the modernist designer's belief that he (usually) knew what was good for the consumer, the postmodernist designer was creating a space for women which they could inhabit, enjoy and use as means of discovering their individual and collective identities. Equally, if they opted not to, there were other goods on offer which invited them to adopt a range of alternative cultural identities – a relative freedom of choice which had been denied women hitherto.

In addition to a liberal use of historical quotation and pastiche – strategies for undermining modernism's constant search for the new and its view of itself as sitting in an unquestioned forward-thrusting historical evolution – the aesthetic programme of postmodernism also embraced electicism, and encouraged a use of narrative and symbolism through its employment of surface pattern both traditional and novel in inspiration. These all served to bring it closer to the notion of taste as it had operated within the feminine sphere for well over a century. The architect's wife was a 'throwback' to a time when the dictates of modernism had had much more authority attached to them. While many of her late twentieth-century contemporaries, spared partners like hers for whom the inter- ior was such a significant marker of aesthetic control, could relish the pleasure of a neo-Victorian interior, complete with ruched curtains and gilt-framed mirrors, she was imprisoned within another taste-culture which was not permitted such an indulgence.

While postmodernism was clearly not a cultural route to women's complete emancipation and equality with men nonetheless it offered new challenges and possibilities in terms of their shifting relationship with material culture. Most importantly, it embraced difference and cultural diversity in a new way. Its essentially non-hierarchical view of culture allowed for the possibility of feminine taste finding a new level of acceptance, even if it was not necessarily women who were promoting and benefitting from its values. The real test of whether postmodernism implied a new set of possibilities for women's culture as a whole lay in the way in which it represented women's experience. Women's earlier exclusion from modernism had been largely a result of the fact that the model of modernity had been essentially masculine in nature, rooted in urban experiences and technological progress. Women's experience of modernity had been linked, in contrast, to shifts in the meaning of domesticity, to the rise of consumption, and to the emergence of a modern, feminised product and interior aesthetic. These had not, for the most

The glamour, luxury and nostalgic appeal of ruched curtains made a visible impact in countless interior decor schemes in the 1980s, both élite and popular, demonstrating one of the ways in which the aesthetic and ethical preoccupations of design modernism had finally been overturned. (Photograph by Martin Parr. Magnum Photos Limited)

part, been represented by the cultural forms of modernism. It was not until the 1950s that women's modernity found a form of full expression in the mass-produced material culture of that decade. However, the strength of the attacks upon it as a manifestation of capitalism in a state of decadence were such that it was denied any kind of cultural legitimation at that time.

Arguably, with the advent of postmodernism, women's encounter with modernity found an outlet which was for the first time judged to be culturally legitimate – over a century since the separation of the spheres had created a notion of feminine taste. Women's culture, as represented by the exercising of that taste, had finally come to be recognised as valid. Also, for the first time since the concept of design had been constructed as the masculine equivalent and controller of feminine taste, that taste appeared to be openly controlling design and, what's more, receiving approval for so doing from the high cultural institutions.

On another level the aesthetic liberation achieved within postmodernism can be seen to have brought little more than ruched curtains in reach of women. However, the curtains did not come complete with the social, political, cultural and moral meanings, and highly-valued image of domesticity, they had carried in the Victorian era. In this age of stylistic free-for-all, there was no more 'value' attached to Venetian blinds than to curtains. Both were available, both were disseminated through the media, and consumers could (providing their partners let them) make their own choices. Ideology and aesthetics had parted company to such an extent that feminine taste had lost its power to 'resist'. Just as theoretical postmodernism failed to equip women with an agenda of their own, so its material and aesthetic manifestations were equally unsuccessful in highlighting new values through which women could achieve some kind of victory.

On the face of it, the inclusion of postmodern designs in museums and collections marked an unprecedented victory for feminine taste. In the mid–1980s every major decorative arts museum introduced a brightly-coloured item of furniture produced by the Milan-based Memphis group, headed by Ettore Sottsass, and a piece of highly-styled Japanese electronic leisure equipment (usually a Sony Walkman) into its collection. Inevitably, however, the judgments made of them derived from the all-too-familiar modernist taste canon and there was little evidence of a radical regendering of the criteria used to assess such objects. This was, in the end, an example of the same form of tokenism that underpins the idea of putting a women on every interviewing board. The power of institutionalised modernism to absorb difference proved impressive and postmodernism was ultimately unable to resist its pull. As ever, the victory belonged to high culture, popular culture becoming simply one of the sources from which it drew its new energies. The very act of putting a mass-cultural object into a museum transformed it instantly into an item of high culture and, by implication, extended the modernist canon to include it. This process of masculinisation expanded apace through the 1980s such that by the end of the decade the postmodern design project had lost its power to validate feminine taste and had become little more than an afterword tagged on to the end of modernism. Modernism had quickly recovered its equilibrium, bringing familiar values to bear as a means of discriminating between 'good' and 'bad' postmodernism.

Also, ironically, at the very moment in which feminine taste seemed finally to be finding a level of cultural legitimation, the sexual division of labour which had underpinned the very construction of that taste began to show signs itself of undergoing a transformation. With more and more women, many of them middle class, joining the workforce, with the popularisation of ideas emanating from the women's movement, and technology transforming the workplace and the relationship between home and work, the traditional concept of the separation of the spheres was thrown into question. For a time in the 1970s and 80s it seemed as if traditional notions of femininity and masculinity, as they related to the separate spheres, were a thing of the past. With this opening up of the spheres came a questioning of stereotypical notions of femininity and masculinity and a widening of the possibilities for men and women in which to explore sexual and gender identities others than those determined by their biological destinies. In those same decades, a variety of sexual identities offered themselves up like commodities on the marketplace. Material culture played a role in forming, reinforcing, reflecting and embodying those identities in the way it always had. Now, however, with the apparent demise of the conventional separation of the spheres, there was a greater sense of freedom in being able to take those identities on board. Aided by the non-hierarchical languages of postmodernism, designers helped to provide ready-made cultural identities through the goods they transformed and which consumers appropriated and used.

Most of this, of course, operated on the level of mythology, constructed and disseminated by the media and sustained by the lifestyle ideals that accompanied the marketing of goods.[12] In reality, in spite of women's entry in large numbers into the paid workplace, the ideology of the separate spheres remained as strong as ever and most women's lives simply became ever harder, their identities more confused as they struggled to meet the joint responsibilities of domesticity and the workplace. The minimal provision of childcare, the continuing dominance of the ideology of family life as the basis of a stable society, and inherited expectations about gender roles, meant that the shift in the sexual division of labour was more imagined than real. In spite of a number of advances, both legislative and cultural, gender inequalities were also far from eroded. Stereotypical notions of femininity and masculinity, disseminated through the mass media and sustained by material culture, remained unchanged although variations on the themes abounded. People still defined themselves in relation to those stereotypes: there were simply more to choose from and more combinations to create. Divorced from substantial changes in the sexual division of labour, postmodernism's alignment with feminine taste was, in the end, little more than a gesture in recognition of an alternative viable aesthetic for everyday life.

If modernism had been the manifestation of a culture rooted in the ideals and ideologies of mass production, postmodernism represented one which was dominated by mass consumption, a shift which meant a reordering of the hierarchical relationship between them. While, in reality, little had changed since the late 1920s when General Motors had outwitted the Ford Automobile Company, the cultural validation of consumption had been a long time in coming. Now within postmodernism it was celebrated as a means of focusing on the values of personal pleasure, individual identity and cultural diversity rather than those of the standardised masses. While this may have signalled a reappraisal of feminine culture, this new stance was not without its influential critics.

Some writers moved beyond modernism to embrace the possibilities and liberations that could be seen on the horizon for
the first time; others pulled back from the brink, fearful of
plunging headlong into a bottomless value-free pit. Writers
such as the French cultural theorist Jean Baudrillard[13] and
philosopher Francois Lyotard[14] were at one and the same time
the most perceptive and articulate documenters of postmodernity, and its harshest critics. Recognizing an irreversible
change in the cultural status quo, they longed, nonetheless, for
the ordered value-system that had been lost. For others,
women among them, whose marginality meant that they had
nothing to lose, postmodernity and postmodernism offered a
ray of hope.

But it was a hope not to be realized as postmodernist material culture split into two. Its high cultural manifestations
entered the institutions of modernism and became yet another,
if somewhat decadent, manifestation of that great ideal, and its
popular cultural forms were swallowed up by the world of
commerce, judged in the end to be only superficial passing fads.
Once more the 'trivial' and the feminine were downgraded and
relegated to the sphere of the vulgar and the marginal. The
dream of a seamless link between high culture and popular
culture, between culture and commerce, and between the
masculine world of design and the feminine world of taste
proved to have been but a temporary illusion. As we approach
the year 2000 postmodernism and a concern for the 'aesthetic'
dimension seems to have been little more than a temporary
interlude; the world of material culture occupies itself in an
essentially neo-rationalist manner with questions about
resources and sustainability, perceived as being of much greater
'significance' than that of taste. Issues of survival have replaced
those of pleasure and identity and in their train comes an
inevitable re-masculinisation of the world of material culture.

In the contemporary industrialised world, women, feminine
taste, desire, pleasure, and material culture make up a stereotypical gendered package. Short of a complete social, economic
and cultural revolution necessary to transform the framework
that constructed that package, the stereotypes we have inherited will remain in place, with only small mutations occurring

to them over the years. Within this framework, however, if women cannot achieve the 'joy' that the feminist writer Rosalind Coward[15] has claimed would come with radical change and the elimination of the 'constructed desires' to which she feels women are held hostage, they can at least experience the pleasure to be had from being at one with their constructed tastes and the material culture that sustains and reinforces them. This does not necessarily mean living a life dominated by 'false consciousness' but represents a form, however minor, of feminine resistance to dominant masculine culture.

In the late twentieth century, one of women's inner frustrations derives from the fact that they are constantly being pulled in two directions at the same time. On one level, they are linked to a stereotypical image of femininity formed by the continuing ideology of the separate spheres; on another they are encouraged to reject that image and to aspire to a stereotypically masculine model as a route to cultural legitimacy. Every time a woman chooses to represent her taste in a material manner she has to decide which one of these pulls she will respond to. While the latter may seem the obvious route to emancipation, it denies the collective identity that women's culture has formed through its relationship with the material and aesthetic world through the exercise of taste. It denies, also, women's self-knowledge, their cultural achievements and their successful encounter with modernity that has transformed their lives in this century. While this may not have brought them equality with men in the public sphere, it has enhanced their understanding of themselves, and of their own culture, significantly.

To deny all that, and not to realize that to a significant extent the material world still transmits different messages to men and to women is to be insensitive to the desperation of the architect's wife, to collude with masculine culture's trivialisation of feminine culture, and to undermine the contribution that this culture has to offer, not only to women, but to culture as a whole in the late-twentieth century. To acknowledge the pull of masculine culture, however, is to demonstrate a commitment to succumb to its moralising pressure to aspire to 'good taste' which is simply an entrance ticket to patriarchy. Until the separate spheres are consigned to the past, and domesticity becomes a valued ideal for both men and for women, the exercising of taste will continue to play a vital role within the sexual politics of everyday life.

Notes

Introduction: The Architect's Wife

1. Simone de Beauvoir. *The Second Sex*, London, Penguin Books, 1972, p. 635.
2. The idea of the 'Separation of the Spheres' has underpinned much feminist historical writing over the last two decades, as in the work, for example, of Leonore Davidoff and Catherine Hall. Recently women's historians have tended to see it as an over-simplification. Where material culture studies are concerned, however, its full implications have yet to be assessed.
3. Alison Light. *Forever England: Femininity, Literature and Conservatism between the Wars*, London and New York, Routledge 1991, p. 10.
4. Betty Friedan, *The Feminine Mystique*, London, Penguin Books 1992 (1963). Friedan titles her first chapter 'The Problem that has No Name'.
5. Sheila Rowbotham. *Woman's Consciousness, Man's World*, Harmondsworth, Penguin Books, 1976 (first published 1973), p. 67.
6. Ann Oakley. *Housewife*, Harmondsworth, Penguin Books, 1985 (1974) p. 5.
7. Recent work focusing on the nature of femininity and masculinity, including studies by Rosalind Coward, Lorraine Gamman, Frank Mort and Sean Nixon, has stressed the influence of culture on the construction of gender.
8. Judith Williamson adopted this neo-Marxist position in her book *Consuming Passions: The Dynamics of Popular Culture*, London, Marion Boyars, 1986. The writers Rosalind Williams and Rachel Bowlby (see Bibliography), in their accounts of nineteenth-century department stores, also saw women playing a passive, 'enslaved' role in this context.
9. The anthropologists, Mary Douglas (in her book written with Baron Isherwood, *The World of Goods: Towards an Anthropology of Consumption*, Harmondsworth, Penguin Books, 1978) and Daniel Miller (in his book *Material Consumption and Mass Consumption*, Oxford, Basil Blackwell 1987) have both described consumption in this positive way.
10. Many social psychologists writing about consumption, among them Peter Lunt and Sonia Livingstone in their book, *Mass Consumption and Personal Identity: Everyday Economic Experience*, Buckingham, Open University Press, 1992, have tended to underplay the role played by gender. Their book, for example, devotes only one section in one chapter

(there are seven in all) to the subject of 'Shopping as a gendered activity'.

11. The most enlightening texts in this context are Rachel Bowlby's *Just Looking: Consumer Culture in Dreiser, Gissing and Zola* (New York: Methuen 1985); W.R. Leach's 'Transformations in a Culture of Consumption': Women and Department Stores 1980–1912' (published in *Journal of American History*, 71, Sept. 1984, pp. 319–342); and Rosalind Williams' *Dream Worlds: Mass Consumption in Late Nineteenth-Century France*, Berkeley, University of California Press, 1982.

12. The discipline of semiotics, and more recently, that of product semantics, have as their goal to read objects as if they constituted a language. Their usefulness to this project is limited by their lack of involvement in the historical, socio-economic and cultural contexts of objects.

13. Dick Hebdige. 'Object as Image: the Italian Scooter Cycle' in Dick Hebdige, *Hiding in the Light*, London and New York, Comedia, Routledge, 1988.

14. This theme is also dealt with by George Basalla in his article 'Transformed Utilitarian Objects,' published in *Wintherthur Portfolio*, 1982, pp. 184–201.

15. The idea that objects can be 'read' in a gendered way parallels similar ideas in other cultural arenas, among them literature (Elaine Showalter); film (Laura Mulvey); and advertising (Diane Barthel). (See Bibliography for titles.)

Chapter 1 'An Institution of God Himself': The Domestic Ideal

1. Thorstein Veblen. *The Theory of the Leisure Class*, London, Unwin Books, 1970, p. 26.
2. Rozsika Parker, *The Subversive Stitch: Embroidery and the Making of the Feminine*, London, The Women's Press, 1984, p. 18.
3. Leonore Davidoff and Catherine Hall. *Family Fortunes: Men and Women of the English Middle Class, 1780–1850*, London, Routledge, 1987, p. 3.
4. Debora Silverman, *Art Nouveau in Fin-de-Siècle France: Politics, Psychology and Style*, Los Angeles, University of California Press, 1989, p. 190.
5. Davidoff and Hall, op, cit., p. 191.
6. Ibid.
7. Ibid., p. 73.
8. Ibid., p. 19.
9. Glenna Matthews. *'Just a Housewife': The Rise and Fall of Domesticity in America*, New York and Oxford, The Open University Press, 1987, p. 34.
10. ibid., pp. 18–19.
11. ibid., p. 89.
12. Neil Mckendrick. 'The Consumer Revolution' in Neil McKendrick, John Brewer, and J.H. Plumb (eds), *The Birth of Consumer Society:*

The Commercialisation of Eighteenth-Century England, London, Hutchinson, 1982, p. 24.

13. Catherine Hall. 'Strains in the "firm of Wife, Children and friends?":
Middle-class women and employment in early 19th century England' in P. Hudson and W.R. Lee, *Woman's Work and the Family Economy in Historical Perspective*, Manchester, Manchester University Press, 1990, p. 109.

14. ibid.

15. Louise Tilly and Joan Scott. *Women, Work and Family*, London and New York, Routledge. 1978, p. 136.

16. Janet Wolff. 'The Culture of Separate Spheres: The Role of Culture in Nineteenth-century Public and Private Lives' in Janet Wolff, *Feminine Sentences: Essays on Women and Culture*, Cambridge, Polity Press, 1990, p. 14.

17. Wolff's account is based on research by Maurice Spiers, *Victoria Park Manchester: a nineteenth-century suburb in its social and administrative context*, Manchester, Manchester University Press, 1976.

18. Davidoff and Hall, op. cit., pp. 13–18.

19. ibid., p. 17.

20. ibid., p. 18.

21. For more detail about working patterns in the pre-industrial household see Tilly and Scott, op. cit.

22. Ruth Schwartz Cowan, *More Work for Mother: The Ironies of Household Technology from the Open Hearth to the Microwave*, New York, Basic Books, 1983, p. 26.

23. Alice Clark, quoted in Anne Oakley. *Housewife*, Harmondsworth, Penguin Books, 1985, p. 15.

24. Amanda Vickery. 'Golden Age to Seperate Spheres? A review of the Categories and Chronology of English Women's History in *The Historical Journal*, 36.2., 1993, p. 383.

25. Veblen, op. cit., p. 28.

26. Friedrich Engels quoted in Oakley, op. cit. p. 47.

27. Marc Girouard quoted in Wolff, op. cit., p. 15.

28. See Patricia Branca's essay, '*Image and Reality: The myth of the idle Victorian woman*' in M. Hartman and L.W. Banner (eds), *Clio's Consciousness Raised*, New York, Harper, 1974, in which she has shown that Victorian women were kept very busy managing the household.

29. Davidoff and Hall, op. cit., p. 375.

30. ibid., p. 381.

31. ibid., p. 387.

32. This is the result of a strong Marxist bias within many social and economic historians' accounts of this period.

33. Abby Diaz quoted in Matthews, op. cit., p. 99.

Chapter 2 'The Things which Surround Us': The Domestic Aesthetic

1. Elsie de Wolfe, quoted in J. Banham, S. Macdonald, and J. Porter, *Victorian Interior Design*, London, Cassell, 1991. p. 12.

2. Harriet and Vetta Goldstein. *Art in Everyday Life*, New York, Macmillan, 1932, pp. 2–5.

3. Leonore Davidoff and Catherine Hall. *Family Fortunes: Men and Women of the English Middle Class, 1780–1850*, London, Routledge, 1987, p. 17.
4. Gwendolyn Wright. *Building The Dream: A Social History of Housing in America* New York, Pantheon, 1981, p. 93.
5. ibid., p. 106.
6. Henry Mayhew quoted in Banham, Macdonald and Porter, op. cit., p. 10.
7. John Gloag. *Victorian Comfort: A Social History of Design from 1830–1900*, London, Adam and Charles, 1961, p. 27.
8. Quoted in Bronner, S. J. (ed), *Consuming Visions: Accumulation and Display of Goods in America 1880–1920*, New York and London, W.W. Norton and Co., 1989, p. 161.
9. Wright, op. cit., p. 107.
10. Gloag, op. cit., p. 36.
11. ibid., p. 35.
12. Rozsika Parker. *The Subversive Stitch: Embroidery and the Making of the Feminine*, London, The Women's Press, 1984, p. 34.
13. ibid., p. 95.
14. ibid., p. 119.
15. ibid.
16. Katherine C. Grier, *Culture and Comfort: People, Parlors and Upholstery, 1850–1930*, New York, The Strong Museum, 1988, p. 9.
17. Quoted in Russell Lynes, *The Tastemakers: the Shaping of American Popular Taste*, New York, Dover, 1980, p. 10.
18. Gloag, op. cit., p. 41.
19. Mrs Orrinsmith's words from her book, *The Drawing Room*, of 1878 are quoted in Banham, Macdonald, and Porter, op. cit., p. 41.
20. While John Gloag attributes the invention of coil springs to the Londoner, Samuel Pratt, in 1828, Katherine Grier concentrates on their appearance in America where, in the subsequent decade they were used first in chairs for invalids.
21. Quoted in Gloag, op. cit., p. 70.
22. Grier, op. cit., p. 121.
23. ibid., p. 89.
24. Quoted in ibid., p. 237.
25. Grier, op. cit., expands this idea, p. 89.
26. Wright, op. cit., pp. 109–110.
27. Gloag, op. cit., p. 93.
28. Charlotte Bronte. *Jane Eyre*, London, Pan Books, 1967, p. 411.
29. The idea of 'the fashion system' is best outlined by Roland Barthes. *Systeme de la Mode*, Paris, Editions du Seuil, 1967.
30. These ideas are all eloquently articulated in Elizabeth Wilson. *Adorned in Dreams: Fashion and Modernity*, London, Virago, 1985.
31. See Thorstein Veblen. *The Theory of the Leisure Class*, London, Unwin Books, 1970, (1899).
32. For an extended discussion of this, see Wilson, op. cit.
33. Gloag, op. cit., p. 41.
34. See Grier, op. cit., for a discussion of this idea.
35. H.B. Stowe. *Pink and White Tyranny*, Boston, Roberts Brothers, 1871.
36. Grier. op. cit., p. 9.

37. Wright, op. cit., p. 109.
38. For an expansion of this idea see Grier, op. cit.
39. These ideas are also elaborated in Grier, op. cit.
40. Adrian Forty. *Objects of Desire: Design and Society 1750–1980*, London, Thames and Hudson, 1986, p. 99.

Chapter 3 'Those Extravagant Draperies': Domesticity Contested

1. Charles Eastlake. *Hints on Household Taste in Furniture, Upholstery and other Details*, London, Longmans, Green and Co., 1872 (1868) p. 7.
2. ibid., p. 8,
3. Quoted in Banham, J., Macdonald, S., and Porter, J. *Victorian Interior Design*, London, Cassell, 1991, p. 63.
4. For further details about the Schools of Design see Quentin Bell. *The Schools of Design*, London, Routledge and Kegan Paul, 1963, and Stuart MacDonald. *The History and Philosophy of Art Education*, London, University of London Press, 1970.
5. Banham, Macdonald and Porter, op. cit., p. 64
6. ibid., p.
7. This was the origins of what became the Victoria and Albert Museum.
8. McKendrick, N., Brewer, J., and Plumb, J.H. *The Birth of a Consumer Society: The Commercialization of Eighteenth-Century England*, London, Hutchinson, 1983, p. 28.
9. Kant is quoted in Hilde Hein and Carolyn Korsmeyer (eds). *Aesthetics in Feminist Perspective*, Bloomington and Indianapolis, Indiana University Press, 1993, p. 181.
10. Rozsika Parker. *The Subversive Stitch: Embroidery and the Making of the Feminine*, London, The Women's Press, 1984, p. 21.
11. Pugin's ideas are expressed in his *True Principles of Pointed or Christian Architecture*, Oxford, St. Barnabas Press, 1969 (1841).
12. Eastlake, op. cit., pp. 136–7.
13. ibid., p. 136.
14. Richard Redgrave. *Manual of Design*, London, Chapman and Hall, 1876, p. 87.
15. The idea of the 'male reader' in the context of literature is discussed in Hein and Korsmeyer, op. cit., pp. 108–10.
16. Russell Lynes. *The Tastemakers: The Shaping of American Popular Taste*, New York, Dover, 1980, p. 26.
17. Glenna Matthews *"Just a Housewife": The Rise and fall of Domesticity in America*, New York, Oxford, Oxford University Press, 1987. p. 38.
18. John Ruskin. 'Of Queens' Gardens' in *Sesame and Lilies – Unto the Last* published in *The Seven Lamps of Architecture*, New York, Lovell, Coryell and Co., 1949, p. 86.
19. ibid., p. 87.
20. Eastlake, op. cit., p. 242.
21. John Ruskin, *The Stones of Venice*, New York, Lovell, Coryell and Co., 1851, p. 394.
22. Eastlake, op. cit., p. 12.
23. ibid., p. 11.
24. ibid., p. 84.

25. Ruskin op cit., p. 89.
26. Eastlake op cit., p. 148.
27. John Ruskin. 'The Lamp of Sacrifice' in *The Seven Lamps of Architecture*, London, George Allen and Unwin Ltd., 1925, p. 31.
28. Pugin, op. cit., p. 28.
29. ibid.
30. Eastlake, op. cit., p. 165.
31. ibid., p. 215.
32. Pugin, op. cit., p. 27.
33. ibid., p. 23.
34. Eastlake, op. cit., p. 116.
35. Redgrave, op. cit., p. 59.
36. The key texts on this subject are Owen Jones. *The Grammar of Ornament*, London, Day and Son, 1856 and Christopher Dresser. *Principles of Decorative Design*, London, Cassell, Petter and Galpin, 1873.
37. Eastlake, op. cit., p. 57.
38. ibid., p. 10.
39. Christopher Dresser is quoted in Stuart Durant's monograph on Dresser, London, Academy Editions, 1992, p. 34.
40. Morris is quoted in Asa Briggs. *Victorian Things* London, Penguin, 1988, p. 222.
41. ibid., p. 230.
42. See Anthea Callen. *Angel in the Studio: Women in the Arts and Crafts Movement*, London, Astragal Books, 1979.
43. Pugin, op. cit., p. 1.

Chapter 4: 'Everything in its Place': Women and Modernity

1. Hermann Bahn is quoted in D. Frisby. *Fragments of Modernity: Theories of Modernity in the work of Simmel, Kracauer and Benjamin*, Cambridge, Polity Press, 1985, p. 11.
2. Janet Wolff elaborates the Weberian idea of rationalisation in *Feminine Sentences: Essays on Women and Culture*, Cambridge, Polity Press, p. 34.
3. ibid., p. 35.
4. Frisby, op. cit., p. 14.
5. ibid., p. 18.
6. ibid.
7. Marshal Berman has developed the idea of Faustian discontent in *All That is Solid Melts into Air: The Experience of Modernity*, London, Verso, 1993, p. 79.
8. Richard Sennett. *The Fall of Public Man*, New York, Knopf, 1976.
9. Women's exclusion from modernism has been discussed by the art historian Griselda Pollock in 'Modernity and the Spaces of Femininity' published in *Vision and Difference: Femininity, Feminism and Histories of Art*, London/New York, Routledge, 1988 and by the sociologist of art, Janet Wolff in 'Feminism and Modernism', op. cit.
10. Berman, op. cit., p. 90.

11. See Kathleen D. McCarthy. *Women's Culture: American Philanthropy and Art 1830–1930*, Chicago and London, The University of Chicago Press, 1991.

12. Elizabeth Wilson. *Adorned in Dreams: Fashion and Modernity*, London, Virago, 1985, p. 5.

13. See Gwendolyn Wright. *Building the Dream: A Social History of Housing in America*, New York, Pantheon, 1981.

14. E. Lupton and J. Abbot Miller. *The Bathroom, the Kitchen and the Aesthetics of Waste: A Process of Elimination*, Cambridge, Mass., MIT List Visual Arts Center, 1992, p. 8.

15. Quoted in Dolores Hayden. *The Grand Domestic Revolution: A History of Feminist Designs for American Homes,Neighborhoods and Cities*, Cambridge, Mass, MIT Press, 1981. p. 58.

16. Mrs. Beeton's advice to housewives had first been published in *The Englishwoman's Domestic Magazine* between 1858 and 1860.

17. The Reverend J.P. Faunthorpe. *Household Science: Readings in Necessary Knowledge for Girls and Young Women*, London, Edward Stanford, 1895 (1879) p. v.

18. ibid., p. 285.

19. ibid., p. 295.

20. ibid., p. 263.

21. ibid., p. 259.

22. ibid., p. 263.

23. ibid., p. 3.

24. See Glenna Matthews. *Just a Housewife: The Rise and Fall of Domesticity in America*, New York and Oxford, Oxford University Press, 1987, p. 147.

25. The Rumford Kitchen which was on display at the latter Exposition was a particularly popular exhibit, being the first 'all-electric' one of its kind.

26. Adrian Forty. *Objects of Desire: Design and Society, 1750–1980*, London, Thames and Hudson, 1986, p. 116.

27. R. Binnie and J.E. Boxall. *Housecraft: Principles and Practice*, London, Sir Isaac Pitman and Sons Ltd., 1926, p. 131.

28. Mary Douglas is quoted in Forty, op. cit., p. 157.

29. Hayden, op. cit., p. 3.

30. Matthews, op. cit., p. 141.

31. J.M. Gries and J. Ford (eds). *Homemaking, Home Furnishing and Information Services*, Washington, DC, National Capital Press Inc., 1932. p. 31.

32. Christine Frederick's first writings appeared as a series of articles entitled 'The New Housekeeping' in *Ladies' Home Journal*, of which she was the home editor, from September 1912. In the following year they were collected together into a publication entitled *The New Housekeeping: Efficiency Studies in Home Management*, New York, Doubleday.

33. Christine Frederick. *Household Engineering and Scientific Management in the Home*, Chicago, American School of Home Economics, 1919, p. 20.

34. ibid., p. 29.

35. For evidence of this see Jane Lewis. *Labour and Love: Women's Experience of Home and Family 1880–1940*, Oxford, Basil Blackwell, 1986, p. 29.

36. Many popular advice books for house-owners, such as H. Bryant Newbold's *The Ideal House* of 1928, London, Practical Building Publishing Co. preached the gospel of scientific management. On page 3 of that text, for instance, the author writes, 'Where every unnecessary step means fatigue, and every additional space an increased necessity for cleaning work, passages and hallways are to be avoided.'

37. Ruth Schartz Cowan. *More Work for Mother: the Ironies of Household Technology from the Open Hearth to the Microwave*, New York, Basic Books, 1983, p. 85.

38. ibid., p. 78.

39. Faunthorpe, op. cit., p. 257.

40. Frederick, op. cit., p. 27.

41. Quoted in Asa Briggs. *Victorian Things*, London, Penguin, 1988, p. 218.

42. Rudi Laermans. 'Learning to Consume: Early Department Stores and the Shaping of the Modern Consumer Culture 1860–1914, *Theory Culture and Society*, Vol. 10., no. 4, Nov. 1993. p. 82.

43. D. Chaney. 'The Department Store as a Cultural Form', *Theory Culture and Society*, Vol. 1, no. 3, 1983, p. 24.

44. Thorstein Veblen. *The Theory of the Leisure Class*, London, Unwin Books, 1970, p.47.

45. The writings of Stuart Ewen (see Bibliography) have concentrated on these themes for the most part.

46. Writers about the American experience of participating in consumer culture, among them Ewen, T.J. Jackson Lears, and Neil Harris have tended to focus on the essential 'Americanness' of this phenomenon rather than its gender implications.

47. Rachel Bowlby. *Shopping with Freud*, London, Routledge, 1993, p. 48.

48. M.B. Miller. *The Bon Marché: Bourgeois Culture and the Department Store, 1869–1920*, New Jersey, Princeton University Press, 1981, pp. 168–9.

49. Laermans, op. cit., p. 91.

50. ibid., p. 82.

51. There was a general consensus, from Zola to Veblen, that women were 'seduced' in the act of consumption and that their role was, in essence, a passive one.

52. Laermans, op. cit., pp. 88–9.

53. See K. Haltunen. 'From Parlor to Living-room; Domestic Space, Interior Decoration, and the Culture of Personality' in S.J. Bronner (ed). *Consuming Visions: Accumulation and Display in America 1880–1920*, New York/ London, W.W. Norton and Co., 1989.

Chapter 5 'Letting in the Air': Women and Modernism

1. Cynthia White. *Women's Magazines 1693–1968*, London, Michael Joseph, 1970, p. 94.

2. Ulrich Conrads (ed.). *Programmes and Manifestoes on Twentieth-Century Architecture*, London, Lund, Humphries, 1970, p. 13.

3. ibid., p. 123.
4. Tim and Charlotte Benton and Dennis Sharp. *Form and Function: A Source Book for a History of Architecture and Design 1980–1939*, London, Crosby, Lockwood and Staples, 1975, p. 6.
5. Conrads, op. cit., p. 110.
6. Le Corbusier. *Towards a New Architecture*, London. The Architectural Press, 1974, p. 106.
7. Walter Gropius. *The New Architecture and the Bauhaus*, London, Faber and Faber, 1968, p. 100.
8. Benton and Sharp, op.,cit., p. 108.
9. ibid.
10. Rioux de Maillou in ibid., p. 5.,
11. Adolf Loos. *Spoken into the Void: Collected Essays 1897– 1900*, Cambridge, Massachussetts, MIT Press, 1982, p. 20.
12. Le Corbusier. *The Decorative Art of Today*, Cambridge, Massachusetts, MIT Press, 1987, p. 27.
13. ibid., p. 52.
14. Loos, op. cit., p. 7.
15. Conrads, op. cit., p. 17.
16. ibid.
17. Benton and Sharp, op. cit., p. 180.
18. Gropius, op. cit., p. 92.
19. Benton and Sharp, op. cit., p. 39.
20. Gropius, op. cit., p. 54.
21. Benton and Sharp, op. cit., p. 2.
22. Loos, op. cit., p. 102.
23. Benton and Sharp, op. cit., p. 42.
24. Le Corbusier, *The Decorative Art of Today*, p. 85.
25. Conrads, op. cit., p. 56.
26. ibid., p. 25.
27. Gropius, op. cit., p. 23.
28. Conrads, op. cit., p. 125.
29. Gropius, op. cit., p. 25. Gropius writes, 'One of the most outstanding achievements of the new constructional technique has been the abolition of the separating function of the wall.'
30. Benton and Sharp, op. cit., p. 237.
31. ibid., p. 236.
32. ibid.
33. ibid., p. 238.
34. Le Corbusier, *The Decorative Art of Today* p.7.
35. ibid., p. 48.
36. ibid., p. 55.
37. ibid., p. 90.
38. ibid., p. 36.
39. Benton and Sharp, op. cit., p. 32.
40. Conrads, op. cit., p. 16.
41. ibid., p. 39.
42. ibid., p. 67.
43. Le Corbusier, *The Decorative Art of Today* p. 17.
44. Conrads, op. cit., p. 103.
45. Loos, op. cit., p. 29.

46. Conrads, op. cit., p. 95.
47. ibid., p. 89.
48. ibid., p. 90.
49. Elizabeth Wilson. *The Sphinx in the City: Urban Life, the Control of Disorder and Women*, London, Virago, 1991.
50. ibid., p. 11.
51. Conrads, op. cit., p. 27
52. Le Corbusier, *Towards a New Architecture*, p. 114.
53. Le Corbusier, *The Decorative Art of Today*, p. 188.

Chapter 6 'The Selling Value of Art': Women and the Moderne

1. Andreas Huyssen. *After the Great Divide: Modernism, Mass Culture and Postmodernism*, London, Macmillan, 1986, p. vii.
2. ibid., p. 46.
3. Debora L. Silverman. *Art Nouveau in Fin-de-Siecle France: Politics, Psychology and Style*, Los Angeles, University of California Press, 1989, pp. 71.
4. ibid., p. 19.
5. ibid., p. 63.
6. ibid., p. 191.
7. Quoted in Rudi Laermans. 'Learning to Consume: Early Department Stores and the Shaping of the Modern Consumer Culture (1860–1914), in *Theory, Culture and Society*, Vol. 10, no. 4., Nov. 1993, p. 81.
8. W.R. Leach. 'Transformations in a Culture of Consumption: Women and Department Stores 1890–1912' in *Journal of American History*, 71, Sept. 1984, p. 324.
9. ibid.,
10. ibid., p. 323.
11. This material was presented in a lecture by Nancy Troy delivered at the Victoria and Albert Museum in London, Spring 1994.
12. Quoted in Tim and Charlotte Benton and Aaron Scharf. *Design 1920s*, Milton Keynes, The Open University Press, 1975, pp. 62–3.
13. Neil Harris. 'The Drama of Consumer Desire' in *Cultural Excursions: Marketing Appetites and Cultural Tastes in Modern America*, Chicago, University of Chicago Press, 1990, p. 184.
14. For details on Teague's *oeuvre* see 'Walter Dorwin Teague: Master of Design' in *Pencil Points*, Sept. 1937, pp. 541–570.
15. See article on Donald Deskey in *Fortune*, Feb. 25, 1933, pp. 22–26.
16. F. Kiesler. *Contemporary Art as applied to the Store and its Display*, London, Sir Isaac Pitman and Sons Ltd., 1930, p. 9.
17. ibid., p. 66
18. ibid., p. 73.
19. Roland Marchand. *Advertising the American Dream: Making way for Modernity 1920–1940*, Berkeley, University of California Press, 1985, p. 66.
20. For more information of the growth of branded goods in the USA see Susan Strasser. *Satisfaction Guaranteed: The Making of the American Mass Market*, New York, Pantheon, 1989.
21. Marchand, op. cit., p. 11.

22. ibid., p. 66.
23. Elmo Calkins. 'Beauty the New Business Tool' in *The Atlantic Monthly* 140, Aug. 1927, pp. 145–6.
24. Quoted in David Gartman. *Auto Opium: A Social History of American Automobile Design*, London and New York, Routledge, 1994, p. 45–46.
25. ibid., p. 46.
26. F.H. Young. *Modern Advertising Art*, New York, Covici, Friede Inc., 1930, p. 117.
27. Gartman, op. cit., p. 48.
28. ibid., p. 82.
29. This is the thesis elucidated by David Gartman, op. cit.
30. ibid., p. 97.
31. The idea is expressed by Terry Smith. *Making the Modern: Industry, Art and Design in the US*, Chicago, University of Chicago Press, 1993.
32. ibid., p. 368.
33. Mary McCarthy. *The Group*, London, Penguin, 1968, pp. 89–90.

Chapter 7 'We are All Creators': Women and Conservative Modernism

1. Margaret Bulley. *Have You Got Good Taste?: A Guide to an Appreciation of the Lesser Arts*, London, Methuen, 1933, p. 16.
2. See D. Beddoe. *Back to Home and Duty: Women between the Wars 1918–1939*, London, Pandora, 1939.
3. ibid., p. 9.
4. Alison Light. *Forever England: Femininity, Literature and Conservatism between the Wars*, London and New York, Routledge, 1991.
5. Isabelle Anscombe. *A Woman's Touch: Women in Design from 1860 to the Present Day*, London, Virago, 1984, p. 133.
6. ibid., p. 135.
7. ibid., p. 134.
8. See Cheryl Buckley. 'Women and Modernism: A Case-Study of Grete Marks (1899–1990)' in Jill Seddon and Suzette Worden. *Women Designing: Redefining Design in Britain between the Wars*, Brighton, University of Brighton, 1994, pp. 104–110.
9. C.R. Richards. *Art in Industry*, New York, Macmillan, 1922, p. 29.
10. Henry Dreyfuss. *Designing for People*, New York, Viking Press, 1955, p. 59.
11. Seddon and Worden, op. cit., p. 135.
12. Charles F. Warner. *Home Decoration*, London, T. Werner Laurie Ltd, 1918, p. 87.
13. This idea was expressed by Lynne Walker in a lecture which formed part of a day seminar organised to accompany the exhibition *Women Designing: Redefining Design in Britain between the Wars*, University of Brighton, 7–31 March 1994.
14. Anscombe, op. cit., p. 105.
15. ibid.
16. Quoted in Julia Bigham. 'Advertising as a Career' in Seddon and Worden, op. cit., p. 22.

17. Edith Wharton and Ogden Codman Jr., *The Decoration of Houses*, London, B.J. Batsford, 1898, p. 21.
18. ibid., p. 27.
19. ibid., p. 24.
20. ibid., p. 185.
21. N. Campbell and C. Seebohm. *Elsie de Wolfe: A Decorative Life*, Aurum Press, London, 1992, p. 2.
22. ibid., p. 3.
23. ibid., p. 17.
24. This is well documented in Anscombe, op. cit.
25. Judy Attfield and Pat Kirkham (eds). *View from the Interior: Feminism, Women and Design*, London, The Women's Press, 1989, p. 156.
26. ibid., p. 156.
27. For more information see Anthea Callen. *Angel in the Studio: Women in the Arts and Crafts Movement 1870–1914*, London, Astragal Books, 1979.
28. Attfield and Kirkham, op. cit., p. 174.
29. ibid., p. 177.
30. ibid., p. 178.
31. The Design and Industries Association was formed in Britain in 1915, on the model of Germany's *Werkbund*, which had been founded eight years earlier. Made up of manufacturers, retailers, designers and other promoters of 'good design', defined for the most part according to principles established by the Arts and Crafts movement, its role was to improve the level of design practice in Britain.
32. See Dryad Leaflet no. 123, 'Doll-making with the Professional Touch', Dryad Handicrafts, Leicester.
33. See Dryad Leaflet no. 124, 'More Felt Flowers', Dryad Handicrafts, Leicester.
34. See Dryad Leaflet no. 92, 'Netting', Dryad Handicrafts, Leicester.
35. The use of this term in the inter-war years served to inject a more positive and productive element into home-based labour than was suggested by the term 'housework' which implied drudgery rather than fulfilment through work.
36. Attfield and Kirkham, op. cit., p. 143.
37. ibid., p. 144.
38. ibid., p. 145.
39. See F.A. Dudden. *Serving Women: Household Service in Nineteenth-Century America*, Middletown, Conn., Wesleyan University Press, 1983.
40. G.L. Hunter. *Home Furnishing*, New York, John Lane co., 1913, p. 82.
41. ibid., p. 81.
42. Warner, op. cit., p. 81.
43. ibid., p. 82.
44. H. Bryant Newbold. *The Ideal House*, London, Practical Building Publishing Co., 1928, p. 3.
45. J.M. Gries and J. Ford (eds). *Homemaking, Home Furnishing and Information Services*, Washington DC, Capital Press Inc., 1932, p. 39.
46. Warner, op. cit., p. 155.
47. Sidney Vant. *Simple Furniture-Making*, London and New York, Frederick Warne and Co. Ltd., 1929, p. 1.

48. Illustrated in *The Home of Today: Its Choice, Planning, Equipment and Organisation*, London, *Daily Express* Publications, 1935.
49. W. Fales. *What's New in Home Decorating?*, New York, Dodd, Mead and Co., 1936, p. 151.
50. ibid., plate xvi.
51. ibid., plate xi.
52. Mrs Beeton. *Hints to Housewives*, London and Melbourne, Ward, Lock and Co. Ltd., 1928, p. 271.
53. *The Housewife's Book*, London, *Daily Express* Publications, 1935, p. 161.
52. Fales,, op.cit., p. 43
55. Walter J. Pearce. *Painting and Decorating*, London, Chas Griffin and Co., 1932, p. 8.
56. ibid.,
57. *The Housewife's Book*, op. cit., p. 72.
58. The cultural critics associated with the 'Frankfurt School', among them Theodor Adorno and Max Horkheimer, were beginning, in the inter-war years to voice their unease about the cultural effects of mass production.

Chapter 8. 'The Happy Housewife': Domesticity Renewed

1. Talcott Parsons. *Essays in Sociological Thought* (revised edition), New York, Free Press, 1964, p. 194.
2. See Betty Friedan. *The Feminine Mystique*, Harmondsworth, Penguin, 1992 (1963).
3. Elizabeth Wilson. *Only Halfway to Paradise: Women in Postwar Britain 1945–1968*, London and New York, Tavistock Publications, 1980, p. 2.
4. The 'experts' in question included Talcott Parsons, Donald Winnicott, Dr Spock and Sigmund Freud.
5. Ruth Schartz Cowan. *More Work for Mother: The Ironies of Household Technology from the Open Hearth to the Microwave*, New York, Basic Books, 1983, p. 201.
6. See Joann Vanek. 'Keeping Busy: Time spent in Housework in the US 1920–1970' (unpublished PhD thesis University of Michigan 1973), and 'Time Spent in Housework' in *Scientific American*, Nov. 1974, pp. 116–120.
7. Norman Macre Quoted in Wilson op. cit., p. 13.
8. ibid., p. 8.
9. Barbara Ehrenreich and Deirdre English. *For Her Own Good: 150 Years of the Experts' Advice to Women*, New York, Garden City, Doubleday, 1978.
10. See Lee Wright. 'Objectifying Gender: The Stiletto Heel' in J. Attfield and P. Kirkham (eds). *A View from the Interior: Feminism, Women and Design*, London. The Women's Press, 1989.
11. ibid., p. 15.
12. See Cynthia White. *Women's Magazines 1693–1968*, London, Michael Joseph, 1970.
13. They are recounted in detail in Ehrenreich and English op. cit.

14. ibid., p. 257.
15. Thomas Hine. *Populuxe*, New York, Alfred A. Knopf, 1986, p. 15.
16. Gwendolyn Wright. *Building the Dream: A Social History of Housing in America*, New York, Pantheon, 1981, p. 251.
17. ibid., p. 252.
18. Russell Lynes. *The Tastemakers: The Shaping of American Popular Taste*, New York, Dover, 1980, p. 251.
19. Wright, op. cit., p. 253.
20. Lynes, op. cit., p. 253.
21. The British 'new towns', among them Harlow, Crawley and Cumbernauld, were built on out-of-town, green field sites and were intended to house the overspill from overcrowded urban areas.
22. This idea is elaborated in Judy Attfield. 'Inside Pram Town: a Case-study of Harlow House interiors 1951–1961' in Attfield and Kirkham, op. cit., pp. 215–238.
23. ibid.
24. G. Nelson and H. Wright. *Tomorrow's House*, New York, Simon and Schuster, 1945, p. 18.
25. The Good Housekeeping Institute *Home Encyclopedia*, London. The National Magazine Company Ltd., 1951, p. 93.
26. Attfield and Kirkham, op. cit., p. 225.
27. The Good Housekeeping Institute *The Happy Home: A Universal Guide to Household Management*, London, The Chiswick Press, 1953, plate 58.
28. Molly Harrison in *Modern Homes Illustrated*, London, Odhams, 1947, p. 227.
29. Hine, op. cit., p. 70.
30. Harrison, op. cit., p. 248.
31. The Festival Pattern Group set out to provide a scientific basis for a form of modern pattern which derived from work they undertook involving looking at natural organisms through microscopes and recording the visual results.
32. Quoted in White, op. cit., p. 179.
33. G. Williams *The Economics of Everyday Life*, Harmondsworth, Penguin, 1965 |(1950), p. 114.
34. The Good Housekeeping Institute *The Book of Good Housekeeping*, London and Chesham, Gramol Publications Ltd., 1946 (1944) p. 322.
35. ibid., p. 387.
36. Women's Weekly, 21 Jan. 1956, p.21.
37. Ehrenreich and English, op. cit., p. 286.
38. ibid., p. 288.

Chapter 9 'A Kind of Golden Age':
Goods and Femininity

1. David Gartman. *Auto Opium: A Social History of American Automobile Design*, London and New York, Routledge, 1994, p. 139.
2. Betty Friedan. *The Feminine Mystique*, Harmondsworth, Penguin, 1993 (1963), p. 63.

3. This idea remained strong into the post-war years and underpins much critical writing about consumption. It is dominant, for example, in Kathy Myers. *Understains*, London, Comedia, 1986.

4. *DIA Yearbook*, London 1953, p. 16.

5. ibid., p. 22.

6. *The Evening News*, June 19 1957, p. 6.

7. Formed in 1944 by the British coalition government, the Council of Industrial design was part of the Board of Trade. Its brief was to improve the quality of design in British goods and to raise the level of public taste.

8. Ernest Race. 'Design in Modern Furniture' in Frances Lake (ed.). *Daily Mail Ideal Home Yearbook 1952/3*, London, *Daily Mail* Publications, 1953, p. 62.

9. Gordon Russell. 'On Buying Furniture' in Frances Lake (ed.). *Daily Mail Ideal Home Yearbook 1953/4*, London, *Daily Mail* Publications, 1954, p. 61.

10. Dorothy Meade in *Design*, London, COID, Aug. 1957, p. 42.

11. Paul Reilly. 'Contemporary Design' in Lake, op. cit., p. 128.

12. Lake, op. cit., p. 59.

13. Paul Reilly. 'Glamour, Glitter and Gloss' in Frances Lake (ed.). *Daily Mail Ideal Home Yearbook 1957*, London, *Daily Mail* Publications, 1957, p. 88.

14. Vivien Hislop. *Evening News*, June 19 1957, p. 8.

15. Vance Packard. *The Waste-Makers*, London, Longmans, 1961, p. 70.

16. Dan Cooper. *Inside Your Home*, New York, Farrar, Straus and Co. Inc., 1946. p. 31.

17. ibid,, p. 96.

18. Thomas Hine. *Populuxe*, New York, Alfred A. Knopf, 1986, p. 22.

19. Friedan, op. cit., p. 32.

20. ibid., p. 57.

21. Noel Carrington. *Colour and Pattern in the Home*, London, Batsford, 1954, p. 99.

22. David Gartman elaborates this point in Gartman, op. cit.

23. An advertisement for a Mercury automobile in *Ladies' Home Journal*, April 1950, p. 31.

24. Gartman, op. cit., p. 167.

25. *Ladies's Home Journal* op. cit., p. 67.

26. Kenwood publicity brochure for its 'Chef' food processor, mid–1950s.

27. Kenwood publicity brochure for its 'Monor' food-mixer, mid–1950s.

28. Paul Reilly. 'The Challenge of Pop' in *Architectural Review*, no. 32. Oct, 1967, p. 257.

Chapter 10 'The Anxiety of Contamination': Highbrow Culture and the Problem of Taste

1. Russell Lynes. *The Tastemakers: The Shaping of American Popular Taste*, New York, Dover, 1980, p. 340.

2. Dick Hebdige, 'Towards a Cartography of Taste 1935–1962' in B. Waites, T. Bennett, and G. Martin (eds). *Popular Culture: Past and Present*, London, Croom Helm, 1982, p. 213.

3. Angela McRobbie in Waites, Bennet and Martin, op. cit., p. 266.
4. Lynes, op. cit., p. 310.
5. Herbert J. Gans. 'Design and the Consumer' in K.B. Heisinger and G.H. Marcus (eds). *Design Since 1945*, London, Thames and Hudson, 1983, p. 32.
6. Gans's ideas parallel those expressed by Pierre Bourdieu in his seminal sociological study of taste, *Distinction: A Social Critique of the Judgment of Taste*, London and New York, Routledge and Kegan Paul, 1986.
7. See his analysis in Lynes, op. cit.
8. ibid., p. 311.
9. Gans includes 'housewifes-mothers' in his middle-brow category in Heisinger and Marcus, op. cit., 5.
10. Andreas Huyssen. *After the Great Divide: Modernism, Mass Culture and Postmodernism*, London, Macmillan, 1986.
11. ibid., p. 47.
12. ibid., p. 18.
13. ibid., p. 50–1.
14. ibid., p. 52.
15. See T. Adorno and M. Horkheimer. *Dialectic of Enlightenment*, London, Verso, 1979 (1944).
16. Huyssen, op. cit., p. 48.
17. ibid., p. 21.
18. Clement Greenberg. 'The Avant-garde and Kitsch (1939)' in Gillo Dorfles (ed.). *Kitsch: An Anthology of Bad Taste*, London, Studio Vista, 1968.
19. For more detail about Adorno's ideas about popular culture see Huyssen, op. cit., p. 19.
20. ibid., p. 54.
21. See H. Marcuse. *One-Dimensional Man*, London, Routledge and Kegan Paul, 1964.
22. Hoggart's ideas are expressed in his book *The Uses of Literacy*, Harmondsworth, Penguin, 1958 (1957).
23. Raymond Williams first articulated his thoughts on this subject in *Culture and Society 1780–1950*, London, Chatto and Windus, 1958.
24. David Riesman. *The Lonely Crowd: A Study of the Changing American Character*, New Haven and London, Yale University Press, revised edition, 1970.
25. Christopher Lasch. *The Culture of Narcissism: American Life in an Age of Diminishing Expectations*, New York, W.W. Norton, 1978.
26. op cit., 340.
27. ibid.,
28. ibid., 341.
29. Margaret Mead is quoted in Marcuse, op. cit. p. 111.
30. Vance Packard. *The Waste-Makers*, London, Longmans, 1961, p. 12.
31. ibid., p. 25.
32. Exhibitions about design which had been held at MOMA since the 1930s included *Machine Art* (1934); *Alvar Aalto* (1938); *Low-Cost Useful Objects* (1938); *Modern Furniture Competition* (1940); and *Charles Eames Furniture* (1946).

33. Edgar Kaufmann Jr. *Industrial Design*, New York, Aug. 1954, p. 23.
34. Edgar Kaufmann Jr. *Introductions to Modern Design*, New York, MOMA 1969 (1950), p. 7.
35. ibid.
36. ibid.
37. Edgar Kaufmann Jr. 'Borax or the Chromium-plate Calf' in *Architectural Review*, London, vol. 6, no. 4., Aug. 1948, p. 89.
38. ibid.
39. Kaufmann, *Introductions to Modern Design*, p. 8.
40. See Dick Hebdige. 'Towards a Cartography of Taste 1935–1962' in B. Waites, T. Bennett and G. Martin (eds). *Popular Culture: Past and Present*, London, Croom Helm, 1982.
41. A. Davis. *Design*, London, Aug. 1953, p. 3.
42. Dorfles, op. cit.
43. Claire Catterall. 'Perceptions of Plastics: A Study of Plastics in Britain 1945–1956' in Penny Sparke (ed.). *The Plastics Age: From Modernity to Postmodernity*, London, Victoria and Albert Museum, 1990, p. 70.
44. ibid., p. 69.
45. Harold Van Doren. 'Streamlining: Fad of Function?' in *Design*, London, Oct. 1949, p. 2.
46. ibid., p. 5.
47. Alan Jarvis. *The Things we See: Inside and Out*, Harmondsworth, Penguin, 1947, p. 29.
48. The Independent Group consisted of a group of individuals linked in various ways to the visual arts, among them Eduardo Paolozzi, Richard Alloway, Reyner Banham, Toni del Renzio, Nigel Henderson, and Alison and Peter Smithson, who came together at The Institute of Contemporary Arts in the mid–1950s to discuss the effects of technology and mass culture upon the arts. Unlike many of their contemporaries, they took a sympathetic approach to the subject, celebrating the products of the mass media, among them advertising, streamlined automobiles, movies and pulp novels.
49. Huyssen, op. cit., p. 46.

Conclusion: Postmodernity, Postmodernism and Feminine Taste

1. Janet Wolff. *Feminine Sentences: Essays in Women and Culture*, Cambridge, Polity Press, 1990, p. 1.
2. ibid.
3. ibid., p. 74. Wolff discusses the ideas of Julia Kristeva concerning women and language.
4. See Andreas Huyssen. *After The Great Divide: Modernism, Mass Culture and Postmodernism*, London, Macmillan, 1986, p. 184.
5. See Janet Wolff and Craig Owens. 'The Discourse of Others: Feminists and Postmodernism' in Hal Foster (ed.). *Postmodern Culture*, London, Pluto Press, 1990 (1983), pp. 57–82.
6. See Janet Wolff and Linda Nicholson (eds). *Feminism/Postmodernism*, London, Routledge, 1990.
7. Wolff, op. cit. p. 87.
8. ibid.

9. Robert Venturi. *Complexity and Contradiction in Architecture*, New York, MOMA, 1966, p. 22.

10. Robert Venturi, Denise Scott-Brown and Steve Izenour. *Learning from Las Vegas*, Cambridge, Mass., MIT Press, 1972.

11. Huyssen op. cit., p. 59.

12. Used in the Barthian sense as articulated by Roland Barthes in *Mythologies*, London, Jonathan Cape, 1972 (1957).

13. For a selection of Baudrillard's writings see Bibliography.

14. Jean-Francois Lyotard. *The Postmodern Condition: A Report on Knowledge*, Manchester, Manchester University Press, 1984 (1979).

15. Rosalind Coward. *Female Desire*, London, Paladin, 1984.

Bibliography

Abelson, E. S. *When Ladies Go A-Thieving: Middle-Class Shoplifters in the Victorian Department Store*, Oxford, Oxford University Press, 1989

Adburnham, A. *Shops and Shopping 1800–1914*, London, Allen and Unwin, 1981

Adler, H. *The New Interior: Modern Decorations for the Modern Home*, New York, The Century Company, 1916

Adorno, T. and Horkheimer, M. *Dialect of Enlightenment*, London, Verso, 1979 (1944)

Albrecht, D. *Designing Dreams: Modern Architecture in the Movies*, New York, Harper and Row, 1986

Ames, K. 'Designed in France; Notes on the Transmission of French Style to America', *Wintherthur Portfolio*, 12, Charlottesville, Va, University of Virginia Press, 1978, pp. 103–114

Ames, K. *Material Culture: A Research Guide*, Kansas, University of Kansas Press, 1983

Ames, K. L. & Ward, W. R. (eds.). *Decorative Arts and Household Furnishings in America 1650–1920: An Annotated Bibliography*, Virginia, University of Virginia Press, 1990

Anscombe, I. *A Woman's Touch: Women in Design from 1860 to the Present Day*, London, Virago, 1984

Apparudai, A. (ed.). *The Social Life of Things: Commodities in Cultural Perspective*, Cambridge, Cambridge University Press, 1986

Arnold, E. & Burr, L. 'Housework and the Appliance of Science' in Faulkner, W. & Arnold, E. (eds.), *Smothered by Invention*, London, Pluto Press, 1985

Ash, J. & Wilson, E. *Chic Thrills*, London, Pandora, 1992

Attfield, J. 'Feminist Critiques of Design' in Walker J., *Design History and the History of Design*, London, Pluto Press, 1989

Attfield, J. & Kirkham, P. *A View from the Interior: Feminism, Women and Design*, London, The Woman's Press, 1989

Baehr, M. & Dyer G. (eds.). *Boxed In: Women and Television*, London, Pandora, 1987

Ballaster, R., Beetham, M., Frazer, E. & Hebron, S. (eds.). *Women's Worlds: Ideology, Femininity and the Woman's Magazine*, London, Macmillan, 1991

Banham, J., Macdonald, S. and Porter, J. *Victorian Interior Design*, London, Cassell, 1991

Banner, L. *American Beauty*, New York, Alfred A Knopf, 1983

Banner, L. & Hartman, M. (eds.). *Clio's Consciousness Raised*, New York, Harper and Row, 1974

Barker, N. & Parr M. *Signs of the Times*, London, BBC Publications, 1992

Barnes, R. (ed.). *Dress and Gender: Making and Meaning in Cultural Contexts*, Providence, Oxford, Berg, 1993

Barrett, H. & Phillips, J. *Suburban Style: The British Home 1840–1960*, Boston, Toronto, London, Little Brown and Company, 1993

Barrett, M. 'Ideology and the Cultural Production of Gender' in Newton, J. & Rosenfelt, D. (eds.). *Feminist Criticism and Social Change*, London, Methuen, 1985

Barthel, D. *Putting on Appearances: Gender and Advertising*, Philadelphia, Temple University Press, 1988

Barthes, R. *Mythologies*, Paris, Editions du Seuil, 1957

Battersby, C. *Gender and Genius: Towards a Feminist Aesthetics*, London, Women's Press, 1990

Battersby, M. *The Decorative Twenties*, London, Studio Vista, 1976

Battersby, M. *The Decorative Thirties*, London, Studio Vista, 1976

Baudrillard, J. *For a Critique of the Political Economy of the Sign*, St Louis, Telos Press, 1981

Baudrillard, J. *La Societé de consommation, ses mythes, ses structures*, Paris, Gallimard, 1970

Baudrillard, J. *Le système des objets*, Paris, Denoel-Gonthier, 1968

Bauman, Z. *Modernity and Ambivalence*, Cambridge, Polity Press, 1990

Bayley, S. *Harley Earl and the Dream Machine*, New York, Knopf, 1983

Bayley, S. *Taste*, London, Faber and Faber, 1991

Beddoe, D. *Back to Home and Duty: Women between the Wars 1918–1939*, London, Pandora, 1989

Beckett Jones, G. *Manual of Smart Housekeeping*, New York, Chester R Heck Ltd., 1946

Beecher, C. E. *A Treatise on Domestic Economy for the Use of Young Ladies at Home and at School*, Boston, Marsh, Capen, Lyon and Webb, 1841

Beecher, C. & Stowe, H. B. *The American Woman's Home*, New York, J. B. Ford and Co., 1870 (1869)

Beeton, Mrs. *Hints to Housewives*, London, Butler and Tanner Ltd., 1928 (1861)

Bel, Geddes, N. *Horizons*, New York, Dover Publications, 1977

Bell, C. *Middle-Class Families*, London, Routledge and Kegan Paul, 1968

Bell, D. *The Cultural Contradictions of Capitalism*, New York, Basic Books, 1976

Benhabib, S. 'Feminism and the Question of Postmodernism' in *The Polity Reader in Gender Studies*, Cambridge, Polity Press, 1994

Bentley, I., Davis, I. and Oliver. *Dunroamin: The Suburban Semi and its Enemies*, London, Barrie and Jenkins, 1981

Benton, C. 'Aventure du mobilier: Le Corbusier's furniture designs of the 1920s', *Decorative Arts Society Journal*, 6, 1982, pp. 7–22

Benton, T. & C. & Sharp, D. (eds.). *Form and Function: A Source book for a History of Architecture and Design 1890–1939*, London, Crosby, Lockwood and Staples, 1975

Bereano, P., Roase, C. & Arnold, E. 'Kitchen Technology and the Liberation of Women from Above' in Faulkner, W. and Arnold, E. (eds.), *Smothered by Invention*, London, Pluto Press, 1985

Berman, M. *All That is Solid Melts into Air: The Experience of Modernity*, London, Verso, 1983

Betterton, R. *Looking On: Images of Femininity in the Visual Arts and Media*, London, Pandora, 1987

Bevier, J. 'The House, Its Plan, Decoration and Care', vol 1, in *The Library of Home Economics*, Chicago, American School of Home Economics, 1907

Bigsby, C. W. E. (ed.), *Superculture: American Popular Culture and Europe*, London, Paul Elek, 1975

Binnie, R. & Boxall, J. E. *Housecraft: Principles and Practice*, London, Sir Isaac Pitman and Sons Ltd., 1926

Boorstin, D. *The Americans: The Democratic Experience*, New York, Random House, 1973

Boorstin, D. J. 'Welcome to the Consumption Community', *Fortune*, 76 (1967), pp. 118–38

Bourdieu, P. *Distinction: A Social Critique of the Judgement of Taste*, London and New York, Routledge and Kegan Paul, 1986

Bowlby, R. *Still Crazy After All These Years*, London, Routledge, 1992

Bowlby, R. *Just Looking: Consumer Culture in Dreiser, Gissing and Zola*, New York, Methuen, 1985

Bowlby, R. *Shopping with Freud*, London, Routledge, 1993

Branca, P. 'Image and reality; the myth of the idle Victorian woman' in Hartman, M. & Banner, L. W. (eds.). *Clio's Consciousness Raised*, New York, Harper, 1974

Branca, P. *Silent Sisterhood: Middle-Class Women in the Victorian Home*, London, Croom Helm, 1975

Briggs, A. *Victorian Things*, Harmondsworth, Penguin, 1988

Brittain, V. *Lady into Woman*, London, Andrew Drakes, 1953

Brookeman, C. *American Culture and Society since the '30s*, London, Macmillan, 1984

Bronner, S. J. (ed.). *Consuming Visions: Accumulation and Display of Goods in America, 1880–1920*, New York and London, W. W. Norton and Co., 1989

Brownmiller, S. *Femininity*, New York, Simon and Schuster, 19984

Bruere, M. & R. *Increasing Home Efficiency*, New York, Macmillan, 1912

Buckley, C. 'Design, Femininity, and Modernism: Interpreting the Work of Susie Cooper' in *Journal of Design History*, Oxford, vol. 7, no. 4, 1994, pp. 277–293

Buckley, C. 'Made in Patriarchy: Towards a Feminist Analysis of Women in Design' in *Design Issues*, vol. 3, no. 2, 1986

Buckley, C. *Potters and Paintresses: Women Designers in the Pottery Industry 1870–1955*, London, The Women's Press, 1990

Buckley, C. 'Women and Modernity: A Case-study of Grete Marks' in Seddon and Worden, *Women Designing: Redefining Design in Britain Between the Wars*, Brighton, University of Brighton, 1994

Bulley, M. *Have You Got Good Taste?: A Guide to the Appreciation of the Lesser Arts*, London, Methuen, 1933

Burman, S. (ed.). *Fit Work for Women*, London, Croom Helm, 1979

Burrows, R. & Marsh, C. *Consumption and Class; Divisions and Change*, Macmillan, London, 1992

Bush, D. *The Streamlined Decade*, New York, George Braziller, 1975

Bushman, R. L. & Bushman, C. L. 'The Early History of Cleanliness in America', *Journal of American History*, vol. 24, March 1988, pp. 1213–1238

Calkins, C. *A Course in House Planning and Furnishing*, Chicago, Scott Foresman and Company, 1916

Calkins, E. 'Advertising: Builder of Taste', *American Magazine of Art*, 21 Sep. 1930, pp. 497–502

Calkins, E. 'Beauty, the New Business Tool', *The Atlantic Monthly*, 14 Aug. 1927, pp. 145–6

Callen, A. A. *Angel in the Studio: Women in the Arts and Crafts Movement*, London, Astragal Books, 1979

Campbell, C. *The Romantic Ethic and the Spirit of Modern Consumerism*, London, Basil Blackwell, 1987

Campbell, H. *Household Economics*, New York, G. P. Putnam's and Sons, 1897

Campbell, N & Seebohm, C. *Elsie de Wolfe: A Decorative Life*, London, Aurum Press, 1992

Carrington, N. *Colour and Pattern in the Home*, London, Batsford, 1954

Chafe, W. H. *The American Woman: Her Changing Social, Economic and Political Roles 1920–1970*, New York, Oxford University Press, 1972

Chafe, W. H. *The Paradox of Change: American Women in the 20th Century*, New York, Oxford University Press, 1991

Chaney, D. 'The Department Store as a Cultural Form', *Theory Culture and Society*, vol. 1, no. 3, 1983, pp. 22–31

Chapman, D. *The Home and Social Status*, London, Routledge and Kegan Paul, 1955

Cheney, S. & M. *Art and the Machine*, New York, McGraw Hill, 1936

Chodrow, N. *The Reproduction of Mothering; Psychoanalysis and the Sociology of Gender*, California, University of Berkeley, 1978

Church, E. R. *How to Furnish a Home*, New York, D. Appleton and Company, 1883

Clark, A. *Working Life of Women in the 17th Century*, London, Routledge and Kegan Paul, 1982 (1919)

Clark, C. E. Jr. *The American Family Home 1800–1960*, Chapel Hill, University of North Carolina Press, 1986

Collins, P. *Changing Ideals in Modern Architecture 1750–1950*, London, Faber and Faber, 1965

Collins, P. *Radios: The Golden Age*, San Francisco, Chronicle Books, 1987

Cook, C. *The House Beautiful*, New York, Scribner, Armstrong and Company, 1878

Conrads, U. (ed.). *Programmes and Manifestoes on Twentieth-Century Architecture*, London, Lund Humphries, 1970 (1964)

Cornforth, J. *English Interiors 1790–1848: The Quest for Comfort*, London, Barrie and Jenkins Ltd., 1978

Council of Industrial Design, *Design in the Festival*, London, HMSO, 1951

Cowan, R. S. *More Work for Mother: The Ironies of Household Technology from the Open Hearth to the Microwave*, Basic Books, New York, 1983

Cowan, R. S. 'The Industrial Revolution in the Home: Household Technology and Social Change in the 20th Century' in *Technology and Culture*, vol. 17, no. 1, January 1976

Cowan. 'Two Washes in the Morning and a Bridge Party at Night: the American housewife between the wars', *Womens's Studies*, vol. 111, no. 2, 1976

Coward, R. *Female Desire*, London, Paladin, 1984

Creed, B. 'From Here to Modernity – Feminism and Postmodernism', *Screen*, vol. 28, no. 2, 1987

Culler, J. *On Deconstruction: Theory and Criticism after Structuralism*, London, Routledge, 1983

Czikszentmihalyi, M. & Rochberg-Halton, E. *The Meaning of Things: Domestic Symbols and the Self*, Cambridge, Cambridge University Press, 1981

Davidoff, L. & Hall, C. *Family fortunes: Men and Women of the English Middle Class 1780–1850*, London, Routledge, 1987

Davidoff, L., L'Esperance, J., & Newby, H. 'Landscapes with Figures: Home and Community in English Society' in Oakley, A. & Mitchell, J. *The Rights and Wrongs of Women*, London, Penguin, 1976

Davidoff, L. 'The Rationalisation of Housework', in *Dependence and Exploitation in Work and Marriage*, London, Longman, 1976, pp. 121–151

Davidson, C. *A Woman's Work is Never Done: A History of Housework in the British Isles 1650–1950*, London, Chatto and Windus, 1982

De Beauvoir, S. *The Second Sex*, London, Penguin, 1972

Debord, G. *Society of Spectacle*, Detroit, Black and Red, 1970

Delamont, S. & Duffin, L. (eds.). *The 19th Century Woman: Her Cultural and Physical World*, London, Croom Helm, 1978

Denvir, B. *The Late Victorians: Art, Design and Society 1852–1910*, Essex, Longmans, 1986

De Syllas, J. 'Stramform', *Architectural Association Quarterly*, April, 1969

De Wolfe, E. *The House in Good Taste*, New York, 1913

De Zurko, E. R. *Origins of Functionalist Theory*, New York, Columbia University Press, 1957

Dittmar, H. 'Gender Identity: relation meanings of personal possessions', *British Journal of Social Psychology*, 28, 1989, pp. 159–171

Dorfles, G. *Kitsch: An Anthology of Bad Taste*, London, Studio Bista, 1973

Douglas, A. *The Feminization of American Culture*, New York, Avon, 1977

Douglas, M. & Isherwood, B. *The World of Goods: Towards an Anthropoly of Consumption*, Harmondsworth, Penguin, 1978

Downing, A. J. *The Architecture of Country Houses*, New York, Dover, 1969 (1850)

Dreyfuss, H. *Designing for People*, New York, Viking Press, 1955

Dudden, F. A. *Serving Women: Household Service in 19th Century America*, Middletown, Conn., Wesleyan University Press, 1983

Duncan, H. D. *Culture and Democracy: The Struggle for Form in Society and Architecture in Chicago and the Middle West during the Life and Times of Louis Sullivan*, New York, Bedminster Press, 1966

Eastlake, C. *Hints on Household Taste in Furniture, Upholstery and Other Details*, London, Longmans, Green and Co., 1872 (1868)

Ecker, G. (ed.). *Feminist Aesthetics*, London, Women's Press, 1985

Edis, R. W. *Decoration and Furniture of Townhouses*, 1881

Ehrenreich, B. & English, D. *For Her Own Good, 150 years of advice to women*, New York, Garden City, Doubleday, 1978

Elinor, G. *Women and Craft*, London, Virago, 1987

Evans, C. & Thornton, M. *Women and Fashion*, London, Quartet, 1989

Ewen, S. *All Consuming Images: The Politics of Style in Contemporary Culture*, New York, Basic Books, 1988

Ewen, S. *Captains of Consciousness: Advertising and the Social Roots of Consumer Culture*, New York, McGraw Hill, 1977

Ewen, E. & Ewen, S. *Channels of Desire: Mass Images and the Shaping of the American Consciousness*, New York/London, McGraw Hill, 1982

Falk, P. *The Consuming Body*, London, Sage, 1994

Fales, W. *What's New in Home Decorating?*, New York, Dodd, Mead and Co., 1936

Faulkner, W. & Arnold, E. (eds.). *Smothered by Invention*, London, Pluto Press, 1985

Faunthorpe, Rev. J.P. (ed.). *Household Science: Readings in Necessary Knowledge for Girls and Young Women*, London, Edward Stanford, 1895 (1879)

Featherstone, M. *Consumer Culture and Postmodernism*, London, Sage Publications, 1983

Featherstone, M. 'The Body in Consumer Culture', *Theory, Culture and Society*, vol. 1, no. 2, pp. 18–33

Felski, R. *Beyond Feminist Aesthetics: Feminist Literature and Social Change*, Cambridge, Mass., Harvard University Press, 1989

Ferguson, M. *Forever Feminine: Women's magazines and the Cult of Femininity*, London, Heinemann, 1983

Ferry, J. W. *A History of the Department Store*, New York, Macmillan, 1960

Finch, J. & Sommerfield, P. 'Social reconstruction and the emergence of companionate marriage 1945–1959' in Clark, D. (ed.), *Marriage, Social Change and Domestic Life: Essays in Honour of Jackie Burgoyne*, London, Routledge, 1991

Fine, B. & Leopold, E. *The World of Consumption*, London and New York, Routledge, 1993

Fraser, R. (ed.). *Work: twenty personal accounts*, Penguin, Harmondsworth, 1968

Flax, J. 'Postmodernism and Gender Relations in Feminist Theory', *Signs*, vol. 12, no. 4, Summer 1987

Flax, J. *Thinking Fragments: Psychoanalysis, Feminism, and Postmodernism in the Contemporary West*, Berkeley, California, University of California Press, 1990

Forty, A. *Objects of Desire: Design and Society 1750–1980*, London, Thames and Hudson, 1986

Foster, H. *Postmodern Culture*, London, Pluto Press, 1990 (1983)

Frampton, K. *Modern Architecture: A Critical History*, London, Thames and Hudson, 1980

Fraser, N. & Nicholson, L. 'Social Criticism without Philosophy: An Encounter between Feminism and Postmodernism', *Theory, Culture and Society*, vol. 5, nos. 2–3, 1988, pp. 380–391

Frederick, C. *Selling Mrs Consumer*, New York, The Business Bourse, 1929

Frederick, C. *Household Engineering and Scientific Management in the Home*, Chicago, American School of Home Economics, 1919

Frederick, C. *The New Housekeeping: Efficiency Studies in Home Management*, New York, Garden City, Doubleday Page, 1913

Friedan, B. *The Feminine Mystique*, Harmondsworth, Penguin, 1992 (1963)

Frisby, D. *Fragments of Modernity: theories of modernity in the work of Simmel, Kracauer and Benjamin*, Cambridge, Polity, 1985

Gablik, S. *Has Modernism Failed?*, London, Thames and Hudson, 1984

Galbraith, K. *The Affluent Society*, Harmondsworth, Penguin, 1958

Gamman, L. & Marshment, M. (eds.). *The Female Gaze: Women as Watchers of Popular Culture*, London, Women's Press, 1988

Gans, H. *Popular Culture and High Culture: An analysis and evaluation of taste*, New York, Basic Books, 1974

Gardner, C. & Sheppard, J. *Consuming Passions: The Rise of Retail Culture*, London, Unwin Hyman Ltd., 1989

Garrett, A. & R. *Suggestions for House Decoration in Painting, Woodwork and Furniture*, London, Macmillan and Co., 1876

Gartman, D. *Auto Opium: A Social History of American Automobile Design*, London and New York, Routledge, 1994

Gasset, O. Y. *The Revolt of the Masses*, London, Allen and Unwin, 1961 (1931)

Gebhard, D. 'The Moderne in the US 1920–41', *Architectural Association Quarterly*, 2 July, 1970

Geertz, C. 'Art as a Cultural System' in *The Interpretation of Cultures*, New York, Basic Books, 1973

Gere, C. *19th Century Decoration: The Art of the Interior*, London, Weidenfeld and Nicholson, 1989

Giedon, S. *Mechanization Takes Command*, New York, Norton, 1949

Gilbreth, L. M. 'Efficiency Methods applied to the Kitchen', *Architectural Record*, vol. 67, March 1930, pp. 291–294

Gilbreth, L. M. *The Home-Maker and Her Job*, New York, D. Appleton, 1927

Gilligan, C. *In a Different Voice: Psychological Theory and Women's Development*, Cambridge, Mass., Harvard University Press, 1982

Girouard, M. *The Victorian Country House*, Oxford, Oxford University Press, 1971

Gloag, J. *Victorian Taste*, Devon, David and Charles, 1962

Gloag, J. *Victorian Comfort: A Social History of Design from 1830–1900*, London, Adam and Charles Black, 1961

Goffman, E. *Gender Advertisements*, London, Macmillan,1976

Good Housekeeping Institute. *The Book of Good Housekeeping*, London, Gramol Publications Ltd., 1946 (1944)

Good Housekeeping Institute. *The Happy Home*, London, Rainbird Mclean Ltd., 1950s

Goodal, P. 'Design and Gender', *Block*, vol. 9, London, Middlesex Polytechnic, 1983

Green, H. *The Light of the Home: An Intimate View of the Lives of Women in Victorian America*, New York, Pantheon Books, 1983

Greenhalgh, P. *Ephemeral Vistas: The Expositions Universelles, Great Exhibitions, and World's Fairs 1851–1939*, Manchester, Manchester University Press, 1988

Greenhalgh, P. (ed.). *Modernism in Design*, London, Reaktion Books, 1990

Greenhough, H. *Forms and Function: Remarks on Art, Design and Architecture*, Los Angeles, University of California Press, 1969

Grief, M. *Depression Modern – the '30s Style in America*, New York, Universe Books, 1975

Grier, K. C. *Culture and Comfort: People, Parlors and Upholstery 1850–1930*, New York, The Strong Museum, 1988

Gries, J. M & Ford, J. (eds.). *Household Management and Kitchens*, Washington DC, National Capital Press Inc., 1932

Gries, J. M & Ford, J. (eds.). *Homemaking, Home Furnishing and Information Services*, Washington DC, National Capital Press Inc., 1932

Gropius, W. *The New Architecture and the Bauhaus*, London, Faber and Faber, 1968

Haber, S. *Efficiency and Uplift: Scientific Management in the Progressive Era 1890–1920*, Chicago, University of Chicago Press, 1964

Hall, C. 'Married Women at Home in Birmingham in the '20s and '30s', *Oral History Society Journal*, vol. 5, no. 2, Autumn 1977, pp. 62–83

Hall, C. 'Strains in the "firm of Wife, Children and Friends"? Middle-class women and employment in early 19th century England' in Hudson, P. & Lee, W. R. *Women's Work and the Family Economy in Historical Perspective*, Manchester, Manchester University Press, 1990

Hall, C. 'The History of the Housewife' in Malos, E. (ed.), *The Politics of Housework*, London, New York, Allison and Busby, 1982

Hall, C. *White and Middle-Class: explorations in feminism and history*, Oxford, Oxford University Press, 1992

Haltenen, K. 'From Parlor to Living Room: Domestic Space, Interior Decoration, and the Culture of Personality' in Bronner, S. J. (ed.), *Consuming Visions: Accumulation and Display in America 1880–1920*, New York/London, W. W. Norton and Co., 1989

Haltunen, K. *Confidence Men and Painter Women: A Study of Middle-Class Culture in America 1830–1870*, New Haven, Yale University Press, 1982

Hamish, Fraser, W. *The Coming of the Mass Market 1850–1914*, London, Macmillan, 1981

Hansen, J & Reed, A. *Cosmetics, Fashion and the Exploitation of Women*, New York, Pathfinder Press, 1986

Harris, N. 'Museums, Merchandising and Popular Taste: The Struggle for Influence' in Quimby, A. M., *Material Culture and the Study of Everyday Life*, New York, W. W. Norton and Co., 1978

Harris, N. 'The Drama of Consumer Desire' in *Cultural Excursions: Marketing Appetites and Cultural Tastes in Modern America*, Chicago, University of Chicago Press, 1990

Harrison, H. A. (ed.). *Dawn of a New Day: the New York World's Fair 1939/40*, New York, New York University Press, 1981

Hartman, S. M. *The Home Front and Beyond: American Women in the 1940s*, Boston, Twaune, 1982

Harvey, B. *The Fifties: an Oral History*, New York, HarperCollins, 1993

Harvey, D. *The Condition of Postmodernity*, Oxford, Basil Blackwell, 1989

Haweis, Mrs. M. E. *The Art of Decoration*, London, Chatto and Windus, 1889

Hayden, D. *Redesigning the American Dream: The Future of Housing, Work and Family*, New York, W. W. Norton, 1984

Hayden, D. *The Grand Domestic Revolution: A History of Feminist Designs for American Homes, Neighbourhoods and Cities*, Cambridge, Mass., MIT Press, 1981

Haug, W. F. *Critique of Commodity Aesthetics*, Cambridge, Polity Press, 1986

Hebdige, D. *Hiding in the Light: on images and things*, London/New York, Routledge, 1988

Hebdige, D. *Subculture: The Meaning of Style*, London, Methuen, 1979

Hein, H. & Korsmeyer, C. (eds.). *Aesthetics in Feminist Perspective*, Bloomington and Indianapolis, Indiana University Press, 1993

Henderson, K. (ed.). *The Great Divide: The Sexual Division of Labour, or 'Is It Art?'*, Milton Keynes, Open University, 1979

Heskett, J. *Design in Germany 1870–1918*, London, Trefoil, 1986

Hill, G. *Women in English Life*, London, Richard Bentley and Son, 1896

Hine, T. *Populuxe*, New York, Alfred A. Knopf, 1986

Hoggart, R. *The Uses of Literacy*, Harmondsworth, Penguin, 1958

Hoke, D. *Ingenious Yankees*, New York, Columbia University Press, 1990

Hole, C. *English Home Life 1500–1800*, London, Barsford, 1947

Holt, J. M. *Housecraft Science*, London, G. Bell and Sons Ltd., 1953

Horowitz, D. *The Morality of Spending: Attitudes towards the Consumer Society in America 1875–1940*, Baltimore, John Hopkins University Press, 1985

Houghton, W. E. *The Victorian Frame of Mind 1830–1900*, New York, Yale University Press, 1957

Hounshell, D. *From the American System to Mass Production 1800–1932: The Development of Manufacturing Technology in the U.S.*, Baltimore and London, John Hopkins University Press, 1982

Hollander, A. *Seeing Through Clothes*, New York, Viking Press, 1978

Hower, J. *History of Macy's of New York 1858–1919*, Cambridge, Mass., Harvard University Press, 1943

Hudson, P. & Lee, W. R. (eds.). *Women's Work and the Family Economy in Historical Perspective*, Manchester, Manchester University Press, 1990

Hunter, G. L. *Home Furnishing*, New York, John Lane Company, 1913

Hutcheon, L. *The Politics of Postmodernism*, London/New York, Routledge, 1989

Huyssen, A. *After the Great Divide: Modernism, Mass Culture and Postmodernism*, London, Macmillan, 1986

Jackson Lears, T. J. *No Place of Grace: Antimodernism and the Transformation of American Culture 1880–1920*, New York, Pantheon Books, 1981

Jamieson, F. 'Postmodernism, or the Logic of Late Capitalism', *New Left Review*, vol. 146, 1984, pp. 53–92

Jeffreys, J. B. *Retail Trading in Britain 1850–1950*, Cambridge, Cambridge University Press, 1954

Jencks, C. *Modern Movements in Architecture*, Harmondsworth, Penguin, 1973

Jervis, S. *High Victorian Design*, Woodbridge, Suffolk, Boydell, 1983

Katz, S. *Plastics: Design and Materials*, London, Studio Vista, 1978

Katzman, D. M. *Seven Days a Week: Women and Domestic Service in Industrializing America*, Chicago, University of Illinois Press, 1981

Kaufmann, Jr. E. *Introduction to Modern Design*, New York, Museum of Modern Art, 1969 (1950)

Keats, J. *The Insolent Chariots*, New York, Lippincott, 1958

Kellner, D. 'Critical Theory, Commodities and the Consumer Society', *Theory, Culture and Society*, vol. 1, no. 3, pp. 66–83

Kerr, R. *The Gentleman's House*, London, J. Murray, 1864

Kiesler, F. *Contemporary Art as applied to the Store and its Display*, London, Sir Isaac Pitman and Sons Ltd., 1930

Kouwenhoven, J. A. *Made in America: The Arts in Modern Civilisation*, New York, Doubleday, 1949

Kramarae, C. (ed.). *Technology and Women's Voices*, London/New York, Routledge, 1988

Kuhn, A. *Women's Pictures: Feminism and Cinema*, London, Routledge, 1982

Laermans, R. 'Learning to Consume: Early Department Stores and the Shaping of the Modern Consumer Culture (1860–1914)', *Theory, Culture and Society*, vol. 10, no. 4, November 1993, pp. 79–102

Lake, F. (ed.). *Daily Mail Ideal Home Yearbook*, London, Daily Mail, 1948/9; 1949/50; 1950/51; 1952/3; 1953/4; 1957

Landes, J. *Women and the Public Sphere: A Study in the Representation of Gender Relations 1750–1850*, Indiana University Press, 1986

Lasch, C. *The Culture of Narcissism: American life in an Age of Diminishing Expectations*, New York, W. W. Norton, 1978

Leach, W. R. 'Transformations in a Culture of Consumption: Women and Department Stores 1890–1912', *Journal of American History*, 71, September 1984, pp. 319–342

Le Corbusier. *The Decorative Art of Today*, Cambridge, Mass., MIT Press, 1987

Le Corbusier. *Towards a New Architecture*, London, The Architectural Press, 1974

Lee, M. J. *Consumer Culture Reborn: the cultural politics of consumption*, London and New York, Routledge, 1993

Levine, D. N. (ed.). *George Simmel on Individuality and Social Forms: Selected Writings*, Chicago, University of Chicago Press, 1971

Lewis, J. *Labour and Love: Women's Experience of Home and Family 1880–1940*, Oxford, Basil Blackwell, 1986

Lewis, J. *Women in Britain Since 1945: Women, Family, Work and the State in the Post-war Years*, Oxford, Blackwell, 1992

Lewis, J. *Women in England 1870–1950: Sexual Divisions and Social Change*, Brighton, Wheatsheaf, 1984

Lifshey, E. *The Housewares Story*, Chicago, National Housewares Manufacturers Association, 1973

Light, A. *Forever England: femininity, literature and conservatism between the wars*, London/New York, Routledge, 1991

Ling, P. J. *America and the Automobile: technology, reform and social change 1893–1923*, Manchester, Manchester University Press, 1990

Lloyd Jones, P. *Taste Today: The Role of Appreciation in Consumerism and Design*, Oxford, Pergamon Press, 1991

Loewy, R. *Never Leave Well Enough Alone*, New York, Simon and Schuster, 1951

Loos, A. *Spoken into the Void: Collected Essays 1897–1900*, Cambridge, Mass., MIT Press, 1982

Lundberg, F. & Farnham, M. *Modern Women: The Lost Sex*, New York, Harper and Brothers, 1947

Lunt, P. & Livingstone, S. M. *Mass Consumption and Personal Identity: Everyday Economic Experience*, Buckingham and Philadelphia, Open University Press, 1992

Lupton, E. & Abbott Miller, J. *The Bathroom, the Kitchen and the Aesthetics of Waste: A Process of Elimination*, Cambridge, Mass., MIT List Visual Arts Center, 1992

Lynd, R. & H. *Middletown: A Study in Contemporary American Culture*, New York, Harcourt, Brace and World, 1929

Lynde, C. J. *Physics of the Household*, New York, Macmillan, 1914

Lynes, R. *Good Old Modern: an Intimate Portrait of the Museum of Modern Art*, New York, Atheneum,. 1973

Lynes, R. *The Tastemakers: The Shaping of American Popular Taste*, New York, Dover, 1980

McAuley, F. 'The Science of Consumption', *Journal of Home Economics*, vol. xii, no. 7, July 1920

McBride, T. M. 'A Woman's World: Department Stores and the Evolution of Women's Employment 1870–1970', *French Historical Studies*, vol. 10, no. 4, 1978

McBride, T. *The Domestic Revolution*, London, Croom Helm, 1976

McCarthy, K. *Women's Culture: American Philanthropy and Art 1830–1930*, Chicago, University of Chicago Press, 1991

McClaugherty. 'Household Art: Creating the Artistic home 1868–1893', *Wintherthur Portfolio*, 18 (1983), pp. 1–26

McCracken, G. *Culture and Consumption: New Approaches to the Symbolic Character of Consumer Goods*, Bloomington and Indianapolis, Indiana University Press, 1988

MacDonald, D. *Against the American Grain*, London, Victor Gollanz, 1963

McRobbie, A. & Nava, M. (eds.). *Gender and Generation*, London, Macmillan, 1984

Malos, E. *The Politics of Housework*, London/New York, Allison and Busby, 1980

Manzini, E. *The Material of Invention*, Milan, Arcadia, 1986

Marcuse, H. *One Dimensional Man; Studies in the Ideology of Advanced Industrial Society*, Boston, Beacon Press, 1964

Marcuse, H. *Eros and Civilization*, Boston, Beacon Press, 1964

Marrey, B. *Les Grands Magasins des origines à 1939*, Paris, Picard, 1979

Marchand, R. *Advertising the American Dream: Making Way for Modernity 1920–1940*, Berkeley, University of California Press, 1985

Marcus, L. S. *The American Store Window*, New York/London, Whitney Library of Design, 1978

Matthews, G. *'Just a Housewife': The Rise and Fall of Domesticity in America*, New York/Oxford, Oxford University Press, 1987

May, L (ed.). *Recasting America: Culture and Politics in the Age of the Cold War*, Chicago, Chicago University Press, 1989

Mayr, O. & Post, R. C. (eds.). *Yankee Enterprise: The Rise of the American System of Manufactures*, Washington, Smithsonian Institution Press, 1981

Meikle, J. *Twentieth-Century Limited: Industrial Design in America 1925–1939*, Philadelphia, Temple University Press, 1979

Mendus, S. & Rendall, J. (eds.). *Sexuality and Subordination: Interdisciplinary Studies in Gender in the 19th Century*, London, Routledge, 1989

Merivale, M. *Furnishing the Small House*, London, The Studio Publications, 1938

Miller, D. *Material Culture and Mass Consumption*, Basil Blackwell, Oxford, 1987

Miller, M. B. *The Bon Marche: Bourgeois Culture and the Department Store 1869–1920*, New Jersey, Princeton University Press, 1981

Millet, K. *Sexual Politics*, London, Virago, 1977 (1971)

Mills, S. (ed). *Gendering the Reader*, Hemel Hempstead, Harvester Wheatsheaf, 1994

Mitarachi, J. F. 'Harley Earl and his Product: the styling section', *Industrial Design*, New York, October 1995

Moles, A. *Psychologie du kitsch: L'art du bonheur*, Paris, Mame, 1971

Morris, B. *Victorian Table Glass and Ornaments*, London, Barrie and Jenkins, 1978

Mulvey, L. 'Visual Pleasure and Narrative Cinema', *Screen*, vol. 16, no. 3, Autumn 1975, pp. 6–18

Mulvey, L. *Visual and other Pleasures*, London, Macmillan, 1987

Mukerji, C. *From Graven Images: Patterns of Modern Materialism*, New York, New Columbia University Press, 1983

Muthesius, H. *Das Englische Haus*, Berlin, E. Wasmuth, 1904

Myers, K. *Understains*, London, Comedia, 1986

National Magazine Company Ltd. *Good Housekeeping's Setting Up Home*, London, Ebury Press, 1963

Nava, M. *Changing Tastes: Feminism, Youth and Consumerism*, London, Sage Publications, 1992

Nava, M. 'Consumerism and its Contradictions', *Cultural Studies*, vol. 1, no. 2, pp. 204–10

Naylor, G. *The Bauhaus Re-assessed: Sources and Design Theory*, London, Herbert Press, 1985

Nead, L. *Myths of Sexuality: Representations of Women in Victorian Britain*, Oxford, Balckwell, 1988

Nearing, N. M. S. 'Four Great Things a Woman Does to a Home that makes her the Greatest Power in America Today', *Ladies Home Journal*, New York, 29, May 1912

Neff, W. F. *Working Women*, London, George Allen and Unwin, 1926

Nelson, G. & Wright, H. *Tomorrow's House*, New York, Simon and Schuster, 1945

Nevins, A. & Hill, F. *Ford, Expansion and Challenge 1915–1935*, New York, Charles Scribners and Sons, 1957

Newson, J. *Education of Girls*, London, Faber and Faber, 1948

Newton, C. & Putnam, T. *Household Choices*, London, Futures Publications, 1990

Nicholson, L. (ed). *Feminism/Postmodernism*, London, Routledge, 1990

Nicholson, S. *A Victorian Household*, Gloucestershire, Alan Sutton Publishing Ltd., 1994

Oakley, A. *Housewife*, London, Allen Lane, 1974

Oakley, A. *Woman's Work: The Housewife, Past and Present*, New York, Pantheon, 1974

Ogden, A. *The Great American Housewife: From Helpmate to Wage Earner 1776–1986*, Westport, Connecticut, Greenwood Press, 1986

Ortner, S. & Whitehead, H. *Sexual Meanings: The Cultural Construction of Gender and Sexuality*, Cambridge, Cambridge University Press, 1993 (1981)

Packard, V. *The Hidden Persuaders*, Harmondsworth, Penguin, 1957ar

Packard, V. *The Status Seekers*, Harmondsworth, Penguin, 1963 (1959)

Packard, V. *The Waste-Makers*, London, Longmans, 1961 (1960)

Palmer, P. *Domesticity and Dirt: Housewives and Domestic Servants in the USA 1920–1945*, Philadelphia, Temple University Press, 1984

Parker, R. *The Subversive Stitch: Embroidery and the Making of the Feminine*, London, Women's Press, 1984

Parker, R. & Pollock, G. *Old Mistresses: Women, Art and Ideology*, London, Routledge, 1981

Partington, A. *Consumption Practices as the Production and Articulation of Differences: Re-thinking Working-class Femininity and Consumer Culture in 1950s Britain*, unpublished PhD thesis, Dept. of Cultural Studies, University of Birmingham, 1990

Pasdermadjian, H. *The Department Store: Its Origins, Evolution and Economics*, London, Newman, 1954

Pattison, M. *The Business of Home Management*, New York, 1915

Pearce, W. J. *Painting and Decorating*, London, Chas Griffin and Co., 1932

Peel, Mrs. *The Labour-Saving Home*, London, John Lane Bodley Head, 1917

Pevsner, N. *High Victorian Design: a Study of the Exhibits of 1851*, London, Architectural Press, 1951

Pitkin, W. B. *The Consumer: His Nature and his Changing Habits*, New York and London, McGraw Hill, 1932

Plummer, K. S. 'The Streamlined Moderne', *Art in America*, Jan/Feb, 1974

Pollock, G. 'Modernity and the Spaces of Femininity' in Pollock, G. *Vision and Difference: Femininity, Feminism and Histories of Art*, London, Routledge, 1988

Poovey, M. 'Feminism and Deconstruction', *Feminist Studies*, vol. 14, no. 1. Spring 1988

Poovey, M. *Uneven Developments: The Ideological Work of Gender in Mid-Victorian England*, University of Chicago Press, Chicago, 1988

Porter Benson, S. *Counter Cultures: Saleswomen, Managers and Customers in American Department Stores 1890–1940*, Urbana Chicago, University of Illinois Press, 1986

Porter Benson, S. 'Palace of Consumption and Machine for Selling: The American Department Store 1880–1940', *Radical History Review*, 21 Fall, 1979, pp. 199–224

Post, R. C. (ed.). *1876- a Centennial Exhibition*, Washington, Smithsonian Institution, 1976

Pribham, D. (ed.). *Female Spectators: Looking at Film and Television*, Verso, London, 1988

Proun, J. D. 'Mind in Matter: An Introduction to Material Culture Theory and Method', *Winterthur Portfolio*, 17 Spring, 1982

Pugin, A. W. *The True Principles of Pointed or Christian Architecture*, London, John Weale, 1841

Pulos, A. *The American Design Adventure 1940–1975*, Cambridge, Mass., The MIT Press, 1988

Pulos, A. *The American Design Ethic*, Cambridge, Mass., The MIT Press, 1983

Radway, J. *Reading the Romance: Women, Patriarchy and Popular Literature*, London, Verso, 1987 (1984)

Rainwater, L., Coleman, R. P. & Handel, G. *Workingman's Wife: Her Personality, World, and Lifestyle*, New York, Oceana Publications, 1959

Redgrave, R. *Manual of Design*, London, Chapman and Hall, 1876

Rees, B. *The Victorian Lady*, London, Gordon and Cremonesi, 1977

Richards, C. R. *Art in Industry*, New York, Macmillan, 1922

Richards, E. 'Housekeeping in the 20th Century', *American Kitchen Magazine*, vol. xii, no. 6, March 1990

Richards, J. M. *The Castles on the Ground: The Anatomy of Suburbia*, London, J. Murray, 1973

Richards, T. *The Commodity Culture of Victorian England: Advertising and Spectacle 1851–1914*, London/New York, Verso, 1990

Rieff, P. *The Triumph of the Therapeutic: uses of Faith after Freud*, New York, Harper and Row, 1966

Riesman, D. *The Lonely Crowd: A Study of the Changing American Character*, New Haven and London, Yale University Press, rev. ed., 1970

Roberts, E. *A Woman's Place: An Oral History of Working-class Women 1890–1940*, Oxford, Basil Blackwell, 1984

Rosenberg, B. & White, D. M. (eds.). *Mass Culture: The Popular Arts in America*, Glencoe III, The Free Press, 1957

Rowbotham, S. *Woman's Consciousness, Man's World*, Harmondsworth, Penguin, 1973

Rowe, P. G. *Making a Middle Landscape*, Cambridge Mass., The MIT Press, 1991

Ruskin, J. *The Seven Lamps of Architecture*, New York, Lovell Coryell and Co., 1900

Ruskin, J. *The Stones of Venice*, New York, Lovell, Coryell and Co., (1951–3)

Ryan, M. 'The Empire of the Mother: American Writing about Domesticity 1830–1860', *Women and History*, vol. 2, no. 3, 1982

Ryan, M. *Womanhood in America: From Colonial Times to the Present*, New York, New Viewpoints, 1975

Saisselin, R. *Bricabracomania: The Bourgeois and the Bibelot*, London, Thames and Hudson, 1985

Schaefer, H. *Nineteenth-Century Modern: The Functional Tradition in Victorian Design*, London, Studio Vista, 1970

Scharf, L. *To Work and to Wed: Female Employment, Feminism and the Great Depression*, Westport, Greenwood, 1980

Schowalter, E. *A Literature of Their Own*, London, Virago, 1982

Scourse, N. *The Victorians and their Flowers*, London, Croom Helm, 1983

Seddon, J. & Worden, S. *Women Designing: Redefining Design in Britain Between the Wars*, Brighton, University of Brighton, 1991

Sennett, R. *The Fall of Public Man*, New York, Knopf, 1976

Sennett, R. *The Conscience of the Eye: The Design and Social Life of Cities*, London, Faber and Faber, 1990

Sheldon, R. & Arens, E. *Consumer Engineering: A New Technique for Prosperity*, New York, Harper, 1932

Shields, R. (ed.). *Lifestyle Shopping: The Subject of Consumption*, London and New York, Routledge, 1992

Silverman, D. L. *Art Nouveau in Fin-de-Siecle France: Politics, Psychology and Style*, Los Angeles, University of California Press, 1989

Sklar, K. K. *Catherine Beecher: A Study in American Domesticity*, New Haven, Conn., Yale University Press, 1973

Smith, D. 'Femininity as Discourse' in Roman, L., Christian-Smith, E., & Ellsworth, K. (eds.), *Becoming Feminine: The Politics of Popular Culture*, London and New York, Falmer, 1988, pp. 37–59

Smith, T. *Making the Modern: Industry, Art and Design in the US*, Chicago, University of Chicago Press, 1993

Sparke, P. (ed.). *Did Britain Make It?: British Design in Context 1946–1986*, London, Design Council, 1986

Sparke, P. *Electrical Appliances*, London, Unwin Hyman, 1987

Sparke, P. 'From a Lipstick to a Steamship: The Growth of the American Industrial Design Profession' in Bishop, T. (ed.), *Design History: Fad or Function?*, London, Design Council, 1978

Sparke, P. (ed.). *The Plastic Age: From Modernity to Post-Modernity*, London, Victoria and Albert Museum, 1990

Steedman, C. *Landscape for a Good Woman: A Story of Two Lives*, London, Virago, 1986

Steele, V. *Fashion and Eroticism: Ideals of Feminine Beauty from the Victorian Era to the Jazz Age*, Oxford, Oxford University Press, 1983

Steegman, J. *Victorian Taste: A Study of the Arts and Architecture 1830–1870*, London, Nelson, 1970

Stowe, H. B. *Pink and White Tyranny*, Boston, Roberts Brothers, 1871

Strasser, S. *Never Done: A History of American Housework*, New York, Pantheon Books, 1982

Strasser, S. *Satisfaction Guaranteed: The Making of the American Mass Market*, New York, Pantheon, 1989

Talbot, M. & Breckenridge, S. *The Modern Household*, Boston, Whitcomb and Barrows, 1912

Teague. W. D. *Design This Day: The Technique of Order in the Machine Age*, London, The Studio Publications, 1946

Tedlow, R. S. *New and Improved; The Story of Mass Marketing in America*, New York, Basic Books, 1990

Terrill, B. M. *Household Management*, Chicago, Wesleyan University Press, 1983

Thackera, J. *Design after Modernism: Beyond the Object*, London, Thames and Hudson, 1988

The Home of Today: Its Choice, Planning, Equipment and Organisation, London, Daily Express Publications, 1935

The National Magazine Company Ltd. *Good Housekeeping's Home Encyclopaedia*, London, 1951

Thompson, D. (ed.). *Discrimination and Popular Culture*, Harmondsworth, Penguin, 1964

Tilly, L. & Scott, J. *Women, Work and Family*, London and New York, Routledge, 1978

Tomlinson, A. *Consumption, Identity and Style: Marketing Meanings and The Packaging of Pleasure*, London, Comedia, 1990

Troy, N. *Modernism and the Decorative Arts in France: Art Nouveau to le Corbusier*, New Haven, Yale University Press, 1991

Troy, N. *The De Stijl Environment*, Cambridge, Mass., The MIT Press, 1983

Tuchaman, G., Daniels, M. K. & Benet, J. (eds.). *Hearth and Home: Images of Women in the Mass Media*, New York, Oxford University Press, 1978

Turner, B.S. (ed.). *Theories of Modernity and Postmodernity*, London, Sage Publications, 1993 (1990)

Van Doren, H. *Industrial Design: A Practical Guide*, New York, McGraw Hill, 1940

Van Doren, H. 'Streamlining: Fad or Function?', *Design*, October 1949

Vanek, J. *Keeping Busy: Time spent in Housework in the US 1920–1970*, unpublished PhD thesis, University of Michigan, 1973

Vanek, J. 'Time Spent in Housework', *Scientific American*, November 1974, pp. 116–120

Vant, S. *Simple Furniture-Making*, London/New York, Frederick Warne and Co. Ltd., 1929

Veblen, T. *The Theory of the Leisure Class*, London, Unwin Books, 1970 (1899)

Venturi, R. *Complexity and Contradiction in Architecture*, New York, Museum of Modern Art, 1966

Vicinus, M. (ed.). *A Widening Sphere: Changing roles of Victorian Women*, Bloomington, Indiana University Press, 1973

Vickery, A. 'Golden Age to Separate Spheres? A Review of the Categories and Chronology of English Women's History', *The Historical Review*, Cambridge, Cambridge University Press, vol. 36, no. 2, 1993, pp. 383–414

Wahlberg, H. *Everyday Elegance: 1950s Plastic Design*, Atglen, Schiffer Publishing Ltd., 1994

Waites, B., Bennet, T., & Martin, G. (eds.). *Popular Culture: Past and Present*, London, Croom Helm, 1982

Wajcman, J. *Feminism Confronts Technology*, Cambridge, Polity Press, 1991

Wakefield, H. *19th Century British Glass*, London, Faber, 1982

Walkowitz, J. *Prostitution and Victorian Society*, Cambridge, Cambridge University Press, 1980

Walton, W. 'To Triumph before Feminine Taste: bourgeois women's consumption and hand methods of production in mid nineteenth-century Paris', *Business History Review*, 60, 1986

Warner, Prof. D. F. *Home Decoration*, London, T. Werner Laurie Ltd., 1920

Watson, R. M. *The Art of the House*, London, G. Bell and Sons, 1897

Welter, B. 'The Cult of True Womanhood 1820–1860', *American Quarterly*, xviii, 1966, pp. 151–174

Wendt, L. & Hogan, H. *Give the Lady What She wants: The Story of Marshall Field and Company*, Chicago, Rand McNally, 1952

Wharton, E. & Codman, O. *The Decoration of Houses*, London, B. J. Batsford, 1897

White, C. *The Women's Periodical Press in Britain 1946–1976*, Royal Commission on the Press, Working Paper no. 4, London, HMSO 1977

White, C. *Women's Magazines 1693–1968*, London, Michael Joseph, 1970

Whitelegg, E. (ed.). *The Changing Experience of Women*, Oxford, Martin Robertson, 1982

Wightman Fox, R. & Jackson Lears, T. J. *The Culture of Consumption: Critical Essays in American History 1880–1980*, New York, Pantheon, 1983

Williams, H. T. & Jones, Mrs. C. S. *Beautiful Homes or Hints on House Furnishing*, New York, Henry T. Williams, 1875

Williams, G. *The Economics of Everyday Life*, Harmondsworth, Penguin, 1965 (1950)

Williams, R. *Culture and Society 1780–1950*, London, Chatto and Windus, 1958

Williams, R. *The Long Revolution*, London, Chatto and Windus, 1961

Williams, R. *Dream Worlds: Mass Consumption in late 19th Century France*, Berkeley, University of California Press, 1982

Williamson, J. *Consuming Passions: The Dynamics of Popular Culture*, London, Marion Boyars, 1986

Williamson, J. *Decoding Advertisements: Ideology and Meaning in Advertisements*, London, Marion Boyars, 1975

Willis, E. 'Consumerism and Women', *Socialist Revolution*, 3, 1970, pp. 76–82

Willis, S. *A Primer for Everyday Life*, London and New York, Routledge, 1991

Wilson, E. *Adorned in Dreams: Fashion and Modernity*, London, Virago, 1985

Wilson, E. *Only Halfway to Paradise: Women in Post-War Britain 1945–1968*, London/New York, Tavistock Publications, 1980

Wilson, E. *The Sphinx in the City: Urban Life, the Control of Disorder and Women*, London, Virago, 1991

Wilson, R. G., Pilgrim, D. H. & Tashjian, D. *The Machine Age in America 1918–1941*, New York, Abrams, 1986

Winship, J. *Inside Women's Magazines*, London, Pandora, 1987

Winship, J. 'Sexuality for Sale' in Hall, S., Hobson, D. Lowe, A., & Willis, P. (eds.), *Culture, Media, Language*, London, Hutchinson, 1980

Winship, J. 'Woman Becomes and Individual – feminism and consumption in women's magazines 1954–69', *Stencilled Occasional Paper*, 65 Birmingham, CCS, 1981

Wolf, N. *The Beauty Myth*, Cambridge, Mass., The MIT Press, 1989

Wolfe, A. R. 'Women, Consumerism and the National Consumer's League in the Progressive Era 1900–1923', *Labour History*, 6, Summer 1975, pp. 378–392

Wolfe, T. *From Bauhaus to Our House*, London, Abacus, 1991

Wolff, J. 'Feminism and Modernism' in *Feminine Sentences: Essays on Women and Culture*, Cambridge, Polity, 1990

Wolff, J. 'The Culture of Separate Spheres: The Role of culture in 19th public and private life' in *Feminine Sentences Essays on Women and Culture*, Cambridge, Polity, 1990

Worden, S. 'Powerful Women: Electricity in the Home 1919–1940' in
    Attfield, J. & Kirkham, P. *A View from the Interior: Feminism, Women
    and Design*, London, The Women's Press, 1989
Wright, G. *Building The Dream: A Social History of Housing in America*,
    New York, Pantheon, 1981
Wright, G. *Moralism and the Model Home: Domestic Architecture and
    Cultural Conflict in Chicago 1873–1913*, Chicago, University of Chicago
    Press, 1980
Wright, J. M. *The Complete Home: An Encyclopaedia of Domestic Life and
    Affairs*, Philadelphia, Bradley Garretson and Co., 1879
Wright, R. & Wright, M. *Guide to Easier Living*, New York, Simon and
    Schuster, 1950
Young, F. H. *Modern Advertising Art*, New York, Covici, Friede Inc., 1930

Index